The Secret Ring

Other Works by Phyllis Grosskurth

John Addington Symonds: The Woeful Victorian
Gabrielle Roy: A Critical Study
(Ed.) *The Memoirs of John Addington Symonds*
Havelock Ellis: A Biography
Melanie Klein: Her World and Her Work
Margaret Mead: A Life of Controversy

The Secret Ring

Freud's Inner Circle and the Politics of Psychoanalysis

Phyllis Grosskurth

Addison-Wesley Publishing Company, Inc.

Reading, Massachusetts   Menlo Park, California   New York
Don Mills, Ontario   Wokingham, England   Amsterdam
Bonn   Sydney   Singapore   Tokyo   Madrid   San Juan
Paris   Seoul   Milan   Mexico City   Taipei

The lines on page 17 from *Dire Mastery: Discipleship from Freud to Lacan*, by François Roustang, reprinted by permission of the Johns Hopkins University Press, Baltimore/London, 1982.

The lines on pages 31 and 33 from *The Complete Letters of Sigmund Freud to Wilhelm Fliess, 1887–1904*, by J. M. Masson, reprinted by permission of Harvard University Press, Cambridge, Mass. Copyright 1985 and under the Bern Convention Sigmund Freud Copyrights, Ltd. Copyright 1985 by J.M. Masson for translation and editorial matter.

The lines on page 83 from *The Life and Work of Sigmund Freud*, by Ernest Jones, reprinted by permission of HarperCollins Publishers, New York, 1952.

The lines on page 175–176 from *The Letters of Sigmund Freud and Karl Abraham*, edited by Hilda C. Abraham and Ernst L. Freud. Copyright 1964 by Sigmund Freud Copyrights Ltd. and Dr. Hilda Abraham. Reprinted by permission of Basic Books, a division of HarperCollins Publishers, Inc.

Library of Congress Cataloging-in-Publication Data

Grosskurth, Phyllis.
The secret ring : Freud's inner circle and the politics of
psychoanalysis / Phyllis Grosskurth.
p. cm.
Includes bibliographical references and index.
ISBN 0-201-09037-6
1. Freud, Sigmund, 1856–1939. 2. Psychoanalysts—Austria—
Biography. 3. Psychoanalysis—History. I. Title.
BF109.F74G76 1991
150.19′52—dc20
[B]
91-11575
CIP

Jacket design by Julie Metz
Text design by Janis Owens
Set in 11-point Janson by NK Graphics
1 2 3 4 5 6 7 8 9-MA-9594939291
First printing, September 1991

For Bob

Contents

List of illustrations

10. Carl Jung, who refused to be subdued (courtesy Sigmund Freud Copyrights).

11. Loe Kann, who captivated both Ernest Jones and Sigmund Freud.

12. Elma Palos, loved by Ferenczi but rejected by Freud as a surrogate daughter-in-law (courtesy Dr. Judith Dupont).

13. Anna Freud in 1914 on the eve of her flight from Ernest Jones and enemy territory (courtesy the Freud Museum).

14. Ferenczi (on right) visiting Freud during his vacation in Hungary, 1917 (courtesy Sigmund Freud Copyrights).

15. A good cigar, at last. With Jones in 1919 (courtesy the Freud Museum).

16. Freud with his beloved Sophie who died in January 1920 (courtesy the Freud Museum).

Section 3

(FOLLOWING PAGE 168)

17. Freud with Anna at the Sixth International Congress at the Hague in September 1920 (courtesy the Sigmund Freud Archives).

18. The first Rundbrief, written by Ferenczi on September 20, 1920 (courtesy Columbia University).

19. A. A. Brill of New York, What did Jones say about Rank that Brill repeated to Ferenczi? (Courtesy the Sigmund Freud Archives.)

20. The quiet interior of the Hotel du Lac at Lavarone, far above the squabbles at San Christoforo in August 1923.

21. Abraham with his family in summer of 1925 (courtesy Grant Allan).

22. Rank is banished to the far right at the Bad Homburg Conference in September 1925. Jones, Abraham, Eitingon and Ferenczi seated in the middle, Melanie Klein standing in center behind balustrade (courtesy the Freud Museum).

23. Anna and her father in 1927 at Ernst Simmel's sanatorium at Tegel where Freud sought relief from his prosthesis for his cancer of the jaw (courtesy the Freud Museum).

Section 4

Chronology

1887	First meeting of Wilhelm Fliess and Sigmund Freud in Vienna.
1899	Freud's *The Interpretation of Dreams* published November 4, 1899.
1901	*The Psychopathology of Everyday Life* published.
1902	Formation of Wednesday Psychological Society.
1905	*Jokes and Their Relation to the Unconscious, Three Essays on Sexuality,* and *Fragment of an Analysis of a Case of Hysteria* published. Otto Rank meets Freud.
1906	Rank appointed Secretary of Wednesday Psychological Society.
1907	Max Eitingon meets Freud, January 23. Carl Jung visits Freud, February 27. Freud formally reestablishes Wednesday Society as Vienna Psychoanalytic Society, April 15. Rank becomes Secretary of Vienna Psychoanalytic Society.

	Freud meets Jones in Amsterdam in September.
	Jones visits Jung in Zurich, November 25.
	Karl Abraham meets Freud December 15; moves to Berlin same month.
1908	Sandor Ferenczi meets Freud, February 2.
	Ernest Jones meets Freud at Salzburg Congress, April 26.
	First International Psychoanalytic Congress in Salzburg, April 27.
	Jahrbuch für Psychoanalytische und Psychopathologische Forschungen launched (with Jung as editor).
	Jones accepts post at University of Toronto.
1909	Freud, accompanied by Jung and Ferenczi, travels to America to receive honorary degree at Clark University, Worcester, Massachusetts, in September.
	Eitingon moves to Berlin in November.
1910	Hanns Sachs calls on Freud in January.
	International Association of Psychoanalysis founded at Second Psychoanalytic Congress at Nuremberg, March 30–31; Jung becomes president.
	Zentralblatt für Psychoanalyse founded at Nuremberg, edited by Alfred Adler and Wilhelm Stekel.
	Abraham founds Berlin Psychoanalytic Society, March 31.
	Freud and Ferenczi travel together to Italy in September.

Adler elected president, Stekel vice-president of Vienna Psychoanalytic Society, October 12.

Freud publishes *Psycho-Analytic Notes on an Autobiographical Account of a Case of Paranoia* (Schreber case).

1911   A.A. Brill founds New York Psychoanalytic Society, February 12.

Adler resigns as president of Vienna Psychoanalytic Society, Stekel as vice-president, February 22.

First meeting of American Psychoanalytic Society in Baltimore, May 9.

Adler resigns from Vienna Society in early June, followed by nine supporters.

Adler resigns as coeditor of *Zentralblatt*, July.

Third International Psychoanalytic Congress at Weimar, September 21–22.

Imago founded, coeditors Rank and Sachs. First number appears, January, 1912.

1912   Publication of Jung's *Wandlungen und Symbole der Libido*, 1911–12.

Wilhelm Stekel resigns from Vienna Psychoanalytic Society, November 6.

Jones suggests Secret Committee in June.

Internationale Zeitschrift für Psychoanalyse, edited by Ferenczi, Rank, and Jones, founded in November.

Meeting in Munich of Freud, Jung, and Stekel, November 24.

1913	Jones returns to Europe from Canada. Analyzed by Ferenczi during summer.
	Ferenczi founds Hungarian Psychoanalytic Society, May 19.
	Freud presents rings to members of Committee—Jones, Ferenczi, Rank, Abraham, and Sachs—in Vienna on May 25.
	Fourth International Psychoanalytic Congress held at Munich, September 7.
	Jones founds London Psycho-Analytical Society, October 30.
	Freud publishes *Totem and Taboo*.
1914	Jung resigns editorship of *Jahrbuch* and presidency of the International Association on April 20. Abraham becomes interim president.
	Assassination of Archduke Franz Ferdinand on June 28 at Sarajevo, Bosnia (now Yugoslavia).
	Germany declares war on France and invades Belgium on August 3.
	Britain declares war on Germany on August 4.
	Ferenczi conscripted as a doctor in the Hungarian hussars in October.
	Jahrbuch ceases publication.
	Freud publishes *On Narcissism* and *The History of the Psychoanalytic Movement*.
1915	Eitingon enlists in Hungarian Medical Corps.

Sachs conscripted in August, but released.

Abraham posted to army hospital in Allenstein, East Prussia, March 13.

Freud visits Ferenczi at his regimental headquarters in Pápa, Hungary, in September.

1916 Rank transferred to Krakow as editor of official army newspaper, *Krakauer Zeitung*, in January for remainder of the war.

1917 Freud family holiday in Csorbato, Hungary, July 30 to August 31.

Rank visits Freud on Christmas furlough.

Freud publishes *Mourning and Melancholia*.

1918 Anton von Freund sets up *Fond* for furtherance of psychoanalysis.

Fifth International Psychoanalytic Congress in Budapest, September 28–29.

Ferenczi becomes president of International Psychoanalytic Association.

Armistice signed, November 11.

1919 *Internationale Psychoanalytischer Verlag* founded in Vienna, mid-January.

Jones re-forms English group as British Psycho-Analytical Society, February 20.

Rank returns to Vienna.

	Jones meets Rank and Sachs in Switzerland, March 17.
	Ferenczi expelled from Medical Society of Budapest during "White Terror," May.
	Freud reunited with Abraham and Eitingon in Berlin in August.
	Jones reunited with Freud in Vienna in September.
	Eitingon joins Committee, October 13.
	Jones founds International Psycho-Analytical Press and *International Journal of Psycho-Analysis.*
1920	Death of Anton von Freund, January 20.
	Death of Sophie Freud Halberstadt, January 23.
	Opening of Berlin Poliklinik, February 14.
	Sixth International Psychoanalytic Congress at The Hague, September 8–12. Jones becomes president.
	Sachs moves to Berlin in summer.
	Initiation of *Rundbriefe*, September 20.
	Freud publishes *Beyond the Pleasure Principle.*
1921	Freud publishes *Group Psychology and the Analysis of the Ego* in March.
1922	Seventh International Congress of Psychoanalysis in Berlin, September 25–27; last Congress attended by Freud.
1923	Freud publishes *The Ego and the Id* in April.

	Freud's cancer diagnosed.
	Committee meeting on August 26–28 at San Cristoforo, Italy.
1924	Jones makes publishing arrangement with Hogarth Press for publication of psychoanalytic books in English.
	Eighth International Psychoanalytic Congress in Salzburg, April 21–23. Abraham becomes president.
	Rank publishes *The Trauma of Birth*.
	Joint publication of *The Development of Psychoanalysis* by Ferenczi and Rank.
	Ferenczi publishes *Thalassa: The Theory of Genitality*.
	Rank sails for America, April 27.
	Freud publishes *The Dissolution of the Oedipus Complex* in July. Persuaded by Ferenczi to omit criticism of Rank's birth theory.
1925	Rank in New York, January 25 until mid-February.
	Freud's *Autobiography* published in February.
	Ninth International Psychoanalytic Congress at Bad Homburg, Germany, September 3–5.
	Rank in New York, September–December.
	Abraham dies, December 25.
1926	Eitingon succeeds Abraham as President of International Psychoanalytic Association.

Freud's *Inhibitions, Symptoms and Anxiety* published in February.

Rank leaves Vienna permanently, mid-April.

Last meeting of Committee with Freud in Vienna, May 7.

Anna Freud replaces Rank on Committee.

Freud's *The Question of Lay Analysis* published in September.

Ferenczi sails for America, September 22.

Melanie Klein moves from Berlin to London in September.

1927	Tenth International Psychoanalytic Congress at Innsbruck, Austria, first week of September.
	Committee converted into a group of officials of the International Association.
	Ferenczi visits Freud at Semmering, Austria, after Congress, a year after their last meeting.
1929	Eleventh International Psychoanalytic Congress at Oxford, first week in September.
1930	Freud's *Civilization and Its Discontents* published, January 1.
1931	Congress cancelled because of economic situation.
1932	Eitingon suffers cerebral thrombosis, April.

	Ferenczi reads his paper "The Confusion of Tongues Between Adults and Children" at Twelfth International Psychoanalytic Congress at Wiesbaden in September.
	Jones elected President of International Psychoanalytic Association.
1933	Ferenczi dies on May 24. Eitingon moves to Palestine in August.
1938	Freud arrives in England, June 6.
1939	Freud dies in London, September 23.
	Rank dies in New York, October 31.
1943	Eitingon dies in Jerusalem, July 30.
1947	Sachs dies in Boston, January 10 (66th birthday).
1953 -57	Jones writes three volumes of *The Life and Work of Sigmund Freud*.
1957	Jones dies in London, February 11.

Sigmund Freud
(1856–1939)

Sigmund Freud was born on May 6, 1856, in Freiburg, Moravia (now Pribor, Czechoslovakia). His father, Jakob, was a merchant, and his mother, Amalia, 21 years her husband's junior, was Jakob's third wife. Sigmund was their firstborn, followed by Julius (who died as an infant), four sisters, and a brother, Alexander, ten years younger than Sigmund. When Sigmund was three, the family moved to Vienna.

In 1873, Freud entered the medical faculty of the University of Vienna, where he studied in the physiological laboratory of Ernst von Brücke. In 1882 he became engaged to Martha Bernays. That same year Freud turned his attention to psychiatry, with Theodore Meynert as his mentor. In 1885 he spent four months in Paris studying under the famous neurologist, Jean Martin Charcot, at the Sâlpetrière Hospital, where he witnessed Charcot's famous demonstrations of hypnosis, and became involved in the microscopic study of children's brains.

Married in 1886, he started in private practice as a neurologist. In 1883 an older colleague, Josef Breuer, had related to him the story of "Anna O," who had recovered painful memories while under hypnosis. Freud concluded from this that unacceptable wishes were repressed, and he gradually abandoned the use of hypnosis, which was not always effective. He adopted the random method of free association, through which he discovered patients divulged repressed desires. This observation was Freud's first step in developing the theory of psychoanalysis. In 1895 Freud and Breuer cooperated in publishing *Studies in Hysteria*, although Breuer found that he could not support Freud's conviction that sex formed the basis of all neuroses.

In 1897 Freud started his self-analysis, which culminated in *The Interpretation of Dreams* two years later. This book was based on the revolutionary thesis that in dreams unacceptable material was disguised by repression, condensation, and displacement, and that even a young child's mind was animated by sexual and hostile motives.

In 1902 Freud invited a few friends to join him in discussions on the pioneering work he was carrying out. This group, the Wednesday Psychological Society, later became the Vienna Psychoanalytic Society. Alfred Adler and Wilhelm Stekel were among its earliest members.

In 1904 Freud published *The Psychopathology of Everyday Life*, a study of the reasons for slips of the tongue and the act of forgetting. This was followed the next year by three momentous studies: the Dora case (published as "Fragment of an Analysis of a Case of Hysteria"), which illuminated how dream analysis could explain psychoneurotic symptoms; *Jokes and Their Relation to the Unconscious*, a study of how unconscious motives can find indirect expression; and, most important, *Three Essays on the Theory of Sexuality*, an exploration of infantile sexuality and an explanation of adult perversion.

In 1902 Freud had been made a professor extraordinary at the University of Vienna, although he never held any official teaching position. In October 1919 he was given the title of full professor, but was permitted to give only private lectures.

Karl Abraham
(1877–1925)

Karl Abraham was born into a well-established family in Bremen, Germany, on May 3, 1877. He trained as a doctor in various German universities. In 1904 he was appointed by Eugen Bleuler to the Burghölzli Mental Hospital where Carl Jung introduced him to Freud's work. His first meeting with Freud took place in 1907, the same year Abraham moved to Berlin, partly due to his differences with Jung. The first German to practice psychoanalysis, he founded the Berlin Psychoanalytic Society in 1910.

Max Eitingon
(1881–1943)

Max Eitingon was born on June 26, 1881, in Mohilev, Russia. When he was twelve his wealthy family moved to Leipzig. Before obtaining his medical degree, he worked as a volunteer at the Burghölzli where he first heard about Freud. He came as a visitor to the Vienna Psychoanalytic Society on January 23, 1907. After obtaining his medical degree in 1909, he joined Abraham in Berlin. From an early age he was an ardent Zionist; in recent years rumors have circulated that he had associations with the KGB.

Sandor Ferenczi
(1873–1933)

Sandor Ferenczi was born on July 7, 1873, in Miskolc, Hungary. He was the fifth son in a family of twelve children. His parents ran a bookstore and lending library. After receiving his medical degree in Vienna in 1894, he became chief neurologist for the Elizabeth Poorhouse in Budapest and was subsequently appointed as a psychiatric expert to the Royal Court of Justice. Through a colleague, Dr. Philip Stein, he first met Freud on February 8, 1908.

Ernest Jones
(1879–1958)

Ernest Jones was born on January 1, 1879, in the village of Gowerton, Wales, the son of a colliery engineer. In 1900 he obtained his medical degree from University College Hospital in London. From 1903 to 1908 Jones found himself in constant trouble, ranging from charges of insubordination to complaints by parents that he had discussed sex with a young girl patient. He first met Freud at the Salzburg Congress in April 1908. In October 1908, he moved to the University of Toronto, Canada, at the invitation of Dr. C. K. Clarke, to help him set up a new psychiatric clinic.

He made important psychiatric connections in America, but after a sexual scandal he left the university in May 1913.

Otto Rank
(1884–1939)

Otto Rank was born Otto Rosenfeld on April 22, 1884, in Vienna. His relationship with his father was stormy, and at the age of nineteen he changed his name. In the spring of 1905 he met Freud through his family doctor, Alfred Adler. Freud was impressed by his encyclopedic reading and by his manuscript "Art and Artist," which Rank took to their first meeting. Freud encouraged Rank to obtain his doctorate in literature at the University of Vienna.

Hanns Sachs
(1881–1947)

Hanns Sachs was born in Vienna on January 10, 1881. He obtained his law degree in 1904, the same year in which he read *The Interpretation of Dreams*. After attending several of Freud's lectures, he called on

Freud with a copy of Sachs's own translation of Rudyard Kipling's *Barrack-Room Ballads* (Kipling was one of Freud's favorite English writers). Sachs joined the Wednesday Psychological Society in 1909.

Supporting Cast

Wilhelm Fliess (1858–1928)

Wilhelm Fliess was two years younger than Freud, but was well established as a successful ear, nose, and throat doctor in Berlin when the two men met in Vienna in 1887. Like Freud, he had also made a pilgrimage to Paris to study under Charcot. Freud met Fliess through his then mentor, Josef Breuer, who suggested that Fliess attend Freud's lectures at the university. (By 1893 Freud had begun to estrange himself from Breuer because Breuer failed to support the direction that Freud's work was taking; Freud also resented the fact that he had to borrow money from Breuer.) Freud was immediately attracted to Fliess, whom he saw as the ideal friend in whom to confide his researches, since Fliess agreed on the need to preserve a connection between psychological and physiological conceptions.

For several years the two men met regularly. In 1892 Fliess married a Viennese woman, Ida Bondy. It was Fliess who first suggested to Freud the principle of innate bisexuality, which builds upon the finding that each sex contains rudimentary anatomical representations of the opposite sex. Freud, at the urging of Fliess, developed the principle in a psychological direction by claiming that both male and female elements are represented in the unconscious. Fliess also drew a connection between the nose and the female genitalia, asserting, for example, that nose bleeding during pregnancy was a vicarious expression of the menstrual cycle. He traced various neurotic symptoms in women, including painful menstruation, to pathological disturbances of what he called "the genital spot" in the nose. He also claimed that men were affected by this "nasal reflex" syndrome. Freud even allowed Fliess to operate on his own nose several times in an attempt to dispel "neurotic disturbances."

Fliess also attempted to link biology to mathematics. He regarded the key numbers in the human cycle to be 23 and 28, and for some years Freud supplied information to support Fliess's ideas, such as the correlation between his wife's migraine headaches and the dates of her menstrual periods.

In a sense Fliess acted as Freud's analyst, to whom Freud transferred ideal qualities. This intense idealization eventually floundered. At their last meeting in August 1900, the two men quarreled fiercely when Fliess accused Freud of projecting his own ideas onto the minds of his patients. Their friendship had become a competitive rivalry. Unfortunately, most of Fliess's letters to Freud have not survived. Fliess's version of events would undoubtedly be helpful in gaining a perspective on Freud.

Alfred Adler
(1870–1937)

Alfred Adler was born in a suburb of Vienna on February 7, 1870. He completed his medical studies in 1895. He was one of the original members of the Wednesday psychological discussion group. By 1910, Adler was in serious disagreement with Freud. Adler had begun to view the Oedipal struggle as purely symbolic, in which the boy, weak and defenseless, overcompensates in order to achieve superiority over his father and dominance over his mother. Adler was infuriated by Freud's choice of Jung as president of the International Psychoanalytic Association in 1910, and in compensation Freud appointed Adler president of the Vienna Psychoanalytic Society, despite their disagreements.

Adler and Stekel founded and became coeditors of the *Zentralblatt für Psychoanalyse* (Central Newspaper of Psychoanalysis). In 1911 Adler, with nine of the 35 members of the Vienna Society, resigned to found the Society for Free Psychoanalysis, which soon became the Society for Individual Psychology.

Wilhelm Stekel
(1868–1940)

Wilhelm Stekel was born near Czernowitz, Poland (now Chernovtsy in the Soviet Union). He had a brief analysis with Freud in 1902. At the Weimar Congress the *Zentralblatt für Psychoanalyse* had been founded by Stekel and Adler. Freud insisted that he be given the right to veto the appearance of any paper in this journal. In 1912 Stekel refused to accept Freud's demand that Victor Tausk be put in charge of the reviews in the *Zentralblatt*. Stekel resigned from the Vienna Society on November 6, 1912, but, despite Freud's attempts to wrest the *Zentralblatt* from him, Stekel continued to edit it until the outbreak of the war. Freud resisted Stekel's many attempts at reconciliation.

Carl Gustav Jung
(1875–1961)

The son of a pastor, Jung was born in the Swiss village of Kesswil. While a student of psychiatry in 1900 he went to the Burghölzli Medical Hospital in Zurich to work under the direction of Eugen Bleuler. His early writings included a number of references to *The Interpretation of Dreams* and *Studies in Hysteria*. In this early work he also indicated his interest in word association. In 1906 he published *The Psychology of Dementia Praecox*, in which he argued that in dementia praecox a toxin attacks the brain so that repressed material is released. In this work he praised Freud and declared that no real refutation of Freud's theories had yet been made. In 1907, in the company of Ludwig Binswanger (then a volunteer physician at the Burghölzli) he traveled to Vienna to meet Freud, with whom he had thirteen hours of uninterrupted talk. Freud hoped that the Zurich group would provide a wider base for the practice of psychoanalysis.

Georg Groddeck
(1866–1934)

Groddeck, the son of a physician, was born in Baden-Baden, Germany. After army service, he became director of a small sanitorium in Baden-Baden, where he began to develop the theory that illness could be a manifestation of unknown forces, which he called "Das Es," a term later adopted by Freud as "the id." In 1912, Groddeck published a novel attacking psychoanalysis, but he admitted in a letter to Freud dated May 1917 that he had not understood psychoanalysis at the time. At the Hague Congress in 1920 he described himself as a "wild analyst," which shocked many in the audience, although he was nevertheless made a member of the Berlin Psychoanalytic Society. In his clinic he encouraged his patients to trust their doctor with childlike innocence, an approach that greatly influenced Ferenczi, who paid annual visits to Groddeck's clinic after 1921.

A. A. Brill
(1874–1948)

Abraham Arden Brill was the first practicing psychoanalyst in the United States. Born in Austria, he came to America at the age of fifteen and by 1903 had acquired his medical degree from Columbia University College of Physicians and Surgeons. He subsequently specialized in neurology. In 1907 he worked in Zurich under Eugen Bleuler and took Karl Abraham's place when the latter moved to Berlin. Here he was introduced to Freud's work, and on a visit to Vienna, he and Freud took long walks together, all the time discussing psychoanalysis. Brill met Jones and Ferenczi the following year. On his return to New York, he took on two pupils, James J. Putnam, a professor at Harvard University, and Smith Ely Jelliffe. His translations of Freud's work have been widely criticized, the first criticism being transmitted to Freud by Jones. Brill founded the New York Psychoanalytic Society in 1911 and was instrumental in the formation of the American Psychoanalytic Association several months later. He was adamant in his belief that only medically trained people were qualified to be psychoanalysts.

Anna Freud
(1895–1982)

Anna Freud was the youngest of Freud's six children. She did not get along with her sister Sophie, and Freud arranged for her to stay in Merano in the southern Tyrol when Sophie was married in early 1913 in Vienna. Anna became an elementary schoolteacher. In 1918 Freud took her into the first of two analyses. Her membership paper to the Vienna Society, "Beating Fantasies and Daydreams," (1922) was based on herself. She entered the field of child analysis, and her first publication, *The Psycho-Analytic Treatment of Children* [*Einführung in die Technik der Kinderanalyse*, (1927)] was an attack on Melanie Klein's more radical approach.

Melanie Klein
(1882–1960)

Melanie Klein was born in Vienna, the youngest child of a Galician doctor. She married young and had three children. Suffering from chronic depression, after the family settled in Budapest in 1910 she went into analysis with Sandor Ferenczi. He encouraged her to become a child analyst, and her first patients were her own children. In 1920 she moved to Berlin, where Karl Abraham became her training analyst.

Introduction

Why has Sigmund Freud's life and work commanded such undiminished interest? Today—as we approach the end of the century—he appears to have been its leading intellectual force, a far more tenacious influence than Karl Marx.

In the past decade a whole school of revisionist Freudian scholars has emerged, and while they may be critical of Freud, they continue to be fascinated by his personality and by the reasons why the psychoanalytic movement has survived. At the Third Hannah Conference on Freud and the History of Psychoanalysis, held at Trinity College, University of Toronto, October 12 to 14, 1990, scholars as disparate as Steven Marcus, Edward Shorter, and Peter Swales discussed these questions. On Saturday, October 13, a sensationalist article appeared in the Toronto *Globe and Mail* with the headline "Freud Undergoes Analysis and Is Found Inadequate." The conference participants were disturbed because the article had been written before the proceedings had even begun. The same day, however, a student circulated a letter protesting the "Freud-bashing" tone of the conference's first session. "Why not?", one distinguished participant, Frank Sulloway, responded. "If we can't do it in academia, where can we do it? It certainly wouldn't happen within a psychoanalytic society."

In the course of the conference the participants grouped and re-grouped themselves. Paul Roazen, once the *enfant terrible* of psychoanalysis, was attacked fiercely by the American philosopher of science, Adolph Grünbaum. Peter Swales, the reigning *enfant terrible*, was surprisingly subdued. Grünbaum in turn was the target of a member of the audience who argued that Grünbaum's approach was so Jesuitical that whatever argument was raised in favor of Freud, he would find logical reasons to demolish it. The conference had such a highly charged atmosphere that one felt that at any moment people might run up and down the aisles in protest.

Why should Freud be able at this date to inspire such turbulent emotions? At the conclusion of the conference, all the participants gathered on the platform to answer questions from the audience. To the query as to why Freud was still being discussed (even negatively), Sulloway replied: "Freud had a genius for selecting the right questions . . . many people have become famous in science for asking important questions even though they haven't been able to answer them." But why do people continue to react so emotionally to Freud's ideas? Does it have something to do with the intrusion of psychoanalysis into their inner lives?

At the time of the conference, I had recently completed the first draft of this book, and I found myself reflecting on the relationship between the conference and the Secret Committee, which had been formed by Freud to ensure the perpetuation of psychoanalysis. In the course of my research on the Committee, I had become greatly interested in group dynamics. Although the Third Hannah Conference seemed to be a group without a leader, was it possible that all this turbulence was caused by the imposing ghost of Freud hovering above us?

I began to rethink the inherent significance of the Committee, whose members had each received a special ring of friendship from Freud. It occurred to me that the story of the Committee might serve as a metaphor for the psychoanalytic movement itself. The force of Freud's personality and ideas had engendered a cult of personality in which Freud, as guru, had demanded complete personal and professional loyalty. In bestowing the rings on the members of the Committee, he hoped to become their ringmaster, exerting absolute control over them.

The subtext of psychoanalytic history is the story of how Freud manipulated and influenced his followers and successors. Their general passivity caused them to remain in thrall to an interminable analysis. By insisting that the Committee must be *absolutely secret*, Freud enshrined the principle of confidentiality. The various psychoanalytic societies that emerged from the Committee were like Communist cells, in which the members vowed eternal obedience to their leader. Psychoanalysis became institutionalized by the founding of journals and the training of candidates; in short, an extraordinarily effective political entity.

Great leaders may be venerated, or idolized, but the cult of leadership demands that they be remote. Freud was just such a leader. The early psychoanalytic movement took the form of an extended family whose origin was the idealized family of the Committee. It was a male family of sons led by a patriarchal father, but conspicuous in its lack of a nurturing mother.

Undoubtedly Freud's own early family life—a cold, strong mother, a shadowy father, and four younger sisters to whom he felt superior— explains something about the dynamic of the self-created family, the Committee. Freud was a withholding parent, whose "adopted" children (the Committee) hungered for his attention. Quarreling among themselves in their rivalry for Freud's attention, the members of the Committee were bound even more closely to him. Freud ultimately chose as his successor his own daughter, Anna, who had a will as strong as his own, and who possessed the same agile, political instincts. For years she operated as the palace guard.

Here we encounter a paradox. Psychoanalysis had to be codified at this point in its early history in order to survive. There were figures in the psychoanalytic movement, such as Melanie Klein, who insisted that their theories were simply developments of Freud's thinking, but were nevertheless branded as heretics. The tragedy of psychoanalysis as a science has been its rigidity, which made it unable to accommodate an Adler or a Rank. But, in an early playful letter to his young friend Eduard Silberstein, Freud remarked: "An old suspicion has it that no building is sound whose foundations have not cost a human sacrifice."[1]

The members of the Committee constantly spoke of their "debt" to Freud, as though they were driven by an inner need to repay him for an inestimable gift. Through experience they had learned that gratitude was one of the few ways in which they could extract a response from Freud.

Not everyone is capable of being a disciple. We shall see how Jones was almost masochistic in the way he submitted to Freud's bullying, how Abraham was intent on destroying Rank, and how Rank was almost destroyed. For Freud it was imperative to lead; for the others it was necessary to be led. Freud had to create a persona, an image that would demand recognition and attention. In his book on psychoanalytic discipleship, *Dire Mastery*, François Roustang argues that one becomes a disciple to prevent oneself from going mad:

> . . . discipleship demands a harassing amount of work and tireless vigilance. A disciple works, he must work enormously to fill in all the questions that can unexpectedly arise, all the cracks that can open concerning his master's peculiarity; he also has to work to justify and try to understand statements whose principles of coherence are by

definition unknown to him. If he is a disciple it is basically because he is afraid of bearing his own name, of speaking in his own name, of thinking about his fantasies and dreams or, in other words, of flying on a trapeze without a net.[2]

In fact, name changes were not uncommon among the Committee. Ferenczi's father had changed his name from Fränkel. Rank, who had been born "Rosenfeld," transformed himself into "Rank," from a kindly character in Ibsen's *A Doll's House*. Jones wanted to change his name to Beddow-Jones (although Freud dissuaded him). Even Freud, early in his career had shortened his birth name, Sigismund, to Sigmund.

It could be argued that the members of the Committee were essentially displaced Jews—people without a homeland. Jones, a Welshman, constantly emphasized that he was an outsider. By considering changing his name he was attempting to join an English club from which he felt excluded.

In his book, Roustang speaks of the tireless energy required of a disciple. He emphasizes the identification that must take place with the leader, the strained vigilance needed to follow his train of thought. In addition, disciplines must serve as lookouts to watch for enemies outside the ramparts and, more important, to deter the insidious traitors within the fortress.

Freud constantly discouraged the Committee members from burdening him with their ideas on the pretense that he found it difficult to follow another's train of thought. In reality, he believed that cracks would appear in the foundation of his theory if foreign matter was allowed to seep through. Sometimes a little buttressing or patching up was necessary, perhaps, but the superstructure must remain fixed and firm.

The Committee can be viewed as a circus ring in the center of which the ringmaster stands, brandishing his whip. Occasionally one of the animals roars defiantly and skulks off into a corner. Swiftly he is persuaded to remount his stool. Or the Committee can be viewed as a gleaming ring, with Freud himself the precious jewel set in a circle of eternal unity. But if the center could not hold (i.e., if Freud was devalued), the ring would lose its potency and chaos would ensue—as indeed it did. Despite Freud's careful control as the center, his Secret Committee was destined to collapse. In reality, the rings he had given each member failed to ensure eternal unity. Abraham and Jones felt embarrassed wearing their rings (in fact, Jones's ring was stolen from the trunk of his car!), and Freud eventually surrendered his own ring to Eitingon.

The story of the Secret Committee is one of devotion and betrayal, diligence and carelessness, altruism and selfishness. It is a story about people who believed they were reshaping human lives, but their human frailty could not carry the burden of this self-imposed responsibility.

Prologue

Idyll in the Harz Mountains

In the late afternoon of Wednesday, September 21, 1921, the seven members of the Secret Committee met at the Hotel d'Angleterre in Hildesheim, a large medieval town in Lower Saxony, just north of the Harz Mountains.

The arrangements for the meeting had been left in the capable hands of Karl Abraham, president of the Berlin Psychoanalytic Society.

Abraham had coordinated the arrivals of the members like a military maneuver. Freud's daughter Sophie had died in January of the devastating flu that had swept the post-war world. In September Freud went to visit his orphaned grandchildren in Hamburg, proceeding then to Berlin, where he was met at the station by Max Eitingon. Freud, Eitingon, and Hanns Sachs were to depart from the Potsdam railway station at 12:20 on the direct train to their meetingplace in Hildesheim. They would lunch on the train and arrive in the city at 5:22.

From Vienna Otto Rank would take a fast train through Bavaria, change at Leipzig, and arrive at Hildesheim at 5:25.

Ernest Jones was to make his way from the Hook of Holland to Leipzig, where he would accompany Rank to Hildesheim. (These two men were not the happiest of traveling companions, as relations between them had been usually extremely tense, although for some months prior to the meeting the situation had been contained.)

Sandor Ferenczi's journey entailed the most complicated route. He had been complaining of constant ill health and had been having treatment at Georg Groddeck's clinic in Baden-Baden. He had to spend the night in Frankfurt, departing on September 21 for Hanover, where he would change to the Cassel train, arriving at 6:39 in Hildesheim.

Abraham himself was visiting relatives in his hometown of Bremen; traveling from Hamburg, he arrived earlier than the others, at 4:55.

There were so many railway strikes following the war that it was re-markable that all of the group's members were able to converge at one place at the same time. Indeed, Ferenczi was delayed on his return journey and did not reach Budapest until October 4. Adding to the difficulties of travel, a state of emergency had been proclaimed in Germany in August due to a financial crisis.

The psychoanalytic pioneers made a point of staying at excellent hotels, and the Hotel d'Angleterre was the most distinguished hostelry in Hil-desheim. It stood on the Hoher Weg, a curving street at the summit of a maze of medieval passages. It had been an inn since 1827, was rebuilt in 1892, and became famous for its comfort and cuisine. Laurel trees flanked its facade, the entryway was covered in red carpet, and the headwaiter, with a napkin on his arm, stood at the door of the dining room. The set-ting must have reminded the group of their pre-war meetings at the Bristol in Salzburg or the Park in Munich.

The Hildesheim city archives reveal that shortly after the end of the war the name of the hotel had been changed to The Grape, and a large grape was hung over the entrance. Presumably cab drivers, picking up members of the Committee at the railway station, simply took them to what had always been known as the Hotel d'Angleterre. There had been an attempt to restore the hotel's former splendid cuisine, although food was still difficult to obtain.*

In Hildesheim the group visited the two great churches, one Roman-esque, the other Gothic. Freud was captivated by the small Egyptian museum, where he entered into a discussion with the curator about the burial customs of the Egyptians. The young man was puzzled as to why the corpses were placed in a crouching position resembling the embryo in the womb, and Freud informed him that primitive tribes had done the same thing, having learned about the fetal position from the evisceration of animals. (The collection of Egyptian artifacts at this museum is now considered second only to that of the great Charlottenburg museum in Berlin.)

From Hildesheim they moved on to the enchanting town of Goslar, about thirty miles away. Here they probably stayed at the major hotel, the Kaiserworth. Just around the corner was the house where Freud's hero Goethe lived during his tour of the Harz Mountains in the early

---

*In 1934 Hitler visited Hildesheim, whose medieval houses were then swathed in Nazi flags. In 1935 The Grape was converted to business offices. In March 1945 it was destroyed in a massive bombing raid. Today a multistoried parking garage occupies the site.

1770s, a sojourn that inspired him to write *Harz Journey in Winter* and the famous Walpurgisnacht section of *Faust*. (During the 1930s the house was occupied by Field Marshal Erwin Rommel.)

The Oberharz, or Upper Harz, which the group explored, is a region of dense forests of pine and spruce. For centuries silver was mined there, and the last mines were closed in the early 1930s. Much of the older architecture seems to have incorporated the vertical shape of the mine shaft, most strikingly displayed in the wonderful Marktkirche in Claustal-Zellerfeld.

In Freud's day the region was crisscrossed by a splendid network of trains and buses, so that the group was able to explore the area easily. Apparently they also stayed at Schiercke, the sprawling town at the foot of the legendary Brocken, at 3747 feet the highest mountain in the Harz.

The Witches' Sabbath was supposed to be held on the summit of the Brocken on the night before May 1. According to the legend, the witches—that is, women who were believed to have sexual intercourse with the devil—would arrive on broomsticks to perform their evil rites, to induge in orgies, to affirm their allegiance to their master the devil (who would be there in person or in the form of a goat or some other animal), and to receive their assignments for the coming year. Fires were lighted by inhabitants to drive the witches away and anti-hex signs were hammered into the barns by the local peasants. (It is interesting that when Freud referred to sex in his letters, he often added three crosses, the symbol frequently used by peasants to fend off the witches. These he would surely have seen on numerous buildings in this area.)

A railway ascended the Brocken, but Jones tells us that the group climbed the mountain and believed they caught a glimpse of the "Brocken specter," a mirage sometimes seen at sunset. They also ascended a tower whose platform was surrounded by an iron rail at hip level. Freud suggested that they all lean forward against the railing with their hands behind their backs, their feet well back, and imagine that there was nothing there to prevent them from falling. This was an exercise Freud had devised for overcoming the fear of heights, from which he had suffered as a young man. Jones teased him that it didn't seem very psychoanalytic.

(Until recently the Brocken was part of East Germany, a site of heavy military installations. It can be viewed best from the Wurmburg, the second highest peak, from which one also can catch a glimpse of the town of Schiercke, which appealed so much to Freud, in the valley below. A high barbed wire fence used to cut through the Harz, and until recently West German tourists stood behind it in silent fascination, staring at the watchtowers.)

Despite the fact that all the Committee members were suffering from colds, they maintained a strenuous schedule of hiking and sightseeing. Freud seemed indefatigable, although throughout his correspondence he was constantly forecasting an early death for himself. In the evenings the group gathered for scientific discussion and to make plans for a Congress in Berlin the following year.

I have described this meeting in the Harz Mountains as an "idyll" because it was the only real holiday the group ever took together. A spirit of comradeship was established through exercise, hearty eating, and lively discussion. Sachs entertained them with his vast store of Jewish jokes. In November 1920 Freud had complained to Jones, "Business is devouring science. *Die Kunst geht nach Brot* ("Art does not provide bread.") is more true than ever."[1] Now the group reaffirmed their passionate commitment to a revered leader and to a cause that governed their lives. The war was behind them, and the future looked promising.

In his section of the first circular letter after his return to Budapest, Ferenczi wrote: "Greetings on the beginning of a new working year for which we all have found new energy. The unforgettable and full days— the Harz mountains provided a fresh impetus for work. The pleasant memories of those days will help me in hours of depression and tiredness. I am grateful to all of you for many new ideas."[2]

Jones started his section of the letter by "again expressing warm thanks to Abraham for the excellent way in which he conducted our tour and smoothed out all our difficulties. For my part I found the Congress both exceedingly enjoyable and instructive; it will be for ever a pleasant memory, and is one more proof of the practical value of our Committee."[3]

Rank—a man not overburdened with charm—commented curtly, "We hope that everybody returned home safely and already started working again as is the case here."[4]

On their return to their respective homes, the members were once more plunged into hours of analysis and the innumerable administrative details connected with their respective psychoanalytic societies. In a letter of November 6, 1921, Freud remarked wistfully to Ferenczi: "How far away Hildesheim and Schiercke seem!"

But these men did not have time to indulge themselves in sentimentality. Their main task was to preserve the purity of psychoanalytic theory. The

Committee had been formed in 1912, at the instigation of Ernest Jones. The circumstances in which Freud felt it necessary to gather about him a small group of henchmen in order to maintain the faith and to search out deviance is the subject of this book. Historically the chief importance of the Committee is that, despite its turbulent existence, it established psychoanalysis on a firm international basis.

Chapter One

Freud's Early Friendships

FREUD WAS a highly complex man, modified and changed by the disappointments, failures, and successes of his life. In trying to understand this man, who has been such an important influence on our culture, one ponders the question: Why, at a crucial point in the history of psychoanalysis, did the Committee mean so much to him? In fact, what did friendship—as played out with such great drama and intensity by the members of the Committee—mean to Freud?

One might assume that someone who wrote as many letters as Freud did was capable of great friendship. But such an assumption is questionable. For instance, it is clear that for Freud letters were more important than actual encounters. In an early letter to Eduard Silberstein (September 4, 1874), he suggested that they write each other every Sunday with a full account of their activities during the previous week. "In that way, each of us may come to know the surroundings and conditions of his friend most precisely, perhaps more precisely than was possible even at the time when we could meet in the same city."[1] Letters were a means of access to the soul without the sometimes irritating presence of the other person, and the possibility of the other person's interrupting one's train of thought.

A striking feature of Freud's correspondence is the fact that the bulk of it was limited almost exclusively to his professional colleagues. A touching exception is his letters to his friend Eduard Silberstein, a young Romanian from the town of Brăila whom he met in his early teens when both were students at the gymnasium in Vienna.

Because much of our knowledge of Freud comes from the letters of his mature years, it is difficult to imagine him as young. But we see him in these letters as very young and high-spirited, delighting in the vagaries of life ("Isn't life one of the strangest things in the world?"),[2] even suffering from a hangover occasionally. Above all, the letters reveal Freud's adolescent longing to pour out his ambitions and fears to a single, intimate friend. He saw the letters with Silberstein as forging a deeper bond between them. Freud had little inclination for making other friends. He confessed to being bored by his contemporaries; no one could fill Silberstein's place when he was away, although Freud had "enemies by the dozen and of all shapes and sizes" (December 11, 1874). What time he had, he admitted, "I should prefer to spend it with you alone. I suspect we have enough to tell each other to dispense with a third for an audience."[3]

In a much later letter of 1884, Freud gave his fiancée, Martha Bernays, a long account of his early friendship with Silberstein, whom he had seen that very day and whom he found "as devoted to me as ever."

> We became friends at a time when one doesn't look upon friendship as a sport or an asset, but when one needs a friend with whom to share things.

They had spent almost every waking hour together, taking "secret walks." They learned Spanish, which they made into a secret code, taking names from Cervantes with which to address each other, Silberstein becoming Berganza, Freud Cipion. In retrospect, Freud admitted to Martha that he realized that Silberstein "did not like soaring very high; he remained in the human domain; his outlook, his reading, his humor, all were bourgeois and somewhat prosaic."[4] In the early days of the friendship, however, he frequently told Silberstein that he was attracted to the poet in him.

Silberstein and Freud comprised the entire faculty of the ima-

ginary "Academia Castellana" (also called "Academia Espanola")—
"the two sole luminaries of the A.E."[5]—and they addressed each
other formally as "Your Honor." Girls were known as "principles,"
and European cities were given the names of their Spanish coun-
terparts. (Madrid stood for Berlin, Seville for Vienna.)

Since we do not possess Silberstein's side of the correspondence,
it is difficult to gauge his personality. The correspondence starts
out as one between two equals, but later a subtle shift takes place
as Freud attempts to assume dominance. Silberstein's father was a
well-to-do banker, and unlike the impecunious Jakob Freud, he was
able to send his son to any university he chose. Freud gave vent to
his own fantasies when he urged Silberstein to attend "beautiful
Heidelberg" or "merry old Göttingen," but Silberstein asserted his
independence by enrolling, without consulting Freud, in Leipzig,
which his friend considered "dreary."

Apart from a brief crush on the twelve-year-old Gisela Fluss,
the daughter of a family known to both the Freud and Silberstein
households, Freud, unlike his more lighthearted friend, never seems
to have been involved with girls his own age. Freud teased Silberstein about his passing infatuations. "But then," he rationalized, "a
man cannot aspire to everything, and if I am going to continue
feeling awkward in the company of ladies, I am all the more glad
that you should feel at your ease with them" (January 17, 1875).
So long as Silberstein seemed to be indulging only in frivolous
flirtations, Freud could tolerate them. However, when he threatened to become seriously involved with a young woman in the
winter of 1875, Freud suddenly wrote him an urgent letter, totally
different in tone from anything that had preceded it. The language
is no longer boyish pig-Latin, but rather like that of a sermon from
a moral superior (February 27, 1875), warning Silberstein of the
consequences of his behavior.

A thinking man is his own legislator, confessor, absolver. But a
woman, let alone a girl, has no inherent ethical standard; she can act
correctly only if she keeps within the bounds of convention, observing
what society deems to be proper.

Freud was wild with jealousy; he complained that his friend was involved with a girl who "cannot even have enjoyed a proper education." How could he stoop so low when he already had the friendship of the cultivated Cipion? Quite clearly, according to Freud, the girl had a calculating mother who was shrewdly manipulating Silberstein into marriage by sending her daughter to dancing class and in other ways cultivating her feminine wiles.

The infatuation apparently petered out, and gradually Freud began to resume his old bantering tone and to feel free to tell Silberstein about his classes at the University of Vienna and about his professors, such as the charismatic professor of philosophy, Franz Brentano. In 1875 Freud traveled to England to visit his older stepbrothers; and en route he stopped off at Leipzig, where he had to borrow some money from Silberstein, although he was mortified to have to put himself in his friend's debt. On his return to Vienna he was shocked to learn that Silberstein had actually communicated with someone else in Spanish. He longed for a reunion so that their relationship could be reestablished on the old basis:

> I really believe that we shall never be rid of each other; though we became friends from free choice, we are as attached to one another as if nature had put [us] on this earth as blood relations; I believe that we have come so far that the one loves the very person of the other and not, as before, merely his good qualities, and I am afraid that were you, by an unworthy act, to prove quite different tomorrow from the image I keep of you, I could still not cease to wish you well. That is a weakness, and I have taken myself to task for it several times.[6]

Freud was already beginning to worry that Silberstein is going to let him down.

That same winter Silberstein returned to Vienna to enter the law faculty. He was made a Doctor of Jurisprudence in 1879. At an emotional gathering on the eve of Silberstein's departure from Vienna to Brăila, where he chose to settle, Freud made a little speech in which he declared that Silberstein was taking his own youth away with him. And indeed this seems to have been the case. Freud shed his gaiety in the sobering reality of marriage, poverty, and thwarted ambition.

Silberstein never practiced law, choosing instead to become a banker like his father, and to marry a woman he fell deeply in love with between 1881 and 1891. To his dowerless fiancée, Martha Bernays, Freud later described Silberstein's wife as "a stupid rich girl."[7]

Although the letters between Freud and Silberstein ended abruptly in 1881 (Freud ascribed their drifting apart as due to his engagement to Martha), the story of the relationship between the two men did not end there. Silberstein's wife, Pauline, suffered from severe depression. There must have been an exchange of letters (which have since disappeared) when Silberstein wrote to arrange for Pauline to go to Vienna to be treated by Freud, who was by then specializing in hysterical patients. How long she was in treatment we have no way of knowing. What we do know is that on May 14, 1891, she fell to her death in Freud's apartment building at 8 Maria Theresienstrasse. We do not know whether it was before or after Freud had seen her, and the account in the *Neues Wiener Tagblatt* for May 15, 1891, did not mention any names. According to the newspaper report, she threw herself down the stairwell from the third floor, but we do not know on which floor Freud practiced.*

In any event, Freud must have believed that the incident would be seen by Silberstein as a failure on Freud's part, although Silberstein did not seem to bear him ill will or to hold him responsible for his wife's death. After 1881 there exists a single letter from Freud dated April 28, 1910. Apparently Silberstein had written to him the previous year congratulating him (presumably) on his birthday, but Freud had not bothered to reply. "Now life is running out," Freud commented. His mood was somber as he briefly explained that he had encountered many difficulties in his scientific life; he wrote that he "might now be a well-to-do man had I not preferred a large family." Silberstein had apparently offered to send him some patients, and Freud replied loftily that he would "refer

---

*I am indebted to Dr. Ernst Falzeder for providing me with the text of the newspaper account.

them to my many pupils, who will treat them as I will suggest, but I myself cannot take on anything more this season." He possibly felt that he could not risk another failure; but lest Silberstein was in any doubt about Freud's stature, he assured him that he was the leader of a great movement in the interpretation of nervous diseases, a movement that was gaining widespread recognition and on which he had lectured in America the previous year. The letter was signed "Your old Freud." Freud never mentioned Silberstein to anyone else, except in 1928 when the B'nai B'rith in Brăila asked him to send a few words to commemorate Silberstein's death in 1925.

What had happened to the joyous Freud of the early letters? When he became engaged to Martha, he seemed to try to turn her into a substitute for Silberstein. In his long letters to her, Freud used her as a sounding board, and the priggish pomposity with which he occasionally lectured his friend became more pronounced as he tried to mold his future wife by supervising her reading and all her activities. When they married in 1886, the young woman whom he was able to idealize through his letters turned out to be a rather petulant and boring Hausfrau. She bore him six children, and the worry of supporting them was constantly on his mind. The intensity with which he entered into his largely epistolary friendship with Wilhelm Fliess must have been a reflection of his disappointment with reality and his need to seek an idealized friend who existed only as a projection of his own needs. For Freud the ideal friend had to be an extension of himself. His grand passion for Fliess came to a disastrous end nearly six years before his last somber letter to Silberstein. For Freud, falling in love led inevitably to total disenchantment.

At the time of their meeting, Wilhelm Fliess was twenty-nine, a successful ear, nose, and throat specialist in Berlin. In the autumn of 1887 he went to Vienna for some further study with specialists, and the eminent Josef Breuer (1842–1925), at that time Freud's mentor, suggestd that Fliess attend some of Freud's lectures. After Fliess returned to Berlin, Freud initiated the correspondence in November by using a patient's condition as an excuse to tell Fliess "outright in what category of men I place you."[8] His next letter is positively effusive. "I still do not know how I won you," he exults.

"So far I have always had the good fortune of finding my friends among the best of men, and I have always been particularly proud of this good fortune."9

So the relationship began with a *coup de foudre*, and certainly on Freud's part it was a case of intense idealization. In August of the following year Fliess offered some unsolicited advice—namely, that Freud consider going into general practice. In Freud's reply, he evinces an envy that would eventually unravel the very fabric of their relationship:

> The whole atmosphere of Vienna is such that it does little to steel one's will or to foster that confidence of success which is characteristic of you Berliners and without which a mature man cannot think of changing the basis of his existence. So it seems I must remain what I am, but I have no illusions about the inadequacy of the state of affairs.10

The passage conveys frustration and a somewhat unconvincing modesty. At this stage of their relationship Freud was awed by his friend. Fliess had established professional credentials and, unlike Freud with his dowerless bride, had married a woman of substance. It could be argued that Freud was driven to surpass his friend. While each used the other as a sounding board, the direction of their thinking was so different that a real dialogue could not be created. When they did meet, they quarreled fiercely. The tone of passionate self-effacement in Freud's letter of January 1, 1896, is unique, and cannot be found in his correspondence with anyone else.

> How much I owe you: solace, understanding, stimulation in my loneliness, meaning to my life that I gained through you, and finally even health that no one else could have given back to me. It is primarily through your example that intellectually I gained the strength to trust my judgment, even when I am left alone—though not by you—and, like you, to face with lofty humility all the difficulties that the future may bring. For all that, accept my humble thanks! I know that you do not need me as much as I need you, but I also know that I have a secure place in your affections.

He seems uncertain that he actually does occupy such a "secure place." Repeatedly he pleads with Fliess for a meeting, and is beside himself with anxiety when Fliess is slow to write. Yet, on reading through the complete correspondence, it is startling to discover how early in their relationship the disastrous operation on Emma Eckstein's nose occurred. This incident was actually the peripateia in the friendship, the point at which Freud had an abrupt encounter with reality. While the two men had written sporadically since their first meeting in 1887, the friendship intensified in 1895 when Fliess traveled to Vienna at Freud's suggestion to operate on a woman whose hysterical symptoms Freud linked (at Fliess's suggestion) to a blockage in the nose. After Fliess's departure the woman began to bleed profusely, and the situation became so critical that Freud called in another doctor, who discovered that the genius from Berlin had mistakenly left half a meter of surgical gauze in the cavity created by the removal of the turbinate bone. Freud was clearly shaken by the incident, although he assured Fliess that "Of course no one is blaming you. Nor would I know why they should."[11] His denial of his friend's responsibility was so extreme that he displaced the blame onto the hapless woman, whom he began to depict as a chronic hysterical bleeder.

Freud was obsessed with Fliess, who he sometimes called his "Demon," his other half. His ambivalence toward Fliess and his self-reproach for entrusting a delicate operation to a man whom he had over-estimated surface in the constant references to the Eckstein episode as "the dream of Irma's injection." This dream is referred to both in letters to Fliess and in the *Interpretation of Dreams*, which was written during the course of the friendship and while Freud was embarked on his self-analysis. Evidently he saw Fliess as both his intimate friend and his hated enemy.

In the famous photograph of Freud and Fliess standing side by side, the dark resemblance between the two men is striking. Freud both idealized and envied his alter ego. A strong transference was established as Freud poured out his dreams to the man who served, in James Strachey's later phrase, as Freud's "auxiliary super-ego." In its most intensely pathological stage, the relationship—on Freud's part, at any rate—was a case of projective identification.

As Freud gained increasing confidence, he began to want to discard Fliess. Fliess had apparently shown open contempt for Freud's newly discovered theory of psychoanalysis, and, in order to irritate his friend, Freud began telling him about numerous works he had encountered in which people were working on exactly the same theory of numbers with which Fliess was preoccupied. Freud continued to express himself effusively in his letters, but the warmth seems forced.

In March 1900, for once it was Fliess who proposed that they meet. In earlier years Freud would have responded ecstatically to the suggestion. On March 23 he replied:

> There has never been a six-month period in which I so constantly and so ardently longed to be living in the same place with you and that which is yours as the one that has just passed. You know that I have been going through a deep inner crisis; you would see how it has aged me. I was therefore deeply moved when I heard of your proposal that we meet again this Easter. Anyone who did not understand the more subtle resolution of contradictions would think it incomprehensible that I am not rushing to assent to the proposal. In fact, it is more likely that I shall avoid you—not only because of my almost childish yearning for spring and the beauties of nature, which I would willingly sacrifice for the gratification of having you near me for three days. But there are other inner reasons, an accumulation of imponderables, which, however, weigh heavily on me (from the natural habitat of madness you will perhaps say). Inwardly I am deeply impoverished, I have had to demolish all my castles in the air, and I am just now mustering enough courage to start rebuilding them again.

He goes on to say that Fliess would have been indispensable to him during a crisis he had been experiencing during the past six months. However, if they met now, Fliess would only "arouse my innermost (impersonal!) envy." Such being the case, a meeting might be so disturbing that he would relinquish his hard-won composure and the summer would be intolerable as a result. "No one can help me in the least with what oppresses me," he concluded; "it is my cross,

I must bear it; and God knows that in adapting to it, my back has become noticeably bent."

What is one to make of this extraordinary letter, with its combination of self-pity and implied reproach? Freud begins by assuring Fliess how much he had longed "to be living with you and *that which is yours*" during the past six months. The editor of the letters, Jeffrey Masson, speculates that *dem Deinigen* is probably a reference to Fliess's work. (I am inclined to agree with him.) The two men had their final meeting in August, when they quarrelled fiercely over the theory of bisexuality, which Freud claimed he had discovered to be the basis for the psyche. Fliess insisted that the idea had originally been his, and Freud did not acknowledge Fliess's claim until a year later.[12]

By now Freud had in fact betrayed Fliess by revealing Fliess's theory of bisexuality through Freud's patient, the psychologist Hermann Swoboda, who passed it on to Otto Weininger. It was only a matter of time before Fliess discovered this. When he read Weininger's book, *Sex and Character* in 1904, he accused Freud of divulging his ideas. Freud at first denied the accusation, then later admitted only that he had read Weininger's work in manuscript. On July 27, 1904, Freud finally revealed that he had "suspected that one of us might come to regret our formerly unrestrained exchange of ideas." He had projected onto Fliess the image of the totally understanding, totally supportive friend. Without Fliess's unqualified admiration, Freud found it impossible to continue the friendship.

In the letter of March 23, 1900, Freud was in effect saying to Fliess that Freud's betrayal of the friendship would never have happened if he had not been deserted by his friend. Freud described himself as a man of sorrows. The cross which Freud and Freud alone must bear was his guilt—and for the rest of his life he was to be haunted by it. Like the Ancient Mariner, he felt impelled to recount to some of his later colleagues Fliess's paranoia, which was in actuality a displacement of his own guilt. Perhaps Fliess *was* paranoid—but no one could claim that Freud acted toward him like a true friend. He claimed that he had exorcised himself of Fliess only by working the relationship through in 1911, in his interpretation of the mad Judge Schreber whose paranoia he interpreted as repressed homosexuality. To what degree Freud was successful or not in exorcising Fliess we can only speculate on, through his relationship with Carl Jung, with whom he often discussed what he described as "the wounds of the Fliess affair."[13]

Freud's relationship with both Silberstein and Fliess was marked by his envy for their material good fortune. How could it be, he must have pondered, that neither Silberstein (in either his first or second marriage) nor Fliess had a wife who presented him with a whole series of children? To Freud, Martha must have begun to symbolize fecundity. Freud's sense of omnipotence was such that he seems to have denied responsibility for Pauline Silberstein's death; his identification with Fliess was so intense that to admit Fliess's culpability in the botched operation on Emma Eckstein would be to accept that he too was to blame. His betrayal of Fliess was projected onto his friend in the form of paranoia. In his future relationships he would suspect possible betrayal from anyone with whom he came into close contact. Only with an unmarried daughter, particularly a daughter whom he had analyzed himself, would Freud finally find safety.

We do not know when Freud destroyed Silberstein's letters. When Fliess's widow wrote to him in December 1928, shortly after the death of her husband, asking if Freud would lend her Fliess's part of the correspondence, Freud replied evasively that he would have to look for the letters. He claimed never to have found them. It is possible that Freud destroyed them over Christmas. His feelings for both Fliess and Silberstein had long been transferred to other men such as Jung and the members of the Committee. His former friends were now expunged from Freud's own version of his personal history.

Chapter Two

The Unruly Son

WITH THE publication of *The Interpretation of Dreams* Freud believed that he had presented the world with a new vision. In the autumn of 1902, at a time when Freud's relationship with Fliess was in its death throes, a general practitioner, Wilhelm Stekel, proposed to Freud that some of his admirers form a discussion group. "I was the apostle of Freud who was my Christ!"[1] he later recalled. Freud liked the idea, and sent out post-cards to three other men, including Dr. Alfred Adler, and the Psychological Wednesday Society was formed. By 1907 the number of members had grown to between ten and twenty, but dissensions and quarrels had begun to mar the Society. In December 1907 Dr. Karl Abraham from Berlin was a guest of the Society and recorded his impressions for his friend Max Eitingon: "I am not too thrilled by the Viennese adherents. . . . *He* is all too far ahead of the others. . . .Stekel is superficial, Adler one-sided. . . . The young Rank seems very intelligent. . . ."[2]

Freud viewed the group as a sounding board for his ideas, and he was disturbed by the intrusion of democratic unruliness. Consequently he dissolved the group and reformed it in April 1908 as the Vienna Psychoanalytic Society. In September, while in Rome, he sent out circular letters to the members, suggesting that this was an opportunity to resign if for any reason any one of the members did not feel as enthusiastic about the discussions as he had in the past—in other words, if he did not fully support Freud's views. Freud did not enjoy groups, nor was he very adept at controlling them. Otto Rank, the young man whom he had appointed as secretary, was too inexperienced to keep the group in check. Moreover, Freud was beginning to envisage a worldwide psychoanalytic movement, far broader than the narrow confines of Vienna. But who had the energy and dedication to serve as his deputy?

On the morning of February 25, 1907, Freud received two Swiss visitors from the Burghölzli Mental Hospital in Zurich. One was Carl Jung, the other Ludwig Binswanger, who would later become the director of the Kreuzlingen Mental Hospital. Jung had written admiringly of Freud's work. They talked for hours, and Freud was mesmerized by Jung's enthusiasm and by his towering good looks. Binswanger later remembered that after Freud's first meeting with Jung, Freud had an anxiety dream that Jung would replace him.

Nevertheless, he needed an appropriate disciple to disseminate his message about sexuality as the basic force in man's nature, a theory he had recently formulated in *Three Essays on Sexuality*. Jung entered his life like an angel of light, a charismatic blond giant. Like Fliess before him, Jung sought out Freud, but Freud must have reassured himself that there was no resemblance between the two men. Jung's interests appeared to be much closer to Freud's own, and Jung seemed eager to espouse psychoanalysis publicly. It seemed almost miraculous that a Gentile, a Swiss, a man who seemed to have strange powers of prediction should sweep into Freud's life at the moment Freud needed him. The mystical side of Freud silenced the cautious materialist.

Not that there weren't warning signs from the beginning. In his very first letter to Freud, Jung stated frankly that it seemed to him that "though the genesis of hysteria is predominantly, it is not exclusively sexual."[3] Freud did not answer this directly, but indicated that it was only a matter of time before Jung would overcome his "inner resistance to the truth."[4] A few weeks later caution reasserted itself when he warned Jung not to "deviate too far from me when you are really so close to me, for if you do, we may one day be played off against one another."[5]

Freud's relationship with Jung can in no obvious way be compared to that with Fliess. Freud and Fliess were of an age, and the intensity of Freud's feelings for Fliess is reflected in the salutations in his letters. "Dearest Wilhelm," "My beloved friend," and even

"Dear Magician" were used; he reverted to "Dear Wilhelm" only after a stormy meeting in Salzburg in September 1896.

Freud was twenty years older than Jung and by 1906 had achieved the honorary title of "Professor." Jung always addressed him formally as "Dear Professor." This respectful distancing makes Jung's final contemptuous attacks on his former mentor even more painful to read than Fliess's cold, pained reproaches in his last letters, which miraculously surfaced later, despite Freud's earlier claim that he had never found them.*

From time to time Jung confessed to feeling anxious about possible rivals such as Jones, Abraham, and Eitingon, all of whom sought Freud out in 1907 and 1908. Freud would hasten to reassure him about his "Berlin rival," urging him to try to get along with Abraham, particularly as "there can be no question of his replacing you in my eyes."[6]

The time came, of course, when Freud felt impelled to confide in Jung about Fliess. On February 17, 1908, Freud's thoughts turned to Fliess in a discussion of the homosexual component in paranoia: "My one-time friend Fliess developed a dreadful case of paranoia after throwing off his affection for me, which was undoubtedly considerable. I owe this idea to him, i.e., to his behavior. One must try to learn something from every experience." What Freud actually owed Fliess was the theory of bisexuality, and in later years he became scrupulous about asking colleagues to check papers for ideas that he had inadvertently picked up from them.

In this letter to Jung Freud for the first time addressed him as "Dear Friend," having previously progressed from "Dear Colleague" to "Dear Friend and Colleague." Jung took alarm. He thanked Freud for his confidence in him—that is, the feeling that he could impart *confidences* to him—and continued:

> The reference to Fliess—surely not accidental—and your relationship with him impels me to ask you to let me enjoy your friendship not as one between equals but as that of father and son. This distance

---

*J.M. Masson explains that Fliess's letters are in the Jewish National and University Library, Jerusalem. See *The Complete Letters of Sigmund Freud to Wilhelm Fliess 1887–1904*, translated and edited by Jeffrey Moussaiff Masson (Harvard University Press, 1985), p. 461.

appears to me fitting and natural. Moreover it alone, so it seems to me strikes a note that would prevent misunderstandings and enable two hard-headed people to exist alongside one another in an easy and unstrained relationship.[7]

Jung indicated a clear-sighted perception of the dangers of too close an intimacy.* Yet why "father and son" rather than simply "colleagues"? He had probably grasped that Freud (not to speak of himself) needed some kind of special relationship that transcended professional bonds. Yet the filial one in which the son remained in respectful awe of his father was one that the explosive and independent Jung was incapable of maintaining.

But the fantasized father-son relationship continued on its uneasy course. Freud, remarking on an incident in which Jung had predicted that Freud's bookcase would emit a startling noise, found it "strange" that it should have happened on the very evening "when I formally adopted you as my eldest son and anointed you—*in partibus infidelium* (in the lands of the unbelievers)—as my successor and crown-prince,—[yet at that time] you should have divested me of my paternal dignity."[8] The tone is playful but the feelings are somber. He then goes into a garrulous account of his superstitious feeling that he will die at the age of 61 (he was then 53). The superstition had begun to take hold of him through "the hidden influence of W. Fliess," and had "erupted in the year of his attack on me." Freud was interpreting his paranoia about dying as the result of Fliess's paranoia about Freud's alleged betrayal of Fliess's ideas to Weininger. This was both a distortion of Fliess's theory and an error in the date he assigns to the beginning of his fear of death.†

In early June 1909 Freud learned from Jung that he had been involved with one of his patients, Sabina Spielrein. Jung wrote him a hypocritical letter describing how the young woman had "systematically planned my seduction which I considered inopportune."[9]

---

*There was a mysterious incident in Jung's childhood when he may have been sexually abused.
†See Frank Sulloway, *Freud, Biologist of the Mind* (Basic Books, 1979), p. 166. On June 22, 1894, Freud made a superstitious prediction to Fliess that he would die at 51. As Sulloway points out, this was a full year before Fliess had even begun to speak about a 23-day cycle.

On one level Freud chose to believe him, confiding sympathetically that he had been close to experiencing the same temptations. "I believe that only grim necessities weighing on my work, and the fact that I was ten years older than yourself when I came to ψA, have saved me from similar experiences." He then goes on to make the amazing statement: "The way these women manage to charm us with every conceivable psychic perfection until they have attained their purposes is one of nature's greatest spectacles."[10]

Freud had held Emma Eckstein responsible for Fliess's botched operation, claiming that she was a hysterical and manipulative bleeder. Now he was willing to accept that poor Jung had barely managed to escape Spielrein's wiles. But within a month Jung was forced to admit the truth, "a piece of knavery which I very reluctantly confess to you as my father."[11] Again Freud told him "it was not your doing but hers."[12] Freud could not afford to acknowledge Jung's perfidy or his unprofessional conduct. For him the analyst was always right, the patient inevitably wrong. In his anxiety to keep Jung close to him, Freud enshrined the tradition of the omniscience of the analyst. Fearing a break between them, Freud supported Jung in an attempt to forge a bond between them. But his idealized image of Jung had been tarnished.

The incident also pointed up the significant age difference between the two men. Is it possible that Freud envied Jung for yielding to a temptation that he had resisted?* Nevertheless, if Freud were to die at the appointed time, it was necessary now to have a successor to proclaim to the world—for the sake of the cause. Yet Freud was convinced—albeit reluctantly—that the son was longing to replace him. In fact, Freud and Jung were destined to fall out from the moment Freud designated him as his successor. He might have appeared to be honoring him, but Freud was in effect castrating the younger man.

The two men were locked in a fatal embrace, and Freud was constantly on the alert for signs that Jung had devious plans to supplant him. Hence the famous fainting episode in the restaurant in Bremen just before Freud, Jung, and Ferenczi set sail for America

---

*Many commentators have remarked on Freud's attraction to Dora.

1. The Secret Committee. This group photograph was taken in September 1922 in Berlin. (*left rear*) Otto Rank, Karl Abraham, Max Eitingon, Ernest Jones; (*left front*) Sigmund Freud, Sandor Ferenczi, Hanns Sachs.

2. Ernest Jones, wearing his ring.

3. Hanns Sachs.

4. Karl Abraham.

5. Sandor Ferenczi.

6. Otto Rank, wearing his ring.

7. Max Eitingon wearing Freud's ring.

in 1909. During lunch Jung had launched into a discussion of the extraordinary phenomenon of corpses preserved in peat bogs that had recently been discovered in northern Germany. Freud interpreted Jung's interest in the topic as a repressed death wish against Freud. Freud was so distressed that he fainted, at which point Jung picked him up and tenderly carried him to a sofa to recover.

During the voyage across the Atlantic Jung and Freud analyzed each other's dreams; yet when Jung pressed Freud for some personal details so that he could gain a better understanding of one of his dreams, Freud drew back into himself, declaring that he could not risk losing his authority.

Irrevocable events that would lead to an eventual split were about to unfold. In the spring of 1910 an International Congress took place in Nuremburg. Freud deputized, his Hungarian supporter, Sandor Ferenczi (two years younger than Jung, and hence a symbolic younger sibling) to announce to the assembly Freud's proposal for an international psychoanalytic association in which Jung was to serve as permanent president and his Swiss relative Franz Riklin as secretary. One explanation for Freud's failure to make the announcement himself is that he hoped to deflect the justified indignation of his Viennese group, who felt that Freud had insulted them by choosing an outsider. The outraged Viennese, whom Adler had gathered in a hotel room, were startled by Freud's sudden entry. He launched into a passionate appeal. He was getting on in years; the movement could survive only if it extended its frontiers beyond the Jewish community. Seizing his coat by the lapels, he cried dramatically, "They won't even leave me a coat to my back. The Swiss will save us—will save me, and all of you as well."[13] In the end a compromise was reached, with Jung's presidency being limited to two years.

My own view is that Freud used Ferenczi as his deputy because he could not bring himself to utter the statement that he would eventually be supplanted. Nevertheless, after Jung had visited him in December, Freud still maintained to Ferenczi that "I am more than ever convinced that he is the man of the future."[14]

Freud felt more dependent than ever on Jung after Alfred Adler and his supporters resigned from the Vienna Society in June 1911, to protest Freud's autocratic control. Nevertheless, Freud began to detect what appeared to be disturbing indications that his disciple was distancing himself from his leader. Freud complained that Jung could not deal with his "father-complex." He was disturbed that Jung neglected the administrative duties of the International Association because they bored him. Then again, Jung would make sudden impulsive trips to America. The intervals between his letters became more prolonged. Freud could forgive a sexual transgression toward a patient, but not Jung's failure to write to him frequently. On February 25, 1912, Jung informed Freud that "I think I am not wrong in expecting that you rather resent my remissness as a correspondent. In this respect my behavior is indeed a little irresponsible, as I have allowed my libido to disappear into my work." Freud replied (February 29, 1912) that "it would be a severe blow to all of us if you were to draw the libido you require for your work from the Association." He went on to list the areas he felt Jung was neglecting, concluding, "But I am less concerned with the present than with the future; I am determined to make all necessary preparations for it, so as to see everything safe in your hands when the time comes." As early as 1909 Freud admitted that his sensitivity toward the dwindling correspondence had its genesis in his relation to Fliess (March 9, 1909); to which Jung responded: "You may rest assured, not only now but for the future, that nothing Fliess-like is going to happen . . . my affection is lasting and reliable" (March 11, 1909).

The relationship between Jung and Freud was a mixed marriage that could not work, and in various oblique ways, they set out to prove this to each other. In 1910 Jung sent Freud a copy of the memoirs of Judge Daniel Paul Schreber,* possibly hoping that it would convince him of the toxic origins of psychosis. It was a provocative attempt to force a confrontation between them. Freud's response was to write "Psycho-Analytic Notes on an Autobiographical Account of a Case of Paranoia," in which he argued that Schreber's disorder was a result of his repressed homosexual fixation on

---

*Schreber was a jurist who had been incarcerated as insane, but he obtained his release by writing the story of his mental delusions.

his father. The Schreber case probably provided both men with a mutual turning point in the relationship. Jung could not accept the sexual foundation on which Freud insisted psychoanalysis stood. Increasingly, Freud had begun to hear disturbing rumors about lectures Jung had given in America in which he discounted the centrality of the sexual impulse. Yet, rather than force a break, Freud decided that things should appear to be normal, and Jung and Riklin were reelected president and secretary of the International Association at Weimar in November 1911.

Although the denouement was rapidly approaching, a resolution had to be found for the time being. Jung was both president of the International Association and editor of the *Jahrbuch*, the official annual publication of the psychoanalytic movement. How was Freud to get rid of him without creating a public scandal and risking the destruction of the movement? To other colleagues—Ernest Jones, Karl Abraham, and Ferenczi—Freud gradually began to voice his increasing anxiety after Jung changed the date of the 1912 Congress from September to August because of a trip he was making to America to give a course of lectures at Fordham University. Freud did not think a Congress was even necessary that year, and he particularly resented having his summer holiday interrupted. In the end, events ruled out any Congress that year.

Freud spoke almost optimistically about a resolution of his difficulties with Jung during the first months of 1912. On January 23 he described himself to Ferenczi as "a sentimental donkey" despite his gray hairs. He did not want to bear malevolence toward Jung, he said; he was willing to forgive his peccadillos. He wrote that from the outset he had been aware of Jung's ambition, but that he had hoped to channel it by making him president of the Association.

> The prospect of having to do everything by myself as long as I live and then to leave a full successor behind is not very comforting. So I do have to confess that I am not happy at all that I will have to carry that burden.

He expressed his growing desperation when he told Ferenczi that he must now turn to him for support, and he hoped that Ferenczi would not disappoint him. The fact is that Freud could not accept any successor, and he used the sexual issue merely as an excuse to rid himself of Jung.

Ferenczi replied (January 27, 1912) that of course he would not disappoint Freud—so long as Freud's expectations were not too high. He assured him that he was totally devoted both to Freud and to psychoanalysis, but that it would be impossible for him to succeed Freud as a "full successor." Repeatedly he emphasized that it was fruitless for Freud to be so obsessed with the conviction that he needed a worthy successor since, in Ferenczi's view, the psychoanalytic movement had reached a secure enough position that it could function without an autocratic leader.

Freud continued to insist that he hoped their mutual interests would keep him and Jung together, "even without developing an intimate or close relationship. I have no rancour."[15] His ambivalence toward collegial closeness was so severe that he constantly oscillated in his attitude toward Jung. Complaining that he always found it difficult to handle people with enlarged egos, he cried plaintively, "Do *I* really always have to be right, always have to be the better one?" Here he is talking as though a rupture with Jung had already taken place.

An alarmed Ferenczi felt impelled to speak as frankly as possible. He feared that Freud might fall too easily into the trap of distrusting those who did not deserve it (February 2, 1912).

> Of course the first one I am thinking of is myself. Otherwise I do agree with you that the interests of psychoanalysis should guarantee the keeping together of the representatives of psychoanalysis even without personal intimacy.

Freud dreaded direct confrontation, but an incident in May indicated that he was unconsciously precipitating a crisis. He made a visit to Lake Constance to see Ludwig Binswanger, a Swiss colleague who was seriously ill at Kreuzlingen. On this occasion the two men had a frank discussion about Jung. Binswanger described Jung as the sort of person who attracts people at first and then repels them with his coldness and lack of consideration. Nevertheless, he felt that Jung was indispensable to the movement.

Prior to leaving Vienna for Kreuzlingen, Freud wrote to Jung informing him of his plans. Although he did not specifically ask Jung to join them, he later reproached Jung for not getting in touch with him when Zurich was such a short distance away. Jung in turn interpreted Freud's failure to contact him as an insult, which he later described as "the Kreuzlingen gesture"—that in fact Freud had deliberately avoided him. Not until months had passed did he confess that he had misread the postmark on Freud's letter. Whatever the truth, both men seemed intent on creating a rupture.

Nevertheless, Freud seemed completely astonished when he received Jung's brief letter of June 18 in which Jung referred to "the Kreuzlingen gesture."

> Whether your policy is the right one will become apparent from the success or failure of my future work. I have always kept my distance, and this will guard against any imitation of Adler's disloyalty.

A bewildered Freud sent copies to Binswanger and Ferenczi for their reactions. "What does he mean by 'the Kreuzlingen gesture'?" Freud asked. "What is my policy that will prove his work right or wrong? The letter seems to me to be a complete rejection" (Freud/Ferenczi; June 28, 1912).

In May, Ernest Jones had arrived in Vienna, accompanied by his enchanting Dutch mistress, Loe Kann, whom Freud had agreed to analyze. Jones was unhappy in his post on the psychiatric staff at the University of Toronto, and it was apparent that he had no future there, since his reputation had been tarnished by sexual scandals. Now was the time to make the move to establish himself in Europe and perhaps step into the breach as the Gentile Freud needed. Jones used the occasion to undermine Jung, complaining that he had been offended by Jung's failure to answer his letters and that he disapproved of Jung's changing the date of the Congress because of his American plans. Moreover, while Jung had led Freud to believe that his American invitation indicated good prospects for psychoanalysis, Freud reported that Jones now assured him that Fordham was "a small and unknown *Catholic* university run by Jesuits and Jones had already turned down an offer from them" (Freud/Ferenczi; June 23, 1912). Jones also informed Freud that three years ago in Zurich Jung had confided in him that Freud would be destroyed by his own theories. But why hadn't Jones passed on this information at the time?

While Jung was away in America, Freud, shaken by Jones's revelations, began to come to terms with the fact that more than an ocean separated them. He decided to break off all communication with Jung; he wrote to Ferenczi that he would probably be very pleased with the way he was handling the matter. "I feel comfortable, not involved at all, and intellectually superior."[16] Ferenczi replied that he was saddened but not surprised by Jung's open declaration of war. He made the shrewd observation that Jung was treating psychoanalysis as though it were a personal matter between himself and Freud. He added that he was thankful that he had been born a Jew so that he had been spared "all this atavistic nonsense" in his childhood.[17] He warned Freud to be on his guard against Jones as well. Freud's calm mood delighted Ferenczi, he wrote, because it indicated that he had finally "completely given up the forcible effort to create a personal successor" (Ferenczi/Freud; August 6, 1912).

In the meantime Jones had made a proposal to Freud that helped him accept the situation with Jung more philosophically. On July 30 he wrote to Freud, who was taking the cure at Karlsbad, that Jung's behavior had become "a complete puzzle to me, altogether inexplicable." Few men, he continued, were capable of identifying themselves completely with the "cause." He went so far as to express doubts about Ferenczi and Rank. Ferenczi had told him that he wished that a small group of men could be analyzed by Freud personally "so that they could represent the pure theory unadulterated by personal complexes, and thus build an official inner circle in the Verein (association) and serve as centres where others (beginners) could come and learn the work." While Jones envisaged this as an ideal solution, he realized that it was hardly practical.

As an alternative, he suggested that a secret committee be formed as a Praetorian guard around Freud. The unstated aim, of course, was to monitor Jung, to maintain a watching brief in which they would report to Freud. Freud's response (August 1, 1912) was highly enthusiastic:

> What took hold of my imagination immediately is your idea of a secret council composed of the best and most trustworthy among our men to take care of the further development of and defend the cause against personalities and accidents when I am no more. *You say it was Ferenczi who expressed this idea, yet it may be mine own shaped in better times, when I hoped Jung would collect such a circle around him composed of the official headman of the local associations. Now I am sorry to say such a union had to be formed independently of Jung and of the elected presidents. I daresay it would make living and dying easier for me if I knew of such an association existing to watch over my creation.* I know there is a boyish, perhaps romantic element too in this conception but perhaps it could be adapted to meet the necessities of reality. I will give my fancy free play and leave to you the part of the Censor.

It is understandable that Freud's fancy was piqued by the "strictly secret" aspect of the Committee when we remember the elaborate Spanish code and rituals in which he and his youthful friend Silberstein had indulged. Freud proposed as members, in addition to Jones and Ferenczi, Hanns Sachs of Vienna and Karl Abraham of Berlin. Abraham had been at loggerheads with Jung when they both worked in the Burghölzli until Abraham's departure for Berlin in 1907.†

Lest Ferenczi receive undue credit, Jones emphasized to Freud that "The idea of a united small body, designed like the Paladins of Charlemagne, to guard the kingdom and policy of their master, was the product of my own romanticism . . ." (August 7, 1912). The Committee should be unofficial, informal, and secret, but "in

---

*The section in italics (mine) was omitted from Jones's life of Freud.
†It is curious that he did not suggest Max Eitingon, considering that on January 7, 1913, Freud wrote to him: "You were the first emissary to reach the lonely man, and if I should ever be deserted again you will surely be the last to remain with me."

the closest possible touch with you for the purposes both of criticism and instruction. Fortunately the last condition is not difficult; for you are delightfully approachable and generous in your knowledge and advice, as I can personally bear witness with the greatest gratitude."

Jones had grasped the fact that to be a friend of Freud's meant being a sycophant. It meant opening oneself up completely to him, to be willing to pour out all one's confidences to him. Jones had earlier confessed ecstatically to Freud that on their first meeting in 1908 he had experienced a reaction that occurred whenever he encountered an authority figure: that he would be found out in some wrongdoing (January 13, 1912). Nevertheless, for the first time in his life, with Freud he had realized that "here was a man who, in spite of his authority and rank, would understand and not blame."

Jones might have wanted Freud as a surrogate father, but Freud was willing to accept him only as a loyal colleague, not as a beloved son. Freud was not altogether convinced that Jones was always the sacrificial victim in his various sexual misadventures. There seemed to be too many of them, both in Britain and in Canada, for sheer coincidence to be responsible. Moreover, Jones lacked Jung's charisma and Ferenczi's endearing charm.

Meanwhile, on Jung's return from America, Jung wrote Freud a cold letter (November 11, 1912), in which he told Freud bluntly that "Your Kreuzlingen gesture has dealt me a lasting wound. I prefer direct confrontation." He assured Freud that "there is no resistance on my side, unless it be my refusal to be treated like a fool riddled with complexes." For some astounding reason this letter gave Freud hope that a continuation of relations might still be possible (Freud/Ferenczi; November 14, 1912). Yet on the same day, November 14, Freud wrote to Jung, for the first time addressing him as "Dr. Jung" and telling him that he found his "harping on the 'Kreuzlingen gesture' both incomprehensible and insulting, but there are things that cannot be straightened out in writing." But he assured him that he felt "the same need to continue our collaboration."

Then another crisis occurred. Wilhelm Stekel, following in Adler's footsteps, severed his ties with the psychoanalytic movement. But Stekel was reluctant to relinquish the editorship of the journal

Zentralblatt, which he and Adler had founded at Nuremberg in 1910.* Jung, as president of the Association, was forced to call a meeting in Munich to decide the fate of the journal.

On this occasion Freud and Jung went for a long morning walk during which they had a dramatic confrontation that Freud reported fully to Ferenczi. Freud said that he had not minced words with Jung: he had been mistaken in his original judgment of him as a born leader and was now convinced that he was so immature that he needed to be curbed (Freud/Ferenczi; November 26, 1912). It is significant that theoretical differences were not emphasized. Against all hope Freud wanted to believe that Jung would remain loyal, but what he called Jung's "centre of insincerity" disturbed him. He also reported fainting after lunch, and Ferenczi reminded him of the similar occasion in Bremen before he and Jung sailed for America with Freud. Jones (who was present on the later occasion) suspected a homosexual element in Freud's relationship with Jung. After Jones returned to England, he recalled in a letter to Freud their parting at the station in Munich, when he told Freud that he believed Freud would find it "difficult to give up your feeling for Jung (meaning that perhaps there was some transference to him of older affects in you)" (December 23, 1912). In his explanations to Ferenczi and Jung, Freud refused to accept that the incident could have had a neurotic cause, but to Jones he finally admitted that "There is some piece of unruly homosexual feeling at the root of the matter" (December 8, 1912). He also added that after things had been thrashed out with Jung during their walk, he expected that Jung would stay within the psychoanalytic movement. He seemed incapable of grasping that Jung had to be his own man.

As for Jung, the meeting enabled him to see clearly how different he was from Freud. He wished that he had gained this insight earlier, for it would have spared Freud many disappointments (November 26, 1912). Freud replied (November 29, 1912) in a conciliatory tone:

---

*Stekel managed to maintain control, and the journal continued to appear until the outbreak of war in 1914.

Believe me, it was not easy for me to moderate my demands on you, but once I had succeeded in doing so, the swing in the other direction was too severe, and for me our relationship will always retain an echo of our past intimacy.

Jung did not want a reconciliation, but he seemed incapable of expressing this to Freud without insulting him. In the next fortnight he sent Freud a series of letters whose insolence ranged from mild to aggressive, culminating in one of December 18 which Freud described to Ferenczi as "incredibly impertinent."

If ever you should rid yourself entirely of your complexes and stop playing the father to your sons and instead of aiming continually at their weak spots took a good look at your own for a change, then I will mend my ways and at one stroke uproot the vice of being in two minds about you.

In these letters, Jung cast doubts on the validity of Freud's self-analysis. Most cutting of all, he speculated that Freud possibly *hated* neurotics, so that he could not treat his patients entirely lovingly. Jung himself would continue to stand by Freud publicly, but would tell him frankly what he thought of him in future letters.

When Ferenczi heard of this exchange, he hastened to assure Freud that he was probably the only man in the group who didn't require analysis. There is no doubt about Ferenczi's sincerity (and dependency), which is sadly ironical in view of the fact that only a few years later he was offering to analyze Freud himself! But at this point Freud was the omniscient father; Ferenczi wrote to Freud, "you were right in everything" (Ferenczi/Freud; December 26, 1912).

Jung tried to explain his dilemma to Jones in a letter of November 15, describing his state of mind while writing *Wandlungen und Symbole der Libido* (Transformations and Symbols of the Libido), in which he broadened the definition of the libido from sexuality to a more generalized *élan vital*.

I clearly felt that this work was destined to destroy my friendship with Freud, because I knew that Freud will never agree with any change in his doctrine.

He had been proved right. Freud, he saw, was convinced that "I am under the domination of a father complex against him and that all is complex-neurosis. It would break me, if I were not prepared for it through the struggle of the past year, where I liberated myself from the regard for the father."[18] Furthermore, simply because he believed the apostate Adler's views should at least be listened to didn't imply that he had become an out-and-out Adlerian supporter, as Freud was quick to assume. Anyone whose ideas differed from his own, Freud described as an "enemy."

On December 22, 1912, Freud responded to Jung's letter of December 18 with surprising restraint. But the charge of treating his colleagues as patients rankled, and on January 3 he wrote proposing that he and Jung break off relations entirely. Within the next few months Jung resigned from the editorship of the annual psychoanalytic journal, the *Jahrbuch*, and in April 1914 he resigned the presidency of the Association.

Freud was determined not to get into an open fight with Jung, but on October 20, 1913, he emphasized to Ferenczi that he expected Ferenczi to attack Jung in print. "Fights are good," Freud told him. "They keep one in a state of tension. Success always has something paralyzing about it; riots on all sides create the same kind of favorable conditions as our former isolation." This was encouragement to his supporters to manifest their loyalty by attacking Jung.

What is clear from the letters is that Ferenczi was very fuzzy about the theoretical differences between Freud and Jung, but if Freud ordered him to write a critique of Jung's work for the newly founded *Internationale Zeitschrift für ärtzliche Psychoanalyse* (International Journal of Medical Psychoanalysis), as a dutiful son he must obey. He now sat down to read the papers collected as *Transformations and Symbols of the Libido*, in which Jung investigated various manifestations of energy. Afterward he reported excitedly that for Jung the unconscious manifested itself only in dreams and that he equated analysis with confession! Not until Jung had formally broken with the psychoanalytic movement did Freud put pen to paper to spell out his theoretical differences with Jung and Adler in "On Narcissism" (1914) and in a more general overview, "On the History of the Psycho-Analytic Movement" (1914).

In May 1913 the five members of the Secret Committee—Jones, Ferenczi, Abraham, Rank, and Sachs—met in Vienna. There they were bound together by their secrecy against the world, their faith in Freud's theory, and their personal devotion to their leader. Freud told Ferenczi he was very happy with his [*angenommene Kinder*] "adopted children."

Chapter Three

Freud's Adopted Children

WHY FREUD had to have surrogate or "adopted" sons raises questions about his relationship with his own three sons.* With Jung he had a fantasized relationship of the ideal father and son—he was Moses, but Joshua would reach the Promised Land. Each of them, through their specific neurotic needs, seriously misjudged the other by failing to recognize that they were totally incompatible. Freud could not separate his creation, the theory of psychoanalysis, from himself, its creator. He used his theory as a kind of loyalty oath. Rejection of any part of the theory meant personal rejection of him.

Freud gave private assurances to each of the members of the newly formed Committee that he would continue to write to each one personally as in the past. Sandor Ferenczi was particularly reluctant to let the Committee interfere with his special relationship with Freud.

Even during its most glowing phase, Freud's relationship with Jung had never been the intimate friendship that Ferenczi and Freud had enjoyed since their first meeting in 1908. Jung had always refrained from opening his heart completely to Freud, and Freud was uneasy about the impenetrable barrier that made Jung a perpetual enigma to him. For years Ferenczi was his most loved, trusted, and indulged confidant. He joined the Freuds on family holidays and often traveled alone with Freud. There were occasions

---

*Martin was born in 1889, Oliver in 1891, and Ernst in 1892. Freud never encouraged any of them to be analysts. The members of the Committee were half a generation older.

when he rebelled against his dependency, but always he returned, repentant and submissive.

Ferenczi's most famous example of early rebelliousness occurred in Palermo in September 1910, when he refused to act as Freud's amanuensis while Freud dictated his interpretation of the Schreber case. In future years Ferenczi was to recall the incident repeatedly, blaming himself until he finally came to terms with his relationship with Freud shortly before his death. At the time Freud described Ferenczi to Jung as

> a dear fellow, but dreamy in a disturbing kind of way, and his attitude towards me is infantile. He never stops admiring me, which I don't like, and is probably sharply critical of me in his unconscious when I am taking it easy. He has been too passive and receptive, letting everything be done for him like a woman and I really haven't got enough homosexuality in me to accept him as one. These trips arouse a great longing for a real woman. (September 24, 1910)

During the crucial year of 1912 Ferenczi was caught up in the most bizarre soap opera that would continue for many years. He had long been involved with an older married woman, Gizella Palos.* In 1911 he began to analyze her daughter Elma, and through the intensity of the analysis the couple became infatuated with each other.† Gizella was distraught but understanding. The only solution they could see was for Freud to take Elma into analysis. Freud was presented with a *fait accompli*, and although he was heavily overworked, as a favor to Ferenczi he accepted the young woman for the first three months of 1912, the two men maintaining an epistolary commentary on her progress. When Elma returned to Budapest in the early spring, she resumed analysis with Ferenczi— with Freud's approval. On a number of occasions Freud told Ferenczi that he must work out his own destiny, but he made it clear that he felt Ferenczi should marry the devoted Gizella, who was

---

*There is some indication that Ferenczi might have analyzed Gizella for a time (Ferenczi/ Freud; October 30, 1909).

†To complicate matters, Gizella's other daughter was married to one of Ferenczi's brothers.

equally devoted to psychoanalysis. Freud's comments suggest jealousy of his youthful rival, and confidence that the mature woman would not destroy the close bond between the two men.

Freud's voyeuristic involvement in the situation is curious. Ferenczi was constantly demanding Freud's attention, and Freud indulged him to a degree that was unthinkable with any other colleague. Perhaps Ferenczi provided him with a *frisson* and a turbulence from which he shrank in his own rather arid emotional life. Ferenczi was Freud's Scheherazade, entertaining him with the neverending saga of his triangular love situation, whose variations and crises seemed endless.

In March 1913, Ferenczi went off on holiday to the island of Corfu. He reported to Freud that he had seen army maneuvers near Trieste. Two Greek warships were in the harbor, and the island was swarming with refugees. It was simply a tourist's observation, and Ferenczi regretted that Freud was not by his side to enjoy the beauty of the sea as they had done on many occasions in the past.

On his return to Budapest Ferenczi was again pulled into Freud's guerilla warfare with Jung. The general tactics were to put Jung into a position in which he was forced to resign, but they were fearful lest he try to keep the *Jahrbuch* as his own (as Stekel had struggled to do with the *Zentralblatt* the previous year). As a result of Stekel's action, Freud had founded the *Internationale Zeitschrift für ärtzliche Psychoanalyse* as the central organ of the psychoanalytic movement, and had appointed Jones, Ferenczi, and Rank as safe coeditors. Jung was excluded from any involvement with the journals, as well as *Imago* (also founded in 1912), which was devoted to the application of psychoanalysis to cultural subjects, and edited by Rank and Hanns Sachs.

In March, Jung left for America for five weeks. By now Freud was describing him to Ferenczi as "dangerously neurotic" (Freud/Ferenczi; January 5, 1913). He would treat Jung with "cool politeness," consoling himself with the knowledge that Jung had generally fulfilled his function of propagating psychoanalysis.

Jung had written to Ferenczi in February trying to explain his position, a letter that the dutiful Ferenczi had sent on to Freud. Freud, who interpreted the letter as "an indirect communication to me," virtually dictated Ferenczi's reply:

> You trust that Jung doesn't want to break off relations because that certainly isn't Freud's intention. Scientific differences are tolerated within the organization unless personal behavior such as Stekel's and Adler's makes these impossible. You personally regret that letters between Jung and Freud have been discontinued. You wonder if Jung has problems in his relationships with people because you yourself have managed to avoid any difficulties with Freud, etc. etc. You are struggling with Jung's interpretation of libido, etc., but perhaps clinical material will resolve the problem. etc.[1]

Ferenczi proposed to found an official psychoanalytic society in Budapest, a move heartily endorsed by Freud as it would give him additional strength against Jung at the forthcoming Congress in Munich in September. Meanwhile, at Abraham's suggestion, Ferenczi circulated his critique of Jung's views on the libido to the Committee members for their comments.

Ferenczi proposed that he come to Vienna in June for the analysis that Freud had long promised him. Freud expressed nervousness about the prospect. Jones's Dutch mistress, Loe Kann, had decided to leave Jones as a result of her analysis, although Freud rationalized that the relationship had deteriorated long before he had taken her into analysis in the summer of 1912 at Jones's request. Freud was fearful that he might jeopardize his relationship with Ferenczi, who meant far more to him than Jones did. In any case, he explained, five or six weeks was far too short a time for an adequate analysis (Freud/Ferenczi; May 4, 1913).

Meanwhile, across the Atlantic, at the University of Toronto, Jones was embroiled in an unpleasant scandal. One of his former patients had reported to the president of the University that Jones had made sexual advances to her. She was supported by her general practitioner, a woman who Jones claimed had a lesbian relationship with his patient; but he also admitted paying blackmail money to the patient in order to keep her quiet. Jones complained to Freud about feeling enormous fatigue as a result of this ordeal.

On a visit to Vienna at Christmas 1912, Jones caused Loe great distress by having a sexual relationship with Loe's (paid?) companion, a woman referred to in the letters as "Lina." A troubled Freud told him that he must learn to "master such dangerous cravings" (Freud/Jones; January 14, 1912). In response to Jones's effusive gratitude for Freud's intense concern in the matter, Freud, in the same letter, explained why he took such a close personal interest in his colleagues. "It makes me positively unhappy not to be able to assist them or to detect a cloud in our personal relations." It was perhaps a weakness in him, "yet I am too old and worn out to change." For Jones, as for Ferenczi, Freud was the all-wise father to whom his troubled son came for help and advice.

In May 1913 Jones left the University of Toronto forever, determined to try to rehabilitate himself in England. Late in the month he joined the other Committee members in Vienna for their first official gathering. On the morning of May 25 Freud had a private talk with his favorite disciple, Ferenczi. In the afternoon he met with the entire Committee: Ferenczi, Rank, Sachs, Jones, and Abraham. Ferenczi led a discussion of the critique Freud had asked him to write of Jung's views on the libido, and the meeting culminated with Freud presenting each of the Committee members with an ancient intaglio from his collection of antiquities. These they subsequently had mounted in gold rings. Freud himself wore one incised with the head of Jupiter. Traditionally intaglios had been used as seals on contracts before written signatures were used to certify important documents. The rings were pledges of eternal union, symbolizing the allegiance of a band of brothers to their symbolic father, Freud the ring-giver.

During Freud's private interview with Ferenczi, apparently Ferenczi was persuaded to postpone his own analysis so that he could analyze Jones. Jones had to be molded into some sort of shape so that he could replace Jung as the necessary Gentile in a position of leadership, and be worthy of the Committee, which he had proposed.

Jones traveled to Budapest, where the analysis started at the beginning of June for two hours daily although not set at a fixed time. It was undertaken in German, which Jones was making a great effort to learn. On June 7 Ferenczi reported to Freud that he thought the analysis would go well because Jones was making a real attempt to be honest. Jones was certain that they would get some good work done, "which I both want and need." Freud was pleased to hear that he was starting out well, and advised Ferenczi: "Be strict and tender with him. He is a very fine person. Feed the pupa (chrysalis) so that it can become a queen bee. . . ."[2] On the same day, Jones wrote Freud that Ferenczi was "very patient with my eccentricities and changes of mood." He enjoyed the informal scientific talks they had together and also the meetings of the Hungarian Psychoanalytic Society, which had been founded on May 19. Somewhat condescendingly he described Ferenczi as having "a beautiful imagination, perhaps not always thoroughly disciplined, but always suggestive."

Throughout June and July Ferenczi provided Freud with a full account of the course of the analysis. Jones, understandably, was anxious lest Ferenczi reveal everything about him; after all, during the previous year Freud had given him a blow-by-blow account of Loe's analysis and neurotic symptoms. Ferenczi found himself growing very fond of Jones, although his patient had scornful dreams about Ferenczi and indicated a marked tendency for intrigue. Nevertheless, Ferenczi assured Freud, "I believe that we can count on him" (Ferenczi/Freud; June 23, 1913). Jones in turn hoped that the analysis would help resolve his father complex (Jones/Freud; July 9, 1913).

During that summer Freud was also pleased with Loe's growing independence, and admitted to having developed an enormous affection for the lively, attractive woman. He assured Ferenczi that he had not been tempted by her, probably because of the difference in their ages. Jones found himself in an awkward position, knowing that Loe had shown his letters to Freud, and not knowing how much Freud was revealing to Ferenczi about his former mistress's analysis. Freud warned Ferenczi not to repeat too much to Jones about Loe.

During these months Freud was putting the finishing touches to the last section of what was to be his most controversial work, *Totem and Taboo.* He was highly excited, confident that it would be as important as *The Interpretation of Dreams.* Here Freud ventured into an explanation about the origins of civilization: In the beginning an all-powerful father had monopolized the women in the tribe. The sons banded together, killed him, and ate his body. Ensuing quarrels among the brothers led to remorse and an acceptance of the father's prohibition against incest.

On May 17, 1912, Jung had written Freud a long letter explaining that in his view "incest is forbidden *not because it is desired* but because the free-floating anxiety regressively reactivates infantile material and turns it into a ceremony of atonement (as though incest had been, or might have been, desired)." Freud's contradictory account was in effect a way of publicly throwing down the gauntlet to Jung.

Totem and Taboo has often been criticized for having no basis in history, but what is interesting is why Freud felt impelled to write it. Was he partly testing the Committee as well as Jung? He seemed to be repeating his pattern of behavior with Fliess by constantly seeking total approval of his work. Jung had been doing massive research in mythology, and Freud obviously felt a need to surpass him with his interpretation of civilization as beginning with the original Oedipus conflict.

After his first elation, Freud began to worry that the work would hasten the split with Jung. To Abraham he wrote, "Jung is crazy, but I have no desire for separation and should like to let him wreck himself first."[3] Freud professed that he would have preferred Jung to leave of his own accord, but on other occasions he said that he hoped the book would force Jung out of the movement.

Galleys were read by all the members of the Committee, from whom Freud claimed he was eliciting suggestions and criticism. Jones was puzzled that Freud seemed to think that the Oedipal event had *actually* happened in the historical past, and he was bold enough to venture that the account suggested "an unusual personal significance for you" (June 25, 1913). *Totem and Taboo* does seem to have had something to do with Freud's fantasy life. By now Sabina Spielrein (with whom Jung had been sexually involved when she was his patient) had become a member of the Vienna

Psychoanalytic Society,* and Freud was on friendly terms with her. By analysing Elma Palos and Loe Kann, Freud was in effect taking the women away from his "sons." Hence Ferenczi and Jones and Jung all must subconsciously want to kill him.

Freud firmly and politely put Jones's objection to *Totem and Taboo* to one side. Ferenczi knew Freud well enough to beg him not to change anything. He described the work as "the nodal point of human science in the history of civilization" (Ferenczi/Freud; June 23, 1913). He also ventured the explanation that Freud's work was in itself a totem meal, in which Freud acted as the Mithras priest who kills the father with his own hands, while his students are the audience at the "holy spectacle"! Freud congratulated himself that he had now discovered that he was capable of accepting criticism, but of course only if it came from sympathetic critics like Jones and Ferenczi (Freud/Ferenczi; June 26, 1913).

An actual celebratory meal was shared on June 30 when Jones and Ferenczi, having traveled together to Vienna, joined Sachs and Rank to give Freud a festive "totemic" dinner at the Konstantinhügel in the Prater. The evening was crowned by Loe Kann's presentation to him of an Egyptian figurine, which Freud adopted as his official totem.

As Jones's analysis drew to a close at the end of July, he spoke warmly about Ferenczi and his analysis: "It has without doubt been successful in making me face more clearly various character traits and dangerous tendencies, and I trust it will prove its value also when it comes to be tested in actual life."[4] Freud was pleased that Jones had learned to appreciate Ferenczi "as he deserves to be" (Freud/Jones; June 20, 1913). After Jones's departure, Ferenczi, in his isolation in Budapest, found himself missing his new friend, whom he had "learned to love and appreciate" (Ferenczi/Freud;

---

*She attended her first meeting on October 11, 1911, as the second female member. Frau Dr. Margarete Hilferding left the Society at the same meeting in sympathy with Adler. Freud and Spielrein agreed in April 1912 that she could be analyzed the following year and that she should make up her mind by October. After she became pregnant, on August 14 Freud wrote discouraging her in view of her condition. (I am indebted to John Kerr for this information.)

August 5, 1913). He could not, however, guarantee that Jones had mastered his neurotic tendencies. Jones continued to be anxious about what Ferenczi had revealed to Freud. Ferenczi had told Jones casually that he had discussed Jones's analysis "in a general way" with Freud, and if Freud had any comments to make about it, Jones would appreciate hearing them. Freud was wise enough to resist the bait.

On his return to London Jones had taken on his first patient by the middle of August, and by late October had formed the London Psycho-Analytical Society, applying through Jung for membership in the Association [*Vereinigung*].

That summer Freud deserted Karlsbad for Marienbad, accompanied by Martha, his sister-in-law Minna, and his daughter Anna. It rained constantly, and he was deeply depressed. The reason usually given for his state of mind at this time was that he was anxious about a probable confrontation with Jung at the Munich Congress to be held in September. Another possibility is that he might have been suffering from post-partum depression after the completion of *Totem and Taboo*, particularly in light of his superstitious conviction that he would not be capable of a major work for another seven years.

It is also possible that Loe Kann had played a significant role in the manic energy that went into the final section of this work. While Jones was in Vienna, Freud, Kann, and Jones had shared a meal at the Cobenzl restaurant in the hills overlooking the city. Freud later told Jones that he had noticed a constraint between them because of Loe's analysis. During the excursion Jones appeared to tire easily, while "I grew fresher with the advancing hour" (Freud/Jones; June 8, 1913). During his analysis with Ferenczi, Jones realized that he was feeling hostile toward Freud for coming between him and Loe (June 17, 1913). In a letter of December 8, 1912, Freud refers to Loe's "sexual anaesthetia." It was at this point that the frustrated Jones seduced Lina. Freud, unwilling to believe that Jones could have done anything "mean and treacherous," (February 10, 1913) warned him against letting anyone else know what was going on. With the future so uncertain, he could not afford to lose

Jones by others suspecting that he might not be an appropriate colleague. Nevertheless, he was not as easy on him as he had been with Jung over Spielrein.

Freud described Loe as "actually a jewel" (Freud/Ferenczi; May 15, 1913). Jones had "had her" for eight years, his argument ran, so he could hardly complain if he had "lost" her through her analysis with Freud. Again and again Freud refers to her warmly, and is at the same time uneasy about the part he has played in weaning her away from Jones. What he hadn't anticipated was that she would start falling in love with another Jones, this time an American named Herbert ("Davey") Jones. Yet despite Freud's misgivings, she decided to return to England to live with Ernest Jones in August, although she returned to Vienna in November. This situation was as much a tragicomedy as Ferenczi's triangular affair in Budapest.

Perhaps more than bad weather prompted Freud to move on restlessly after a couple of weeks in Marienbad to San Martino di Castrozza in the Dolomites. Here he was joined by Ferenczi and Abraham to discuss strategy for the forthcoming Congress. Freud disapproved of the democratic procedure Jung had introduced of having discussions after every paper. He agreed to deliver a paper, "The Predisposition to Obsessional Neurosis," only if no discussion were allowed. The three men traveled together to Munich, making a great show of unity by staying at the same hotel as the Swiss members. They knew that Jung, with the Zurich contingent behind him, could muster enough votes to be reelected President. Abraham suggested that the Committee members express their disapproval for Jung by block abstentions. As a result of pressure by their respective groups, twenty-two of the fifty-two participants at the Congress refrained from voting. This still left Jung with enough votes to become president. Each of the members of the Committee gave a paper containing criticism of Jung. Little by little they were managing to oust him.

Freud departed for Rome in a mood of satisfaction, and while there received a letter from Jones expressing the hope that he was gratified "to see that this time you had an active bodyguard to support you" (Jones/Freud; September 13, 1913). On October 27

Jung formally resigned the editorship of the *Jahrbuch*. He subsequently wrote to Ferenczi protesting the way he had been treated at Munich. Ferenczi replied (after Freud added a few sentences) that the Hungarians, on Freud's advice, had decided to reelect Jung, but were disgusted by his "completely one-sided and biased commentaries" (November 3, 1913) during the proceedings. On November 6 Ferenczi reported his pleasure at the formation of the London Society "so we will be able to stand against Jung as a closed unit." Jones also wrote to Jung, who replied mildly that it seemed only natural that he could not agree with his views. He failed to see why different viewpoints could not be discussed and felt that his own had been entirely misrepresented at Munich. "This isolation is decidedly unhappy," Jung concluded (November 15, 1913).[5]

Freud began writing "The History of the Psycho-Analytic Movement," fully anticipating that before he had completed it, he could include a section describing Jung's defection. During the autumn there was a good deal of discussion among the Committee members as to the wisdom of breaking away from the International Association and forming a new group. Freud, Ferenczi, and Rank were in favor of it, but the caution of Abraham and Jones prevailed. Jones's clinching argument was that they did not want the Americans to regard them as the outsiders (Jones/Freud; November 4, 1913). After all, Jung had a high profile in America, where he was regarded as the most important representative in psychoanalysis after Freud.

Jones proposed a meeting of the Committee in Vienna at Christmas, but Freud had made plans to visit his daughter Sophie in Hamburg. On his return journey he stopped off in Berlin for a few hours of discussion with Abraham. Neither of them knew that this was to be their last meeting until the end of the war.

In early April 1914, Ferenczi had his last pre-war holiday with Freud. Anna was supposed to accompany them, but she came down with whooping cough. Freud suggested Rank as a replacement. The "indispensable" Rank, as Freud often referred to him, had come into Freud's orbit in 1905 when he presented Freud with a copy of his manuscript "The Artist." An autodidact from a poor family, he was small and unprepossessing, but Freud recognized his potential and encouraged him to pursue his doctorate in literature. He soon became secretary of the Wednesday Psychological Society (the forerunner of the Vienna Psychoanalytic Society). Even though they worked closely together, after Rank received his degree Freud always addressed him formally as Dr. Rank. He was always at Freud's side, talking incessantly into his ear. Freud took a very protective attitude toward his protégé, telling the others that they must be financially responsible for him after Freud's death.

The visit to Brioni gave Ferenczi and Rank an opportunity to get to know each other well, and on his return to Budapest Ferenczi told Freud how much he valued Rank. "Gradually out of the *Komité* a circle of real friends is being formed, in which everyone feels confident and safe" (Ferenczi/Freud; April 18, 1914). Ferenczi admitted, however, that in Freud's presence he felt inhibited. Freud had noticed his constraint but had attributed it to Rank's presence. He did not ask him about it because he himself was "afflicted with a withdrawal of the libido" (April 24, 1914). This kind of abstract jargon was a reformulation of the secret code Freud and Silberstein had maintained so many years before. Even more disturbing, language was being used here to mask the expression of real feelings.

Jones was also forming a close friendship with Hanns Sachs, who arrived in England from Vienna in May. After an enthusiastic account of his impressions of Sachs, Jones assured Freud: "My wish has long been to form a ring round you of men who will deal with the opposition while you progress with the work itself; and the outlook for such an ideal situation seems highly promising" (May 25, 1914).

By the middle of February Freud had finished "The History of the Psychoanalytic Movement," which the Committee referred to as "the Bomb" that would explode in the Jungian camp. At this time there was a good deal of discussion among the members about tactics to get rid of Jung. The Committee members exchanged photographs, and on March 16, 1914, Freud told Abraham that his picture would take the place that Jung's had occupied on the wall of his consulting room. Abraham suggested that the presidents of the constituent societies insert a notice in the *Zeitschrift* expressing their loss of confidence in Jung. Again Jones advised caution. On April 20 Jung suddenly submitted his resignation as president of the Association. Abraham was appointed interim president, although he had suggested Jones for the post. What Jung was planning to do was hard to guess, Freud told Ferenczi, "but it is a matter of indifference to us" (April 24, 1914).

This, of course, was not true. Freud assiduously collected information about the Zurich group and for a time even suspected the Swiss pastor Oscar Pfister, who was one of his most devoted followers, of joining the enemy. Jones, who in the past had advised caution in dealing with Jung, now became almost obsessional about following Jung's every move when the latter gave a triumphant series of lectures in England that summer. Freud was compelled to advise him to exercise a little restraint when he proposed following Jung around and taunting him in order to engage him in debate.

Jones seemed to be trying to prove his total loyalty to Freud. This loyalty was severely tested in late May when he learned that Loe was going to marry the other Jones. It was even more severely tested when Jones also learned that Freud and Rank had traveled to Budapest for the wedding ceremony, which Freud had instructed Ferenczi to expedite. Jones had to accept the situation, but some part of him must have regarded the three men as having betrayed him.

In breaking the news to Jones, Freud was mildly sympathetic, recalling how, in a Weimar coffeehouse in September 1911, Jones had confided in him about Loe's morphine addiction and had asked Freud if he would take Jones's troubled "wife" into analysis. (Freud always spoke as though Jones and Kann were actually married, even though he knew they were not.) It had been a remarkable "chain of changes," said Freud, and it was particularly striking to him "that our relations have not been spoiled and that I have learned to like the other man."[6] Freud's sentiments could not have been entirely palatable to Jones, and despite his protestations a certain bitterness breaks through in his reply (June 17, 1914):

> The most remarkable of the chain of events is the way in which our relationship has more than stood the strain—even a psychologically

interesting matter—and I can only ascribe this, with deep gratitude to the truly English sense of fairness you have displayed throughout the whole course and your kindly attitude towards me in spite of having a distorted amount of my failings presented to you. All this has forged a permanent bond in my feeling toward you.

On June 23 Ferenczi remarked briefly to Jones: "About Freud's and the Jones's couple stay in Budapest you already know."[7] Freud continued to be highly nervous about Jones. On June 16 he told Jones that he would do him a "personal favor" by not embarking on marriage without long reflection. Freud's anxiety was aroused by Jones's enthusiastic reaction to the news that Anna Freud was coming on a visit to England in early July. Jones proposed putting aside the time he had allotted for his holidays to spend with her. An agitated Freud informed Jones that he and his "little daughter" had a tacit understanding that marriage for her was out of the question for two or three years (July 10, 1914). The same day he told his daughter that he thought his letter "will discourage any courting yet avoid all personal offence." Aware that Jones was dancing constant attention on her, Freud continued to be nervous that Jones was using Anna to further his political ambitions. To Ferenczi he verbalized his fear that he did "'not want to lose the good child in an act of revenge" (July 17, 1914).

Freud was exhausted after completing "The History of the Psycho-Analytic Movement" and told Ferenczi bluntly that he wanted to be alone during August. Ferenczi in turn informed Jones that it was *his* suggestion that Freud be left alone (June 23, 1914), and he proposed visiting England (accompanied by Rank) on condition that Jones continue his analysis. Jones agreed because, as he told Freud, "There are still some dark places that I cannot unravel alone" (July 27, 1914).

Chapter Four

Years of Hardship

 ON JUNE 28, 1914, in a letter to Ferenczi, Freud commented on "the surprising murder in Sarajevo." While the political consequences could not be foreseen, he did not think they would entail personal involvement, and he proceeded to discuss psychoanalytic matters. Freud tried to focus his thoughts on the Congress to be held in Dresden and whether all the Swiss members would resign in support of Jung before it took place. While in Karlsbad he heard the news of the German-Austrian declaration of war; he also received word from Abraham that the rest of the Swiss had followed Jung. "So we are at last rid of them, the brutal sanctimonious Jung and his disciples" (Freud/Abraham; July 26, 1914). He had been looking for friends who would not exploit and then betray him, and he congratulated himself that he had finally found them in the members of the Committee.

As late as July 29, Abraham was still convinced that the Congress would take place. Freud thought the only hitch would be that some of the *Ausländer* would be deterred from coming. Since no conflagration involving the major powers of Europe had occurred since 1815, the possibility of a general war was widely discounted. But the assassination of the Emperor's heir was to spark off simmering imperialist and economic rivalries. Serbia was supported by Austria's archenemy Russia. Quickly the brushfire spread. On July 28 Austro-Hungary, supported by Germany, declared war on Serbia. Germany then declared war on Russia (August 1) and on France (August 3), and attacked through Belgium. Britain responded with its declaration the following day.

Jones assured Freud that if there were any danger Freud could count on him to escort Anna home (July 27, 1914). On England's declaration of war against Germany, Jones, with questionable tact, informed Freud that no one had any doubt that Germany and Austria would be badly defeated (August 3, 1914). Jones arranged for Anna to return to Austria by a circuitous route, although he felt that she would be safer if she stayed in England. Evidently Freud preferred her to chance the hazards of war rather than to remain in the hands of the predatory Jones for an indefinite period.* Jones felt that it was his duty "to stay by my post" in his practice rather than join the war service (August 13, 1914). This meant, he told Freud, that he would be in a position to give financial help to Rank or any other members of the Committee who might need it.

With the outbreak of hostilities, Ferenczi's trip to England had to be cancelled. He wanted to use the money he had taken out of the bank for the journey for his postponed analysis with Freud. This seemed particularly important, as Elma Palos had just been married and he wasn't sure what his reaction was to her moving to America with her husband. He traveled to Vienna for a long weekend at the end of September, but was called back to Hungary to serve as a doctor in the hussars and was posted to Pápa, about eighty miles from Budapest. Nevertheless, he managed to get leave to go to Vienna for the last fortnight of October, where an analysis of sorts took place. He proposed to undergo self-analysis, but Freud predicted that it would inevitably be a failure. In a sense this was a tacit encouragement for Ferenczi to continue deluging Freud with his confidences.

By the middle of August Freud's composure was so shaken by the war that he was unable to work. To keep his mind occupied he planned to list his antiquities while Rank catalogued his library. With two of his sons in the army, Freud was caught up in patriotic fervor, rejoicing over the spectacular German victories on both the

---

*When reading through the correspondence for his life of Freud, on July 4, 1953, Jones wrote to Anna defending his pursuit of her: "He seems to have forgotten the existence of the sexual instinct, for I found you (and still do) most attractive. It is true I wanted to replace Loe, but felt no resentment against her for her departure, it was a relief from a burden. In any case, I have always loved you, and in quite an honest fashion."

eastern and western fronts. Jones seemed unaware of the moral implications of Germany's invasion of neutral Belgium. On November 15 he wrote to Freud:

> The only real reason that I can give for wanting our side to win is that on the whole the average Englishman is nearer and more sympathetic to me than the average German, especially the average Prussian. It is difficult to see what vital principle is involved in the conflict which is rather a boyish way of waiting to see which side is stronger, and not being able to agree on the point without testing it by force. Beyond a tremendous abreaction of pugnacity I don't suppose much will result from the whole war, for obviously Germany cannot win, nor can she be really crushed. . . .It looks, however, as though Germany will be left with an abiding hatred of England.

Freud affirmed that he could never regard Jones as an enemy. He told Abraham that his whole heart would be with the war "if I did not know England to be on the wrong side" (August 2, 1914). In his high flush of patriotism, he was irritated by Jones's prediction of a German defeat. Jones talked about the war, Freud told Ferenczi, "with the narrowminded outlook of the English" (Freud/ Ferenczi; November 25, 1914). But Jones continued to speak glowingly about how psychoanalysis would be the only salvation out of the nightmare. "That is why I feel that if the future of psychoanalysis had to be weighed with the future of our country I should side with the former."[1]

Freud became gloomier as the year approached its end. In the final months of 1914 the Germans, after the battle of Ypres, failed to break through the French lines, and the Russians stood firm before Krakow. A quick victory no longer seemed possible. The defections of Adler and Stekel had left the psychoanalytic movement shaken; now how would the war affect it? Freud could understand a rat deserting the sinking ship, he announced dramatically to Ferenczi. Germany did not deserve his sympathy for the way it had rejected psychoanalysis, so Freud did not feel that he and Ferenczi could speak of a "mutual fatherland" (Freud/Ferenczi; December 15, 1914). Nevertheless his eldest son, Martin, won a citation for gallantry for fighting in Russia, and Ernst was engaged in the war against the Italians. The third son, Oliver, worked as an army engineer. During this period Freud frequently dreamt of the death of his sons, which he interpreted as envy of their youth.

The members of the Committee did not show an excess of patriotism in joining the war effort. Ferenczi was constantly trying to pull strings in order to be transferred back to Budapest. Sachs was rejected for military service because of nearsightedness. Rank was trying to avoid conscription, "fighting like a lion against his Fatherland" (Freud/Ferenczi; December 2, 1914). Abraham found some consolation in the war. "I often think of how the war saved us from unpleasant discussions with the Swiss members. When it is over we shall go our separate ways" (February 28, 1915). Nevertheless, as a volunteer, in mid-March 1915, he was sent to head a hospital in Allenstein, in a distant part of East Prussia, where he remained for the rest of the war.

In September Freud was able to visit his daughter Sophie in Hamburg. On his return he stopped off in Berlin to pay his respects to Frau Abraham. (The most human aspect of his somewhat distant relationship with Abraham was the great interest Freud took in Abraham's two children.)

At the end of September, Freud finally managed a visit to Ferenczi at his regiment in Pápa, which gave a tremendous boost to Ferenczi's spirits, and he found himself writing short scientific articles again. On December 24 Freud told him about a discovery of plagiarism by Jones in a paper on "War and Sublimation," which he had published in a Swiss journal without proper attribution to Freud. Ferenczi replied (December 26, 1915) that he was aware of Jones's tendency to plagiarize, as Jones had already done it to him. Ferenczi's diagnosis was that Jones was creatively inhibited. "Despite all that, he is a good fellow."

During 1915 Jones managed to get an occasional letter through to Freud by way of Holland or Switzerland, but on June 17 he wrote anxiously that he had heard nothing from any members of the Committee for six months. Originally he had predicted that the war might continue until 1916 but now it appeared that it might stretch on indefinitely. For the time being the London Society was not holding meetings. There was a strong plea for doctors to join the British army, but Jones continued to insist that his first duty was to psychoanalysis, although he was willing to do some parttime volunteer work. Nevertheless, he managed to elude conscription. He was having Ferenczi's papers translated into English, news Ferenczi received through Rank (Ferenczi/Jones; May 15, 1915). Ferenczi was grateful for this gesture of sympathy "strong enough to survive even this isolation."

Rank had obtained his doctorate in 1912 from the University of Vienna with a dissertation on the epic, which led Freud to announce proudly to Abraham that Rank had solved "the riddle of Homer." The most prolific of all Freud's colleagues, Rank turned out one learned paper after another, kept the minutes of the Vienna Society, coedited two journals, and dealt with recalcitrant publishers. During early 1915 he encouraged Freud to work on twenty-eight lectures, which he delivered at the University of Vienna during the winter semesters of 1915–16 and 1916–17 and published as *Introductory Lectures on Psychoanalysis*.

In July 1915 Rank was conscripted into the ranks of the heavy artillery, but did not leave Vienna until January 1916, when he was posted to Krakow. For the next three years he edited the *Krakauer Zeitung*, an experience from which he gained confidence and mounting independence.

The only member of the Committee who was physically close to Freud during the war was Hanns Sachs. A man with a strong literary bent, Sachs had been trained as a lawyer, but had become an early member of the Wednesday evening sessions and had been devoted to Freud since he first attended his lectures in 1904. In July 1915 he was conscripted into the army service corps but was released twelve days later.

Censorship was such that Freud was unable to send manuscripts to Abraham. He now had to write to Jones in German, letters which took months to reach him. Occasionally Jones received a postcard from Rank, but no word at all from Sachs during 1916. In a letter of March 27, 1916, he told Freud that scarcely a day passed without his thinking of them all. He had hoped at one time to see them by Christmas, but trench warfare seemed to drag on interminably.

In Pápa, Ferenczi spent his time translating *Three Essays on Sexuality* into Hungarian and analyzing the company commandant while they rode about on horseback. His correspondence with Freud was hardly interrupted by the war, particularly as Ferenczi got his wish to be transferred back to Budapest, where he was put in charge of a neurological clinic. He also managed to reach Vienna in June 1916, when he finally had three weeks of analysis with Freud. Freud reserved two hours a day for him. Ferenczi shared meager meals with the Freud family and accompanied Freud on his daily walk around the Ringstrasse, but Freud insisted that no personal matters were to be discussed outside the analytic session.

After Ferenczi's departure Freud continued to have doubts about the advisability of the analysis, and in a remarkable letter of July 31, admitted his anxiety about advising Ferenczi to marry Frau Gizella. "Now I feel frightened," he confessed, "and I wish I had not advised anything, not because of cowardice or because of the responsibility, but because I feel insecure, and of course I am too involved to judge imperturbably on what would be best." Nevertheless, he approved Ferenczi's plan to return later in the summer for further analysis, which took place for three hours daily at the end of September. It is perhaps an indication of Freud's loneliness that he urged Ferenczi to resume the analysis, whereas in his precarious state of mind in 1913, he had discouraged him. On Ferenczi's return to Budapest he found it difficult to bridge the transitional role "from the confessing child to the letter writer who regards himself as a friend."

The *Jahrbuch* had to cease publication, but Freud relied on Ferenczi to keep the *Zeitschrift* alive in this difficult period. In addition, his role as Freud's Scheherazade continued with the neverending saga of his love life. Freud was also bombarded with questions. Was Ferenczi's father fixation so strong that he felt inhibited in heterosexual relations? What did Freud think when Ferenczi did not achieve full sexual satisfaction with Frau Gizella? Dreams were analyzed in depth. Freud's letters of advice were read by Frau Gizella, and her reactions reported to Freud, particularly her vow that she would never leave her lover.

In January 1917, Jones received a batch of letters from Freud. He

8. Eduard Silberstein with his wife Pauline, who was one of Freud's early and unfortunate patients.

9. The passionate duo: Freud and Wilhelm Fleiss.

10. Carl Jung, who refused to be subdued.

11. Loe Kann, who captivated both Ernest Jones and Sigmund Freud.

12. Elma Palos, loved by Ferenczi but rejected by Freud as a surrogate daughter-in-law.

13. Anna Freud in 1914 on the eve of her flight from Ernest Jones and enemy territory.

14. Ferenczi (*on right*) visiting Freud during his vacation in Hungary, 1917.

15. A good cigar, at last. With Jones in 1919.

16. Freud with his beloved Sophie who died in January 1920.

announced ecstatically that he actually seemed to hear Freud's voice speaking. After having a relationship with Lina for three years they had parted, and a month later Jones announced his marriage to Morfdd Owen, a musician, to whom he had proposed on their third meeting. Conveying the news to Abraham, Freud told him that Jones now "regards himself as a *reformed character*" (May 20, 1917).

Loe Kann was able to send the Freud family occasional food parcels through her brother in Holland. In Vienna food was scarce and heating was minimal; Freud had to wear his overcoat indoors. With electricity rationed, he could no longer work in the evenings. Hanns Sachs often sat with him, but Freud found him an unstimulating companion as he shivered in the cold. "I'm still the giant," Freud remarked complacently (Freud/Ferenczi; December 29, 1917).

There was an occasional gleam of light. In late 1916 the Dutch Psycho-Analytic Society was founded by Johann van Ophuijsen, who had earlier appeared to be a supporter of Jung's. Abraham's praise of Freud's *Introductory Lectures* gave Freud great satisfaction (January 13, 1917):

> Living in isolation as one does nowadays, one has vigorously to remind oneself that there are still a few people for whom it is worth writing. Otherwise one would forget and, though one would go on working for oneself, one would not commit it to paper.

The war seemed to be going badly, and Freud's sense of betrayal by the German government was such that he complained to Abraham that "Life bears too heavily with me" (May 20, 1917). World events were occurring with such bewildering rapidity that it was hard to have a fixed opinion on anything. On hearing of the outbreak of the Russian Revolution, Freud made the startling observation that he would have liked to have participated in that great change were it not that one's first concern was about peace (Freud/Ferenczi; March 25, 1917).

In February Ferenczi was discovered to have tuberculosis and a goiter disease. Ever reluctant to acknowledge organic disease in others, Freud described this as a flight into illness. He and Ferenczi had been collaborating on an exploration of Lamarck's theory on the inheritance of acquired characteristics to show how need transforms organs, and how the unconscious, through the omnipotence of thought, affects the body. Ferenczi's condition seemed dramatic proof of this. He was sent to a sanatorium in Semmering for three months, and although it was not far from Vienna, Freud could not find the energy or opportunity to visit him.

At one point there had apparently been some possibility of Ferenczi marrying Freud's oldest daughter, Mathilde. To console Ferenczi, who often complained that Frau Gizella was past the childbearing age, Freud told him that Mathilde appeared to be barren (February 3, 1917).

Lonely and ill, in his mountain isolation Ferenczi finally decided to marry Frau Gizella, his mistress of so many years, and again persuaded Freud to write to her with his endorsement of the idea. Freud could find no better solution for them, he wrote (March 23, 1917). He advised Gizella not to turn Ferenczi down in her concern that her daughter Elma might still be infatuated with Ferenczi. Elma was unhappy in her marriage, and her mother wanted to wait until her daughter returned from America before making a final decision about marrying Ferenczi. Freud was annoyed by this further delay: "Both of you have wasted such a large part of your life with hesitation that what remains of it is of special value" (April 9, 1917).

Meanwhile there was the vital question of where Freud would spend his summer holidays. Ferenczi urged him to consider Hungary. He recommended Csorbato, a beautiful spot in the Tatra Mountains, 4,000 feet above sea level. Ferenczi could arrange adequate accommodation for Freud's family, and food would be plentiful. He could not understand Freud's hesitation.

It was a measure of Freud's intimacy with Ferenczi that he was the only member of the Committee to whom Freud had confided his relationship with Fliess. But he did not tell Ferenczi the memories that Csorbato stirred up in him. In the summer of 1893 Fliess and his family had stayed in Csorbato. Freud, whose family was vacationing in Reichenau, had planned to make the eight-hour trip by train to visit his friend, but there had been a domestic crisis and

Martha had dismissed the cook and nurse. It was clear that she had raised a fuss about Freud joining his friend when she could not accompany him. Freud wrote to Fliess:

> The events at home had shown her how difficult it is to make arrangements for leaving the children; and for the past six years, since child followed child, there has been little room for change and relaxation in her life.[2]

As Fliess knew, Freud continued, he and Martha had been living in abstinence. (It is not clear why he had to include this detail in his long, garbled explanation as to why he was unable to come to Csorbato.) Martha had pointed out that Fliess could easily join Freud in Reichenau. But Fliess did not choose to do so, and Freud had had to endure a "terribly incomplete" year without seeing his friend.

Now, twenty-four years later, Freud had to be assured that Martha would find the accommodations in Csorbato to her liking. The two-month holiday, fortunately, was a wonderful respite for the whole family. In a letter to Abraham Freud described the Hungarians as "uncouth and noisy but obliging and hospitable and friendship and loyalty are taking the form of generosity, with the result that we are able to wallow in a superfluity of bread, butter, sausages, eggs, and cigars, rather like the chief of a primitive tribe" (July 21, 1917). Freud was even able to indulge his passion for mushroom hunting.

Freud and his colleagues were like an extended family during this holiday. Sachs and his girlfriend were accommodated nearby. Rank came during a brief furlough, and Max Eitingon, who was running a hospital in Miskolcz, paid Freud a visit. Ferenczi never seemed to see enough of him. Frau Gizella visited twice. Freud told Ferenczi he was shocked to see how old and worn she looked, but probably as a result of Freud's visit, the marriage was definitely decided on. Gizella broke the news to her husband, and she and Ferenczi began living apart for the six months required by Hungarian law before a divorce could take place.

Freud was pleased that a resolution had been found. On

November 20 he wrote Ferenczi a peculiar letter in which he commented on the age difference between Ferenczi and his fiancée:

> You emphasize that Frau G's signs of aging have frightened you. Those cannot be denied but are viewed from the wrong perspective by you. Maybe you will think that I, because I have grown old myself and no longer have access to youth, think you deserve an old woman. No, I wouldn't impose that on you, but it isn't a matter of choosing a woman.

Fifteen years before she had been a young, beautiful woman; she had aged with Ferenczi; and now they would simply have a comfortable relationship with each other (perhaps something like Freud's marriage). Besides, she had wonderful qualities Ferenczi wouldn't find in a young woman. Freud continued as though he had forgotten whether he was writing about Ferenczi or himself. He felt "used up" and the world was "repulsively disgusting" to him. If the war continued, all he could envisage was complete ruin for Germany (October 9, 1917). His superstitious idea that he was going to die in February 1918 was almost welcome.

Ferenczi dismissed Freud's mood of gloom in a letter dated December 13, 1917. He had experienced any number of "farewell moods" in Freud. "After that, there always followed a rejuvenation, and something beautiful for us, your students."

But 1918 was not a productive year for Freud. The food shortage in Vienna was critical, and his favorite meat and cigars were almost impossible to obtain. The Freuds occasionally received food parcels from Loe Kann or from Ferenczi and a rich Hungarian brewer, Anton von Freund, whom Freud had come to know the previous year while treating him for a neurosis following the removal of a sarcoma of the testicle. Freud feared that there would be a famine and was filled with gloom when he anticipated the future. Even the thought of a German victory was to be feared.[3]

In Budapest there was a general strike in January, with the workers demanding a peace settlement, universal suffrage, and the end of profiteering in foodstuffs. A recurrent theme of Ferenczi's letters was his difficulty in finding adequate housing. In March he visited

Eitingon at his hospital in Miskolcz, which he was running with his new wife, a former actress from Moscow. Ferenczi was very impressed by the dedication of this man with the stammer who had been introduced to psychoanalysis through Jung while working at the Burghölzli. Freud always remembered that Eitingon was the first person from a foreign country to arrive at the Vienna Psychoanalytic Society on January 23, 1907.

Ferenczi wrote to Freud regarding the energetic activity within the Hungarian Psychoanalytic Society, particularly with the introduction of some promising new members such as Michael Balint.

Rank continued to suffer from depression in Krakow, but the amazingly resilient Abraham reported from Allenstein that as soon as there was any hope of peace he had all sorts of scientific plans to put into motion. Freud replied (January 18, 1918) that "Your equable temperament and indestructible vitality stand up well to my alternations between cheerfulness and resignation." Freud admitted that there were some signs of hope, as the Dutch Society was attacking Jung effectively. Abraham was enormously impressed by Ferenczi's paper, "Two Types of War Neurosis," which he thought might well be the best thing he had yet produced. Abraham himself had already started to write a paper for the next Congress, which he expected to be held before the end of the year.

The summer holiday for 1918 was a return to Csorbato during August, and in September the family moved to nearby Lomnitz. Ferenczi felt disappointed that he and Freud had not been able to cooperate on some joint work during this period, "the very opposite of the Palermo situation," when Ferenczi had sullenly refused to work with Freud.[4]

Abraham continued to press for a Congress. At first Breslau was considered; but Ferenczi suggested Budapest, supported by Rank and von Freund, who was by then apparently considered an adjunct member of the Committee. In the form of a *petit comité*, they proceeded to send telegrams all over Europe announcing that the Fifth International Psychoanalytic Congress would be held in the hall of the Hungarian Academy of Sciences on September 28 and 29, 1918. This was remarkable, considering that Austro-Hungary had sued for a separate peace, which had been repudiated by the Allies.

Freud was concerned that the Germans, particularly Abraham, might not be able to attend, but his fears were groundless. Almost all the members at the Congress, except Freud and his Dutch colleagues, were in uniform. The Swiss did not attend. The civic officials granted the members a welcome beyond their wildest expectations. Ferenczi was chosen as the next president of the International Association, and in a paper, "Lines of Advance in Psycho-Analytic Therapy," Freud predicted that Budapest would become the world-center of psychoanalysis. His prognosis was based partly on the fact that von Freund had established a generously endowed foundation for the development of psychoanalysis, primarily as a means of supporting an independent psychoanalytic publishing house.

On his return to Vienna, Freud wrote a deeply emotional letter to Ferenczi (September 30, 1918): "I bask in satisfaction and I am easy at heart to see my frail child of much care, the labor of my life, protected and in safekeeping for the future," thanks to Ferenczi and others. He hoped to see firm cooperation between Ferenczi and von Freund, "the man whom providence has sent to us at the right moment," along with Rank, "who could not be replaced by anyone else." He intended to watch from the sidelines "how well the younger generation is handling things which the finite powers and life-span of age" could not achieve.

For the moment Sachs seemed out of action. On the eve of the Congress he began to spit blood and had to be taken to a Budapest hospital. He had contracted tuberculosis, and Freud believed it was a terminal case. He was moved to Davos, where von Freund arranged to have his expenses paid out of the foundation (Ferenczi/ Freud; October 8, 1918). Freud was not altogether pleased to see the money used this way.[5] A few days later he felt impelled to assure Ferenczi that no ill will was involved in his reaction, simply "the general disinclination as to good deeds ad hominem—and the pedagogic intent not to interfere with aid before the means of the party in question are exhausted" (October 20, 1918). In Hungary he had started to analyze his daughter Anna and reported that her analysis was progressing splendidly, "otherwise my cases are uninteresting." Was there any significance in the fact that he began to analyze Anna at a moment when Ferenczi had been handed over to the mother figure Gizella?

The Ministry of War had approached Ferenczi about establishing some sort of clinic for veterans in Budapest. He suggested Eitingon as his assistant, but there was opposition because he was not a Hungarian. Then in October a petition was circulated with 180 signatures, requesting the rector of the university to allow Ferenczi to give a course on psychoanalysis.

Ferenczi was extremely depressed about what the fate of psychoanalysis would be when Count Mihály Karolyi attempted to dissociate Hungary from Austria. Freud was extremely critical of this "undignified haste" to sever ties with Austria and advised Ferenczi "to retrieve your libido in good time from the fatherland and give it shelter in psychoanalysis, for otherwise you will suffer" (October 27, 1918). He gave Ferenczi a psychoanalytic explanation of his depression which Freud said was

> a neurosis common in wartime. It involves the conflict of two ego-ideals, the customary one and the one forced by the war; the latter is based entirely on new relationships to objects (superiors, comrades) and can be likened to object-fixation, a choice of objects not equitable to the ego, so to speak. Therefore this conflict can be manifested as in a psycho neurosis . . . developing a new ego owing to a libidinous object-fixation, to be overthrown by the former one; a battle with the ego rather than between the ego and the libido, yet fundamentally the same.
>
> A parallel can be drawn to melancholia, where a new ego would also have to be created, but here we do not deal with an ideal but an *abandoned* ego-fixation.

Their world was falling apart. On October 4 the Austro-Hungarian government dispatched a note to the United States, offering to make peace on the basis of President Wilson's Fourteen Points. When Freud wrote to Ferenczi on October 3 he could not have known that on October 18 Wilson would reject the proposal, no longer accepting the autonomy of the nations within the Austro-Hungarian Empire. On October 27 the Emperor agreed to accept an armistice on almost any terms.

But the aborted settlement at the beginning of October indicated that the end of the war was in sight. "How good it is to have one's small interests," Freud sighed, "for the great general ones would yield no satisfaction." He had heard from Rank in Krakow, who wanted to resume his career in Vienna as soon as possible, and Freud planned to put him in charge of the new psychoanalytic publishing venture made possible by von Freund's gift.

On November 9 Freud received a card from Jan van Emden in Holland announcing the death of Jones's young wife. "The poor man," Freud commiserated with Ferenczi. "We do not even have the possibility of conveying our sympathy directly" (November 9, 1918). Freud eventually received a letter from Jones, dated October 4, in which Jones told him of his staggering blow.* He wrote that he hoped that once the war was over Freud would come to England for a rest. Over the years he would urge Freud many times to visit England.

Jones wrote again on December 7. He was looking forward eagerly to a Congress in the autumn of 1919 so that the Association could be reorganized. He also had plans for an English journal or an English edition of the *Zeitschrift*. "There are so many things to talk over," he wrote. As for his own feelings,

> You see I can look forward to life, although I have been through hell itself these last three months. It has been an indescribably terrible experience, signifying more even than a tremendous loss—owing to my inner psychical situation and the poignant circumstances of my wife's death. But I am surely winning through, and have learnt very much by it. Yesterday I read your paper on grief and melancholy, which made a great impression on me. Do you remember talking to me in January 1914 and saying that would be the next advance? I have much analytic experience of it now, and I agree with all you say except one important particular.

On the last day of the year Jones received a letter from Freud posted six weeks earlier. He responded:

---

*Apparently she died of a ruptured appendix. See Jones's incoherent account in *Free Association* (Basic Books, 1959), pp. 254-255.

I was *so* glad to see your handwriting again to know that you are well, and to read your kind words to me. You know that you and psychoanalysis are everything to me, especially now when life is otherwise so drear and empty. Tomorrow, New Year's Day, I shall be forty, and life's greatest happiness is past, forever.

Jones begged Freud, however, not to fear that he would lose heart for psychoanalysis.

Freud was somewhat concerned about Rank's future. In 1908, at the time Rank entered the University of Vienna, he had changed his name from Rosenfeld and had converted to Catholicism. In October 1918 in Krakow, however, he reconverted to Judaism in order to have a Jewish marriage to Beata Mincer, a beautiful young woman who had been helping him with his work on *Imago*, which he had kept alive during the war years.

Both Freud and Ferenczi had misgivings about Rank's marriage.* For a time it looked as though Rank and his new wife would settle in Budapest, since the money for a new publishing venture was being donated by von Freund. Freud was disturbed by this train of events because "I cannot proceed here without him" (November 27, 1918).

Abraham was discharged from the military on December 15 after suffering a severe bout of dysentery. With the future altogether uncertain for all of them, on December 26 Ferenczi wrote to Freud: "The sole consolation which sustains me is the optimism which I owe to belonging to psychoanalysis, a discipline which without any doubt belongs to the future."

---

*Years later Rank told Anaïs Nin that Freud had hoped he would marry Anna Freud.

Chapter Five

Mustering the Troops

THE VERSAILLES peace conference ending World War I opened proceedings on January 18, 1919. Three days before this Freud wrote Jones that although the war had ended officially on November 11, the last months were the worst since 1914, and that the armistice conditions were such that they seemed tantamount to a continuation of hostilities. The closing of the borders made the Austrians feel like rats caught in a trap. Czechoslovakian coal could not be shipped across the frontier. Hungry and half-frozen, the Austrians succumbed to influenza and tuberculosis.

Freud reprimanded Jones—so full of blithe plans for resuming the life of the psychoanalytic movement—for being totally ignorant about the abysmal conditions in Austria. It was also unrealistic, he wrote, to talk about a projected Congress when Ferenczi and von Freund were cut off in Hungary. Moreover, von Freund's malignancy had reappeared, and Freud anticipated his almost certain death which would be a terrible blow to the movement and to Freud personally. "I can't remember a time of my life when my horizon was so thickly veiled by dark clouds or if so I was younger then and not vexed by the ailments that come with the onset of old age" (May 23, 1919).

Jones was busy reconstituting his psychoanalytic group, now known as the British Psycho-Analytical Society and purged of Jungian elements. He was attempting by every avenue to reach Vienna. His alleged plan to investigate the work done there on war shock was refused by the British authorities. Eventually he succeeded in reaching Berne on March 15, where he met Rank, who was already in negotiations with a publisher about the possibility of issuing the various psychoanalytic journals. There was a joyful reunion with a reinvigorated Sachs two days later. During the war the Committee had seemed a figment of their collective imagination. The meeting of the three members was reassurance that it actually existed.

In his life of Freud, Jones later described his astonishment at the remarkable changes he had noticed in Rank:

> I had last seen him a weedy youth, timid and deferential, much given to clicking of heels and bowing. Now in stalked a wary, tough man with a masterful air whose first act was to deposit on the table a huge revolver. I asked him what he wanted with it, and he nonchalantly replied: *"Für alle Fälle"* (for any eventuality). How had he got it through the frontier examination? When the official pointed to the bulging pocket Rank had calmly answered "bread." The change had coincided with his resuming his work in Vienna after the war years spent in Krakow. At the time his Viennese friends connected it with some response to his recent marriage, but later on it became plain that it must have been a hypomania reaction to the three severe attacks of melancholia he had suffered while in Krakow.[1]

However, on March 17, 1919, Jones wrote to Freud:

> Rank I find greatly improved, more independent, self-confident, and manly. I admire his quick brains and sure judgment. We get on splendidly together, and I think you may feel safe in leaving things in our hands; we agreed about everything and shall have done a good deal of business before we separate.

Freud sent the letter on to Ferenczi to keep him informed of developments. The "business" Jones and Rank were sharing was the establishment of the international psychoanalytic publishing house (the *Verlag*), with its management to be shared by the two men. An English journal, Jones's pet project, would be printed in Austria or Czechoslovakia where costs were lower (this eventually led to delays and other difficulties). To Freud's great relief, Rank had returned from Budapest to settle permanently in Vienna. In

Freud's weakened condition he found Rank even more indispensable than before the war. The Rank who emerges from Freud's letters to Ferenczi is slightly different from the paragon depicted to Jones. To Ferenczi Freud attributes Rank's frenzied plunge into work to the need "possibly to rehabilitate himself for his marriage" (January 1, 1919). Freud sent patients to Rank to help him eke out a living. (Rank's qualifications as an analyst were later to be questioned by Jones.) Rank's daughter (and only child), Helene, was born in August.

Jones became increasingly exasperated by Freud's constant praise of Rank. On June 19 Freud wrote, "Rank is of great help to me in these times." On July 28, he reported that Rank was "doing all the work, performing the possible and the impossible alike. I dare say, you know him for what he is, the truest, most reliable, most charming of helpers, the column which is bearing the edifice. I have given him full power to decide as I recognise this superiority in managing these intricate practical matters." Jones managed to respond generously (August 7, 1919): "I am fully in accord with your opinion of Rank, and have boundless admiration both for his capacity and his character. We are in regular communication over our mutual affairs, and are both confident about them in spite of the difficulties." Jones too wanted to be indispensable to Freud.

It was almost as though Freud was deliberately trying to stir up sibling rivalry. At the end of the year Rank went to Holland to make initial arrangements for a Congress in 1920 and was held up by a railway strike. On December 8 Jones made the irritable remark that if Rank had to wait over in Holland it was "largely his own fault, but one cannot wonder that so much contact with the political atmosphere of Vienna has impaired his contact with the outer world." Freud replied sharply (December 23, 1919): "In your remarks on Rank I noticed a harshness which reminded me of a similar mood regarding Abraham. You used kinder language during the war. I hope nothing is wrong between you and ours." Jones replied hurriedly: "You may rest quite assured, as you must be already from talking with Rank, that I have no trace of harsh feeling towards him or Abraham. Some momentary impatience on my part, of no importance, must have produced the impressions on you. I am entirely devoted to every member of our committee" (January 16, 1920).

After their joyful reunion in March, Rank, Jones, and Sachs traveled together to Lucerne, Zurich, and Geneva. From the Hotel St. Gothard in Zurich, Jones reported on March 25:

> It has been wonderfully good to be again with such sympathetic and lively spirits as Rank and Sachs, and I am filled with admiration for their qualities. It is a treat to watch how they turn these stupid and confused Swiss round their little finger. And you can imagine what jokes we all have together.

In Zurich they addressed the newly founded Swiss Psychoanalytic Society, where Sachs, with schoolboyish arrogance, rather than twisting the Swiss around his little finger, insulted Oscar Pfister by suggesting that he resign because he did not seem sufficiently emphatic about sexuality forming the basis of psychoanalysis. Freud was not amused because he did not want to lose Pfister. He had to act as umpire, gently chiding Pfister that perhaps Jung's influence had penetrated his thinking deeper than he realized.

Jones returned to London "full of inspiration for the great work in front of us" (April 2, 1919). He was convinced that the *International Journal of Psycho-Analysis*, which was about to be launched, and the projected psychoanalytic bookstore in London could operate without any financial assistance from von Freund's foundation in Budapest. As for the next Congress, the Committee would have an important role to play. Since it existed both to direct the "external side of the movement" and also to coordinate the "internal, scientific side," Jones suggested to Freud a private Committee meeting of their own, lasting about a week, to be held a fortnight before the Congress in order to discuss the programs planned for the Congress and the more difficult scientific issues that were not usually brought before the public. "Remember," he concluded, "that e.g. Abraham and I have not been in close touch with you, and how important it is to be quite clear amongst ourselves and to present a united front (Unity of command; the great cry of the Entente for the last two years!)."

But as 1919 advanced, Freud began to discourage these enthusiastic plans. At the beginning of the year von Freund had arrived in Vienna to be treated for the recurrence of his cancer. To Ferenczi, Freud interpreted von Freund's illness as the result of his disappointment over not being able to make his father figure rich (January 6, 1919). Freud had given von Freund one of the precious rings in anticipation of making him a formal member of the Committee. For a time Ferenczi indulged Freud in his view of von Freund's neurosis, but in June, on von Freund's return to Budapest, Ferenczi wrote that he was impressed by the heroic way von Freund was reacting to radium treatment: "He can no longer be described as a neurotic; he is so reasonable, intuitive, wise, coming to terms with things, making real decisions, keeping busy" (June 6, 1919).

Some members of the Committee were making fresh beginnings—or accepting the disappointment that beginnings could not be created. On February 17 Eitingon opened up his heart to Freud:

> May I report something about myself, Professor? A deep depression with severe feelings of inadequacy which has plagued me for years and on my return at the end of the war was particularly bad for a short time, is bound up with a narcissistic condition: that we are denied children.[2]

Ferenczi, who also wanted children, at the beginning of March finally married Gizella, who was beyond the age of childbearing.* Freud, in his congratulatory letter, sounds like a relieved mother: "I have often, when thinking of putting my affairs in order and contemplating taking leave, been anxious with worry about how both of you, who have become so dear to me, will fare in the future, an anxiety which has now been put to rest" (March 4, 1919). Ferenczi in turn was hopeful that the marriage would help his relationship with Freud. "Neurotic inhibitions" that had prevented his feeling sufficiently grateful to Freud might now be removed (March 18, 1919). He also reported the bizarre circumstance of Gizella's former husband dropping dead of a heart attack on the day of the wedding.

---

*The Ferenczi letters indicate a possibility that Freud gave Gizella a ring at this time.

In August Jones returned to Switzerland, confident that this time he and Sachs could manage to get to Vienna. In Basel he met a Viennese Jewish woman, Katharine Jokl, and proposed to her on their third meeting—a remarkable example of his repetition compulsion. On October 11 they were married in Zurich, and the following day he wrote to Freud: "Everything augurs perfectly for a most successful married life, which means for me a new life altogether in both happiness and inspiration to activity."

Ferenczi and Gizella had chosen an awkward time to be married: in March a Communist regime under Béla Kun seized power in Hungary. Doctors were paid a fixed salary, there were severe restrictions on food and all possessions, and Ferenczi moved into Gizella's "Socialized" apartment for the time being. Problems began to arise in regard to von Freund's foundation; the $500,000 that Freud described in a letter to Ferenczi as the "Niebelung-treasure" (October 7, 1919) was rapidly dwindling away with the depreciation of the Hungarian currency. At the end of April Ferenczi was appointed a full professor, a situation that would be changed by a right-wing counterrevolution in August.

Full of anxiety over von Freund and the emotions stirred up by moving to a new home, Ferenczi wrote to Freud that he had discovered the thick bundle of letters Freud had written to him over the past ten years (May 23, 1919).

> Here was the whole new genesis of recent psychoanalysis displayed. At the same time they are a testimony to how much affection, great solicitude, dare I say even love, with which you have supervised, guided, protected *my*, oh so difficult development.

Ferenczi wrote that he realized that he had been very touchy since, as Freud's "devoted son," he had obeyed Freud's advice by resisting the temptation of Elma Palos, and eventually marrying her mother Gizella. But there were still problems in his relationships with both Gizella and Freud. His assumption was that it was his obstinacy that prevented these relationships from being perfect. Nevertheless, he wrote:

I am willing to renew a candid, free relationship with you, devoid of petty feelings—or rather, perhaps to start it. It seems to me that I can only enjoy life and be productive in work if I am in good, or even the best relations with you and can remain that way.

Freud became anxious because letters from Ferenczi were slow in reaching Vienna due to the political situation. They had hoped to have a reunion during the summer, but Ferenczi, like Jones, could not get into Austria. Martha Freud had to go into a sanatorium near Salzburg to recover from the flu, while Minna Bernays and Freud went off on holiday to Badensee in the Bavarian Alps. The money for this trip was lent to Freud by Eitingon. Freud scrupulously repaid him six months later.

Admiral Horthy became regent of Hungary in August, heading an anti-Semitic, ultra-rightist government. Ferenczi wrote Freud that he longed to get out of this "hell," in which a red nightmare was replaced by a white one. Prices were exorbitant, Gizella had difficulty finding food, and one could not go out after dark for fear of arrest as a Bolshevik.

The best way for psychoanalysis to flourish would be in total seclusion and without any fanfare, just continuing to work. Personally this trauma will serve to discard certain prejudged notions, developed in childhood, to come to terms with the bitter truth that as a Jew one is *truly* without a country. Thus the released libido should be divided between the few friends one had managed to save from this debacle, the only devoted soul through thick and thin, and through science. You shall have to forgive me if during the coming times, I shall more often than before search for the opportunity to be able to talk to you intimately, or at least through correspondence.[3]

Both men were longing for a meeting in Vienna at the end of September. As Freud reminded Ferenczi (September 9, 1919), it was the first time they had been separated for a whole year. Forgetting that Ferenczi had been married earlier in the year, Freud remarked that it was probably the worst year in Ferenczi's life, just as it had been for him.

You must know just how much I have missed you during this year. It would have been more painful still had I not been in anguish about the threatened fate of Toni [von Freund] at the same time. He will never know how much he has affected me and how great a part he has played in my aging.

His hopes for the future resided in Ferenczi, whose "Hysterie und Pathoneurosis" (Hysteria and Pathoneurosis) he found "pure analytical gold."

In an entirely different mood, on July 10, Freud sent Ferenczi a report of the suicide of a Viennese Society member, Victor Tausk, who had felt that Freud had deserted him when he handed over Tausk's analysis to Helene Deutsch.* Tausk had suffered a severe vomiting attack at the Budapest Congress the previous year. To Abraham Freud remarked coolly: "He was crushed by his past and his war experiences, was supposed to marry this week, could not pull himself together any more. For all his significant talent he was useless to us" (July 6, 1919). To Ferenczi he wrote: "The reasons [for Tausk's suicide] are obscure, probably impotence and the final act of his infantile battle against the spectre of the father. In spite of crediting his talents I cannot generate much sympathy" (July 10, 1919).

Early in September Freud was reunited with Abraham in Berlin on Freud's return from a visit with his daughter Sophie Halberstadt in Hamburg. Sachs's health seemed to confine him to Switzerland, and it became increasingly clear to Freud that Sachs had no inclination to return to Vienna. In Berne, Jones managed to obtain a travel permit from the Austrian consul, who seemed surprised that anyone would want to go to Vienna. Staying once more at the Hotel Regina, on September 27 Jones made his way to Berggasse 19, where a grayer, thinner Freud greeted him. A few minutes later an excited Ferenczi rushed into the room and kissed Jones on both cheeks. After a separation of six years it was a moving moment for the three men. The next day Jones hosted a luncheon at the

---

*See Paul Roazen, *Brother Animal* (New York: Alfred A. Knopf, 1969).

Hotel Cobenzl. He was saddened to see how emaciated the Freud family had become.

Some major decisions were made at this time by the three men. Because of Hungary's isolated position, it did not seem expedient for Ferenczi to continue as president of the Association, and Jones agreed to take on the acting presidency. He later wrote Freud, "I look forward to my responsibilities very seriously, but without apprehension, being well-informed of the general situation and having the best friends around me" (October 12, 1919).

During this visit Freud suggested that Eitingon take the place on the Committee destined for the dying von Freund. On October 12 this was communicated to Eitingon by Abraham, who was busy reestablishing the Berlin group. On November 1 Eitingon assured Freud of his "constantly growing devotion to you and your work":

> I hope to make good personal contact with those gentlemen [the Committee] whom I have respected for years and have regarded as a small nucleus. I have already with Abraham and Ferenczi; and hope in the meanwhile to build up a personal relationship with the others by correspondence.[4]

Life in Vienna continued to be difficult. In October Freud hired an English teacher. He wrote Eitingon (October 12, 1919): "The situation here is hopeless and will doubtless remain so. I believe that England will be willing to allow former enemies to enter by the time I have spent the last of my savings, in about eighteen months from now. My two brothers already rest in English soil; perhaps I shall also find room there."[5] For the time being he increased the number of his patients and demanded payment in their own currency from the British and American patients Jones sent to him.

Anton von Freund died on January 21, 1920. Freud had been expecting his death, but had grown so fond of him that his loss was very painful. The only consolation was that the foundation appeared strong enough to support the newly established psychoanalytic publishing house, the Internationaler Psychoanalytischer Verlag, until at least the end of the year. Just before his death von

Freund had transferred another 11,000 kronen to Freud, who planned to use it for the furtherance of lay analysis. Von Freund had stipulated that his ring was to be returned to Freud, but von Freund's widow refused to part with it, so Freud gave Eitingon his own ring incised with the head of Jupiter.

On January 26 Freud's beloved daughter Sophie succumbed to complications resulting from post-war influenza. Martha Freud, who was particularly close to her daughter, was overwhelmed with grief, but Freud—who for years had expected the death of one of his sons—withdrew into numb stoicism. To Eitingon, who attended the cremation, he wrote: "I do not know what more there is to say. It is such a paralyzing event, which can stir no afterthoughts when one is not a believer and so is spared all the conflicts that go with that. Blunt necessity, mute submission" (February 3, 1920).[6]

Abraham had ambitious plans for the future of his Society. A Poliklinik opened in Berlin on February 14, with generous support from Eitingon, whose family money was derived from branches of the fur trade. Abraham had the reputation of being the best clinician in the group, and the growth of his Society created considerable envy. Ferenczi, on the other hand, felt deeply discouraged about his own future. Elma had returned from America, and in the same letter in which Freud announced von Freund's death, he informed Ferenczi that "your Elma" had visited them, still "beautiful and blooming," and that he was "overjoyed" to hear that she had reconciled with her husband, who would take her back to America in the summer. When Ferenczi complained about his difficult living conditions, Freud responded that they could not be worse than his. When Ferenczi expressed a longing to emigrate to America, Freud discouraged him with an account of his own difficulties in handling a foreign language (March 15, 1920). He added a clinching argument:

> Analysis has undoubtedly been started very well in Hungary, but with your departure everything would collapse. Your life plan should by no means take me into consideration. I am certainly far too old to face the stress of the situation for long.

In other words, Ferenczi's first priority must always be Freud. After all, the Verlag was suffering from "10,000 additional difficulties." Even Rank, "who is always so brave," appeared depressed and not as efficient as usual, but Freud wanted to believe that it was probably only a temporary state of mind.

But Ferenczi refused to be deterred from his plan to emigrate. In his view psychoanalysis was so well established in Budapest that it could function adequately without him. He wanted Freud to write to A. A. Brill in New York asking him about the steps necessary to settle in America. Ferenczi believed that he would not have to work such punishing hours to make ends meet in America and thus could devote more time to scientific writing. For the moment there seemed no hope of a practice in Vienna, but if Freud thought Holland or Switzerland was a possibility, he would happily change his intentions of moving to America. "What I would really like to do is to move wherever you are"; but since this was an impossibility, America seemed the only alternative. "It would be a frightfully long distance for us to be apart,—but—for years have we not been in the same quandary?—And have we any expectation that things will be different?"[7] Nevertheless, Freud refused to modify his reluctance to Ferenczi's departure from Europe.

During the war most of Freud's patients had been Hungarians referred by Ferenczi. Now he admitted that he could not make ends meet without the patients Jones sent to him. These included James Strachey of the well-known literary family. Jones's view of him was that he was "a good fellow but weak and perhaps lacking in tenacity" (May 7, 1920). But Strachey would prove very valuable to Freud in his later translation of Freud's complete works into English.

There had been hopes of having a full Committee meeting in Vienna at Easter, but Abraham and Eitingon were unable to cut through the red tape to obtain permits to travel from Germany to Austria. Jones joined Rank, Sachs, and Ferenczi for a *petit comité* from March 30 to April 9. There was a wonderful evening during this period in which Freud discoursed on new ideas and plans. Gradually the movement was being reestablished.

Jones had inherited £1,000 from his father, who had died the previous February. With Freud's help, he managed to convince Rank to accept £50 a year as part of Jones's donation to the Verlag. Jones argued that it was far preferable that the money should come from a member of the Committee than from some outside donor such as a rich American. Clearly he was trying to appease Freud for his negative feelings about Rank. He also planned to give the Verlag a substantial portion of his inheritance. After all, as he wrote effusively to Freud:

> To me it is clear that I owe my career, my livelihood, my position, and my capacity of happiness in marriage—in short, everything to you and the work you have done. Besides these outstanding facts the small services I may be able to render must always weigh light in the balance, and I cannot hope to redress it. But gratitude is an emotion I can endure well, which as you know is not always the case.[8]

Among the subjects discussed at the Easter meeting were plans for a Congress in The Hague in September. Abraham was furious when he heard of this. He was determined to have the Congress in Berlin, and he accused Jones of imposing his will on the Committee. Jones reminded him that the possibility of The Hague had been raised at the Budapest Congress, and that the other members of the Committee had supported the idea when he elicited their views. It was important to have it in The Hague in order to attract "the Westerners":

> Rank would tell you that the Verlag is nearly at the end of its resources, and the existence of the *Zeitschrift*, the new journal, and Rank's own livelihood (what would our investment be without him?) depends to a very great extent on widening the support of the Westerners.
> One cannot balance the preferences of the Easterners and Westerners fairly, for the psychological situation is different in the two cases. The loyalty of the former is well-established, that of the latter is not, and though it may seem unjust to put a further strain on the former, yet it is definitely in our interests to do so provided only that it is at all possible.
> . . . I think it highly desirable to make the whole movement and

Association as international as possible, which would be well served by holding our Congress in a neutral country.

Jones informed Freud of the contents of this letter to Abraham. He added that at a meeting of the British Society he had raised the matter, and that the members had been of the opinion that a Berlin Congress "would harm the cause greatly in England by reinforcing the view of psychoanalysis as a German decadent science, and not an international movement which we want it to be" (January 16, 1920). He gently hinted that if Freud stood behind him, he was convinced that he could "put things objectively to Abraham in such a way as to appease him, for he is a very reasonable and clear man." Freud agreed with Jones that it was essential to attract the Westerners and that he would "struggle with you against Abraham" (January 6, 1920). Rank lent his support, and Jones pleaded with Abraham once more:

> Ask yourself how Germans would feel spending some days in Paris in hotels, restaurants, etc., and remember that Berlin is to us what Paris doubtless is to you. There are very few Jewish Internationals in American Ps.A., and none in England. It is hard to say how far this feeling would operate in fact, but it exists . . . .[9]

Abraham was not so much moved by his argument as by Freud's decision that von Freund's foundation would pay the travel expenses of the European members, while the Dutch would provide their lodging.

The diminishing funds of the foundation received an infusion of 1,000 kronen given to Eitingon by his relatives in New York. In his announcement of the joyful news, Freud warned Ferenczi that "it must not be known beyond our intimate circle and Eitingon himself demanded that his name should not be connected with it" (May 14, 1920). It meant, too, that Freud was finally able to raise the salaries of Rank and Theodore Reik, who was assisting Rank with the editorial work.

By May opposition to psychoanalysis in official medical circles in Budapest had grown to the point that Ferenczi was expelled from the Medical Society. Freud congratulated him ironically on his "public distinction" and hoped that he would not be too downcast (June 17, 1920). Personal and professional questions were as intertwined for Ferenczi as they had been before the war, and he continued to pine after Elma; and in what seemed an attempt to impose guilt on Freud, he confessed to feeling badly that he could not love his wife as he should.

Ferenczi was plunged into a deep depression all that summer. He and Gizella booked rooms in Aussee, hoping that Freud might lift his spirits by joining them. But since Ferenczi's marriage, Freud was more elusive than he had been in the past. He had already arranged to go to Gastein with Minna and to accompany Anna to Hamburg to visit his grandchildren at the end of August before proceeding to The Hague. On hearing this disappointing news, Ferenczi wrote plaintively, "Do you think it will ever be possible to spend the summer close to each other?" Even their correspondence, which was supposed to complement their personal talks, was slackening off.[10]

Abraham, frustrated by the rejection of Berlin as the site for the Congress, was determined to entice Freud to deliver some lectures there before Freud departed for Holland. On August 2 Freud wrote peevishly to Jones: "Really I am not in a condition now to woo for the affection of the prudish intellectual beauties of Berlin. I see you were right, Prussianity is very strong with Abraham." Jones, too, was pressing Freud to visit England after the Congress. Freud sighed, "I feel so tired." After the domestic peace of the war years, Freud was finding the return of his adopted sons a mixed blessing.

Chapter Six

A Band of Brothers

THE SIXTH Congress of the International Psychoanalytic Association was held September 8 through 12, 1920, with fifty-seven guests attending. Jones was confirmed as president, and Abraham, a gifted linguist, gave the opening address in Latin in order to avoid offending any national sensibilities. Freud presented a paper on "Supplements to the Theory of Dreams," and Ferenczi gave one on "Further Developments of an Active Therapy in Psycho-Analysis," based in part on his recent analysis of the Polish woman, Eugenia Sokolnicka, whose progress Ferenczi had reported in detail to Freud.*

Since Freud arrived in The Hague on the eve of the Congress, the Committee meeting was held after the departure of the other members. It was the first complete gathering of the current group, which now counted Eitingon as a full-fledged member. Jones, as the initiator of the Committee, was named chairman. On this occasion Freud proposed that they exchange *Rundbriefe*, or circular letters, on a regular basis. The letters would be written at weekly intervals, each writing on the same day. Jones would write from London (in English); Abraham and Eitingon, with Sachs (who was soon to join them) from Berlin; Rank (after discussion with Freud) from Vienna; and Ferenczi from Budapest. The initiation of the *Rundbriefe* was the first practical act of the Committee. During his tenure as president of the International Association, Jung had oc-

---

*Freud thoroughly approved of the technique Ferenczi was using with her, but described her as an intelligent but "repulsive person," who could not accept that she was growing old (June 6, 1920). She was forty-three years old at the time.

casionally sent official circular letters to members of the branch societies, letters that served as prototypes for the *Rundbriefe*. Freud had learned a profound lesson from his experience with Jung: only by some such centralizing device could Freud be sure that the business of the International Association was being conducted effectively. With his neurotic anxiety about receiving mail, the circular letters were a means of allaying concern about what might be happening and of maintaining control over the whole organization. These round-robin letters were in effect a means of keeping the troops in line, for each correspondent was actually reporting to the commander.

The letters ranged from two to seven typewritten pages. After a number of general comments and an account of the situation in each society, the questions raised by the respective members would be answered in turn. Abraham soon suggested that they address each other with the familiar *du*, since they were all brothers. Each member was assigned an area of psychoanalytic literature to review.

Ferenczi was the first to write on September 20. His letter took only three days to reach London. The faithful Gizella had transcribed it by hand. Ferenczi set out a proposed agenda: the letters would contain scientific matters and personal information, but politics were to be excluded. He also suggested that all the societies have a common set of admission standards and that all members should be consulted when a new member was to be introduced. Jones disagreed strongly with the proposal for common standards, objecting that it would introduce difficult bureaucratic procedures. In addition, there was the unstated fact that he and Abraham, who were building up strong local societies, did not want any interference with their autonomy. As a final note, Jones announced that his wife had given birth to a daughter the previous day (October 7, 1920).*

On October 4 Freud wrote to Jones that the previous evening, while driving along the Danube with Rank and Sachs, the three men had decided on the content of their first letter:

---

*In a previous letter to Jones, Freud had described the birth of one's first child as "one of the queerest and most exalted situations in life, the beginning of infinite happiness and endless cares" (October 4, 1920).

I feel very proud of the Congress and as I proclaimed in my improvisation highly relieved by the conviction that men like you, Ferenczi, Abraham, Rank, etc. are apt and ready to supplant me. The remainder of my time and powers I will have to devote to the duty of providing for my family, that is to say to making money, but if scientific interest, which just now is asleep with me, gets aroused in the course of time I may still be able to bring some new contribution to our unfinished work. Scientific interchange among the members of the Committee seems a highly important task for the future; too much of our relations has been taken up by business interests in these last months.

The centre of our activity has now shifted to the English affairs and we hope you will behave cautiously and lead us out of the stress we find ourselves in at the moment. We want more money or more reserve.

Sachs was due to arrive in Berlin on October 8, and Abraham made a special request to Ferenczi that Melanie Klein move to Berlin "for the pedagogical analysis of children" (October 6, 1920). On October 10 the Vienna letter dropped a strong hint that Berlin might take in Ferenczi as well. Abraham made it clear that his Society could handle only one leader, and that they would accept new members from other centers only if such people found themselves in dire financial straits. In a private letter to Freud (July 16, 1920), Abraham suggested that if Ferenczi were in danger from the political regime in Budapest, he would be the ideal person for the projected Poliklinik in Vienna. Ferenczi was no suppliant: in his *Rundbrief* he declared that he had no intention of moving from Budapest (November 11, 1920).* His health was not particularly good, and he described himself as so busy that he could refer patients to his colleagues. It was clear that Abraham wanted a strong society, but not a strong rival within it. After all, he had already asked for Klein, and Franz Alexander left Budapest in 1921 to be analyzed by Sachs, later to be followed by Sandor Rado in 1923. Abraham had also tried to entice Rank to Berlin, but Rank preferred to stay in Vienna (Freud/Abraham; June 2, 1920).

---

*But in a private letter to Freud dated May 30, Ferenczi signed his letter "Warm greetings from someone who would like to emigrate."

Scientific issues were seldom raised in the circular letters, although Freud had given this as an important raison d'être for the letters. Ferenczi sent Freud a copy of a paper he had just written, "Psycho-Analytic Observations on Tic." Freud responded (October 11, 1920) that he had found it "very clever, completely correct and consequential, also full of promise for the future, but its actual point is lacking." When Ferenczi pressed him for more details, Freud evaded the issue (October 31, 1920), claiming that he had not really investigated the subject in any depth because he did not want to hinder Ferenczi's independence. This was a far different attitude than Freud had displayed during the war, when he encouraged Ferenczi to send him everything he was writing. "Also my reaction to foreign ways of thinking usually takes me a long time," he now wrote. Freud expected his colleagues to read his work, but his growing reluctance to read theirs carefully was to have unfortunate consequences for the Committee.

Complaints began to surface almost from the beginning of the circular-letter writing. Why, Rank demanded, were three signatures not to be found on the Berlin letters? In Vienna they made it a practice that Rank would write the letter on Thursday, Freud would sign it on Friday, and it was sent off the same day. Abraham replied snappishly that it was impossible to get the letters off in time if everyone signed, but that he always discussed the contents with Sachs and Eitingon. Jones would blow up over tiny details, such as the British member Joan Riviere being referred to as Frau Riviere instead of Mrs. Riviere by the Viennese typesetter of the *International Journal.* In his life of Freud, Jones defended himself as a perfectionist with an impatience with sloppiness, so that he risked provoking the sensibilities of other people. Rank was already overwhelmed with work "so my occasional protests irritated him beyond measure."[1]

On October 8 Rank sent out an extraordinary *Rundbrief,* quite clearly written without Freud having read it. It included three "confessions" that he felt impelled to disclose to his brothers. Apparently there was a plan among the members of the Committee to present Freud with a ring to replace the one he had surrendered to Eitingon. Through Rank's "carelessness" Freud had learned of the project and had emphatically vetoed the idea. It was clear that Freud perceived himself alone as the bestower of the symbolic rings.

Freud had also discovered (again through the garrulous Rank) that the Committee members were thinking of presenting him with a testimonial volume on his birthday. Freud's negative response was such that Rank stated candidly that the idea of a *Festschrift* (a commemorative volume) "most certainly stirs touchily his old age complex."

Finally, Theodore Reik, Rank's assistant, "through a blunder for which neither of us is responsible," had discovered and read the last *Rundbrief* from Berlin. Rank hastened to add that there was nothing of consequence in it; and besides, the secrecy of the letters could scarcely be hidden from Reik since they were addressed to Rank, and the two men were working in the same office.

Abraham had objected to the logo of Oedipus consulting the Sphinx on the letterhead of the *Rundbriefe* because it suggested a secret society, yet from the beginning Freud had emphasized the crucial importance of secrecy. And since the secrecy of the *Rundbriefe* was all-important, surely another method could have been devised such as having the letters sent to Freud directly? It is tempting to speculate that Rank, as the youngest member of the Committee—and the one who resented carrying more burdens than anyone else—was unconsciously trying to jeopardize the importance and continuation of the Committee. By revealing "secret" plans to Freud, he was in effect sabotaging the other members. The writing of the *Rundbriefe* imposed an additional burden on him, and whenever a suggestion was made for longer intervals between letters, it was usually either initiated or supported by Rank.

In order to mitigate his "confessions," Rank ended with the suggestion that all of them use the familiar "*du*," a practice that had already been initiated. His letter ended more warmly than usual, with a "handshake in friendship, putting the seal to the Du." It is curious that none of the others objected to this example of Rank's carelessness, possibly because they did not want to offend Freud.

Rank was racing against time with the rapid devaluation of both the Austrian and German currency. He himself wrapped all the parcels containing galleys that were sent to England, rushing back and forth to the post office. The tension under which he was laboring breaks into the formal style of the *Rundbriefe*. On November 17 Abraham remarked that Rank's heavy workload was responsible for "a certain impatience" in the Vienna letters.

Jones had succeeded in setting up an International English Press in London, as well as a separate bookshop selling psychoanalytic books. Jones had been full of enthusiasm for his venture, but as the months passed it was clear that the shop was not generating capital. Rank complained that the English members had not paid their contribution to the upkeep of the shop as they had promised to do. In order to keep the shop going, Jones transferred money from the press to subsidize it. Rank objected to this confusion, particularly since the press already owed money to the Verlag in Vienna. Rank insisted that the shop be closed.

Jones was very much on the defensive with Freud over the situation. He assured Freud that he considered himself an excellent accountant: "It was always a point of emulation between me and my father who was very talented in such work, and I would like to think I inherit it" (October 28, 1920). Jones complained because the English galleys were slow in being returned from Vienna, and Rank explained that both type and paper were scarce. He never received replies to his queries about the number of subscribers to the *International Journal of Psychoanalysis*, etc. His detailed accounts of the difficulties of publishing in Vienna were remarkably patient, and in desperation, he finally suggested that Jones's assistant, Eric Hiller, come to Vienna, learn the language, and oversee the British interests.

In an extremely long *Rundbrief* (October 21, 1920), Rank attempted to clarify the situation. In addition to the touchiness Abraham had detected in Rank, Abraham had complained that Vienna was behind in its contributions of reviews of psychoanalytic literature. "This isn't exactly the land of milk and honey," Rank commented ironically, and proceeded to give a detailed explanation for the delays. Finally, he exclaimed:

> Enough of this. We ourselves regret that this correspondence which should serve as a consolation for our personal relationships should be

spoiled right at the beginning by a note of discord. But as friends and analysts you will understand that this honest bitching is necessary because I am losing my patience in the face of continuing difficulties.

He took up the issue again on November 25: "I admit that I am impatient. I am indeed suffering from that because of a congenital defect,—and I am also over-worked." He also recognized that "it is not impossible that we are all overworked and overstrained." He proposed a peace banquet at their next meeting.

In his life of Freud, Jones claimed that he strove to conceal his difficulties with Rank from Freud, whereas Rank, on the spot, "had not the same scruples" and was constantly complaining to Freud about how difficult Jones was to deal with.[2] Yet Jones was determined that Freud be made aware of his problems with Rank. If Freud had detected irritation in Jones's manner, he pointed out that it was simply a reaction to Rank's "dictatorial manner," which made it difficult to deal with him (November 25, 1920).

Jones referred to Abraham's remark in his last letter that "we must make great allowances for the strain Rank is under at present and for the impatient restlessness of his disposition, which has its advantages and its disadvantages." It was tactless of Jones to try to undermine Rank with Freud, for it was inevitable that Freud would support Rank, whom he saw on a daily basis toiling under immense difficulties. "As a rule I agree with you on most relevant points," Freud replied (January 24, 1921). "I do not agree with you when you get moody and harass Rank about trifles like misprints, etc. which can nowhere be avoided." The British press, he added, was notoriously slow, and he hoped the situation would improve with the arrival of Hiller in Vienna, for then galleys would not have to be sent back and forth between London and Vienna. Jones in turn made a gesture of appeasement by appointing Rank and Ferenczi as honorary members of the British Society.

All of the Committee members were undoubtedly overworked, and some of them were suffering from malnutrition. During a strike in Berlin in November, Abraham had to write his letter by candlelight. Everyone agreed to Jones's proposal (November 16, 1920) that the letters be written every ten days instead of once a week. Before the year was out, Abraham began to press for a Congress in Berlin in 1921. Jones replied that he was open to persuasion, but would prefer postponing a Congress in favor of a Committee meeting since they had never had one devoted to scientific discussion. Vienna concurred that a Committee meeting would be preferable, especially because Freud was so exhausted. The meeting could be held at Easter, Whitsun, or at the end of their summer holidays. "The nature of the meeting should emphasize our friendly relationships, and naturally also foster scientific work. Of course everybody is free to express himself and ask questions but there should be no obligation to prepare a talk, etc." Freud suggested a discussion on the significance of telepathy for psychoanalysis.

In his last *Rundbrief* of the year (December 31, 1920), Jones remarked: "It becomes even clearer, as I saw when suggesting in 1912 that the Committee be formed, that our main hope lies in the steadfast holding together of our little group of Paladins, connected by both scientific and personal bonds."

While Ferenczi might have written rather testily to Berlin that he had no intention of leaving Budapest, he asked Freud privately to rethink Ferenczi's position if Vienna was destined to become the center of psychoanalysis (October 16, 1920). Freud dismissed this idea with his usual contempt for the Viennese members: "A raven should not put on a white shirt!" Freud was determined that Ferenczi should hold the Budapest group together, and in his letter of October 16, 1920, he also conveyed the news that he himself had turned down a lucrative offer from America. One of the reasons he often gave to discourage Ferenczi was the problem of speaking English to foreign patients. It took such an effort, Freud wrote, that he was experiencing great torment in his nose and jaw.*

Jones was not the only member of the Committee with whom Rank experienced difficulties. Abraham, after testily responding to a number of minor complaints from Vienna, finally exploded in a *Rundbrief* of January 31, 1921. He issued an ultimatum. If there

---

*This may be the first reference to his incipient cancer.

were any more complaints about the management of the Berlin Society, he would resign immediately. This was a strong announcement that he was master in his own house.

The others scurried to mend the rift. In his *Rundbrief* for February 11, Jones adopted a playful tone, reminding Abraham, "remember that you are not allowed to resign without permission of the Committee, which will be rather hard to obtain! You have been President of a Ps-A [viz. psychoanalytic] society uninterruptedly for longer than anyone in the world, and you know what enormous importance we all attach to your remaining in control." Ferenczi added that Abraham should not consider resigning over "petty little matters." To Freud privately, Ferenczi wrote: "Rank should be more considerate of Abraham's sensitivity in his circular letters, perhaps more in the tenor than in the content of his admonitions" (February 7, 1921). The Vienna letter stated that the Viennese members had not taken seriously Abraham's threat to resign.

After the arrival of Eric Hiller in Vienna, there was a period of peace between Rank and Jones regarding the Verlag. Jones had problems of his own in Britain, which was conducting official investigations of suspected quack therapists. One of Jones's main opponents was Oscar Wilde's former lover, Lord Alfred Douglas, who headed the Catholic Purity League, and who had sworn to uproot psychoanalysis in Britain. Jones had a long struggle ahead of him before he finally achieved official medical recognition.

Ferenczi continued to harp on his dream of emigrating to America. Freud seemed to be playing a rather puzzling cat-and-mouse game with Ferenczi, when he informed him on February 6, 1921, that he had received a request from Philadelphia for an English-speaking analyst, with a guaranteed income of $5,000 for the first year. He even added that Martha had pleaded with him that this was the opportunity Ferenczi had been seeking. Freud proceeded to list the grounds for his opposition:

1. I believe that you do not know enough English to do analytic work in this language, which after my experience this year is deucedly difficult.

2. You can if you want to, go to New York on your own, without guaranteed support.

3. Evidently you are in the process of enormous advance in Budapest.

4. You would feel miserable in America, without pupils or friends, in a totally illiberal society, which is really interested only in the pursuit of the dollar.

5. We cannot do without you here, without losing Hungary and everything that is being achieved there.

6. I would never see or hear from you again, etc. etc.

Ferenczi replied that he was willing to practice his English (if only Freud would send him some English-speaking patients!), and that in a couple of years in America he could save as much as he would earn in Budapest in ten years or more.[3] Freud did not pursue the discussion except to say that Ferenczi's enthusiasm had something to do with Elma's projected return to America (April 17, 1921). But Freud finally acknowledged Ferenczi's financial problems when he asked Jones if he could send some patients to Ferenczi, "who now experiences how impossible it is to live on home patients" (April 12, 1921), as well as to Rank, who, he assured Jones, was as excellent in analysis as he was in mythology (March 18, 1921).

Aware that Freud no longer seemed as interested in him as in the past, Ferenczi desperately continued to try to bind Freud to him by opening his heart in his childlike way. On July 24 he sent him a long account of his mother's final torments before her death. Trying to extract sympathy, he described his heart attack after her death and how Gizella's loving care was all that had sustained him. He was bitterly aware that Freud would undoubtedly suggest that Elma's departure for America was responsible for Ferenczi's condition, and he almost defiantly announced that he was going to Vienna to consult Felix Deutsch about his health before making plans for the summer.

Freud sent a cold reply from Bad Gastein on July 27, 1921. He started out by telling Ferenczi that he was not making him anxious (if that was what he had had in mind), but he was actually "offending" him. If he wanted to consult "a harmless internist," go ahead, but he certainly didn't believe that Ferenczi was suffering from any organic problems. What he did believe was that Ferenczi was indulging in an "unfair contest." Because Freud was constantly discussing the prospect of his own death, Ferenczi felt that he had to do Freud one better!

Finally he turned to the death of Ferenczi's mother: "So you have buried your mother. She was, so far as I know, a very respectable woman, she had something superior about her. I suppose that gives you a peculiar feeling of being alone in the world."

Reverting immediately to himself, Freud wrote that his fear was that his own mother would outlive him and that his death would have to be concealed from her. (Did he suspect that she might be indifferent?) When Jones's father had died the previous year, Freud was able to show a degree of empathy because his own father's death had "revolutionized" his soul. Freud seemed totally incapable of understanding the close bond a son might feel toward his mother.

Ferenczi was undoubtedly devastated by his mother's death and immensely grateful to Rank and Deutsch for their kindness during his visit to Vienna. His hurt and resentment toward Freud break through on August 17 in a letter from Garmisch, where Ferenczi was convalescing. He thanks Freud for his "condolences" and ironically makes the sarcastic comment that he has decided to take longer walks, "disregarding my subjective complaints" and ignoring his doctor's instructions.

Ferenczi wanted to visit Freud in Seefeld, only three stops away by train from Partenkirchen, but a frontier crossing pass was extremely difficult to obtain. On August 23 Freud was furious when he returned to his lodgings after hiking in the woods and discovered that Ferenczi had come and gone during his absence. He demanded advance notice of a visit in future, and a discomfited Ferenczi tried to explain to him that when the pass had come through suddenly that morning, he had decided to seize the chance opportunity of seeing Freud.

On September 6 Ferenczi traveled to Baden-Baden for his first visit to Georg Groddeck's sanatorium. Groddeck had come into

Ferenczi's life at a moment when he needed him. Ferenczi's early doubts about Groddeck's being a "wild" analyst* with his own subjective interpretations were assuaged by the tenderness with which Groddeck cared for his patients. It was the maternal tenderness Ferenczi had sought from Freud, but which he had received only in situations in which Freud's curiosity was aroused or when he desperately needed Ferenczi's company.

Abraham finally agreed to a Committee meeting rather than a Congress—provided that he would be allowed to plan it.† The Committee members could all see the sense in this arrangement, because the real business of the psychoanalytic movement was conducted privately by the Committee rather than in the larger and more democratic Congresses.

The week-long meeting at the end of September, with its hearty companionship and strenuous exercise is described in the prologue to this book. In the evenings, the members gathered for scientific discussion, which usually meant a paper delivered by Freud.

As early as November 1920 Freud had proposed telepathy as a research topic for the next Committee meeting. "If we had to accept the phenomena summarized under the term 'telepathy,' " he asked, "how would it influence the theory and practice of psychoanalysis?" This he attempted to explore in "Psycho-Analysis and Telepathy," a paper delivered one evening in the Harz Mountains, but not published during his lifetime.

Freud began by emphasizing to "the circle that is closest to me"[4] that they were not destined to devote themselves "quietly" to the extension of their science. First, there had been identifiable enemies—Adler, Stekel, Jung—but now they were faced with "something tremendous, something elemental, which threatens not us alone but our enemies, perhaps still more."[5]

It is not clear what Freud meant by these portentous words. He described analysts as "at bottom incorrigible mechanists and materialists."[6] Nevertheless, he proceeded to relate a series of examples of thought transference that clearly impressed him deeply. Indeed,

---

*This was the way Groddeck had described himself at The Hague the previous year.
†Abraham usually organized most of the Congresses.

there was one such case in which the patient had "touched in the most remarkable way on an experience which I had had myself immediately before."[7]

He described his own life as having been "particularly poor in an occult sense."[8] He urged his colleagues, however, to collect examples of cases of thought transference, although he gave no indication of how this would deepen or enlarge the purview of psychoanalysis. He ended by asking them to consider the "momentous step" this would involve; his own nervousness about the possible public reaction to a study of thought transference is evident, for the members of the Committee were the only people ever made privy to the contents of this paper.

Ferenczi was highly enthusiastic about the subject, but Jones made it clear that he was nervous about the "unscientific" nature of telepathy. As late as March 7, 1926, Freud informed Jones that he was convinced of the worth of telepathy, particularly after some striking experiments conducted with Ferenczi and Anna Freud. He recognized, he said, the British animosity toward the subject, and while he regarded occultism as different in nature from psychoanalysis, he emphasized that it was his "private affair." Nevertheless, the caution exhibited in those papers he did publish on the subject perhaps reveals one of the few instances in which Freud was restrained by his colleagues. Certainly he began to advise Ferenczi not to publicize his interest in the occult.

For seven men to be in close proximity for a week inevitably meant that certain personality differences would emerge. A spirit of camaraderie existed; nevertheless, age and status differences were apparent. Jones, Abraham, and Ferenczi were presidents of their respective societies. Eitingon, the secretary of the Berlin Society, was also its rich benefactor. Jones and Abraham usually found themselves in agreement on theoretical and political matters. Ferenczi was still on fairly good terms with everyone despite danger signs in his relationships with Jones and Abraham. Rank and Sachs, the youngest members of the Committee and the only two who were non-medical, were the juniors in every respect. They worked together harmoniously as coeditors of *Imago*, in contrast to the constant disagreements between Rank and Jones over the Verlag and the recently established *International Journal of Psycho-Analysis*. While Sachs simply accepted his place in his usual sunny manner, the overworked Rank, who had been given, as we have seen, to frequent outbursts of pique in the *Rundbriefe*, made it clear that he had the ear of Freud at all times, but was constantly smoldering about too much being expected of him. Sachs, Jones's oldest friend in the group, began to get on Freud's nerves, and Freud regretted that he had ever been made a Committee member. This is puzzling when one remembers Sachs's devotion to Freud throughout the war, when he alone of the other members remained in Vienna, where he eventually contracted tuberculosis.* On his return to Vienna Freud informed Jones that the meeting would have been completely satisfactory apart from "two darker spots" that "somewhat diminished its splendor" (October 2, 1921). In addition to what he described as Sachs's "deterioration," Freud had been disturbed by Jones's sickly appearance and his habit of disappearing once or twice a day without any explanation. Freud asked for some reassurance. Jones blamed his behavior on his cold:

> Partly for toxic reasons and partly from my intolerance to nasopharyngeal irritation (erogene zone I suppose), this trouble always affects me physically, in the direction of a slightly hypochondriacal withdrawal. (Jones/Freud; Oct. 11, 1921.)

He added that he was extremely worried about raising the mortgage for his new house. As for his old friend Sachs, who was acquiring a reputation as something of a playboy in Berlin, he "has evidently some infantile regression and has been behaving in Berlin rather like a youth visiting a Grosstadt for the first time."

One of the major topics of discussion at the reunion was the problem of American opposition to lay analysis. It was difficult to formulate any clear policy on how to deal with the issue as far as Americans were concerned, since Freud lacked the personal control he exerted over the European members. There was suspicion in

---

*Later in the year, when Abraham reported that Sachs was settling in well in Berlin, Freud replied that he was happy to hear it but that unfortunately he and Sachs had become estranged during the past few years (Freud/Abraham; December 9, 1921).

Vienna that Jones supported the Americans in their insistence that analysts must be medically trained. In his *Rundbriefe* during the course of the year, Jones had voiced misgivings about various unofficial non-medical groups that had sprung up in Britain. On June 21 Rank advised him against adhering to his "rigid medical principle" because there might be some valuable people among the non-medical groups. Berlin's position (July 1, 1921) was that it would not be good if the medical people were outnumbered by lay analysts. A distinction should be made between the scientific value of the medical people and the practical usefulness of the lay analysts. On the same day Jones defended the British Society as being more receptive to lay members than any other society. After Rank raised the subject once more on July 22, Jones told him that he was "beating a dead horse." Nevertheless, the question of Jones's equivocal attitude was to surface again in future years.

The issue of allowing homosexuals to become members arose later in the year. Both Jones and Ferenczi opposed allowing them in "because *in most cases they are too abnormal*" (December 1, 1921). Vienna took a far more tolerant stand. On December 11, Rank wrote that they believed "a decision should be reached individually based on the other qualities of applicants." Furthermore, to bar homosexuals from joining the societies seemed to be a form of persecution that should not be tolerated. Berlin dissented. In the *Rundbrief* of January 11, 1921, the consensual view was that of course they disapproved of discrimination against any individuals, but "generally we have had the experience that homosexuals with a non-suppressed inversion cannot go very far with us." Their own neurosis prevented them from analyzing the neuroses of others. The work of a notorious local homosexual figure, the sexologist Magnus Hirschfeld, certainly indicated lack of judgment. Consequently, they would accept only a very exceptional candidate. Rank replied to Berlin in a letter of January 22, 1922:

> We recognize the arguments against the analytical work of homosexuals as correct, but we would warn against applying this as a general rule. We have to take into account the different types of homosexuals and the different mechanisms in the development of homosexuality.

Rank seems to be using the royal "we"; but to the others it must have been galling to accept that a junior person like Rank was speaking with the same voice as Freud.

The affairs of the Verlag were relatively quiescent in 1921. On December 21 Rank reported that Hiller had returned to England for Christmas. "For the past few months he has been more than industrious and really deserves a vacation." Yet almost inevitably the cooperative publishing venture was destined to erupt once more the following year.

Chapter Seven

Squabbles Terminable and Interminable

FREUD'S *Group Psychology and Analysis of the Ego* was published in August 1921, just before the Committee meeting in the Harz Mountains. *Totem and Taboo* had a long gestation period, finally ending in a conclusion close to Freud's current experience. While writing *Totem and Taboo* Freud was constantly brooding that Jung had a compulsion to supplant him. While writing *Group Psychology* he pondered the phenomenon of groups, and the galvanizing force that led him to finish the work was his perception of the Committee.

Group Psychology is a curiously contradictory production, a combination of a rigorous observation of human nature and fantasized wish fulfillment of what human collectivity might be. In its early sections Freud seems to endorse Gustave Le Bon's view of group dynamics.

A group is impulsive, changeable, and irritable. It is led almost exclusively by the unconscious. The impulses which a group obeys may according to circumstances be generous or cruel, heroic or cowardly, but they are always so imperious that no personal interest, not even that of self-preservation, can make itself felt. Nothing about it is premeditated. Though it may desire things passionately, yet this is never so for long, for it is incapable of perseverance. It cannot tolerate any delay between its desire and the fulfillment of what it desires. It has a sense of omnipotence; the notion of impossibility disappears for the individual in a group.[1]

However, by the time Freud reached Section X, he seemed to be holding out hope that within a group the individual's ego could be transformed through the agency of the ego ideal, "just as it is possible for bees in case of necessity to turn a larva into a queen instead of into a worker"*[2] "The primal father of the horde," in his account, was able to force a number of individuals into group psychology, that is, an artificial entity, in which all its members believed that they were equally loved and equally persecuted. They long for an authority figure and invest him with a predominance over them. In an extraordinary postscript, Freud turns to the situation in the Roman Catholic Church, in which each member has "to identify himself with Christ and love all the other Christians as Christ loved them."[3]

The Committee had been operating for just under a year since the inception of the *Rundbriefe*. In the extraordinary passages on identification with the leader in *Group Psychology*, Freud seemed to be creating a manifesto of his hopes and aspirations for the Committee, as well as establishing an omnipotent persona for himself. Regrettably, his group was already indicating characteristics similar to those described in Le Bon's view of group behavior rather than Freud's idealized fantasy.

1922 started out peacefully enough. Both Ferenczi and Abraham lectured in Vienna in January. On Ferenczi's return to Budapest, he wrote to Freud that Freud could no longer reproach him for having a father fixation when his kindness and hospitality had only reinforced it (January 25, 1922). In his reply (February 9, 1922) Freud expressed some extraordinary fantasies. Something in him, he wrote, rebelled against the constant compulsion to make money.

> Strange secret desires emerge, perhaps from the inheritance of the ancestors, for the orient and the Mediterranean and a life of a completely different kind, late childish desires, and not compatible with reality.

---

*Freud used the same image to Ferenczi in his advice to him when he took Jones into analysis: "Feed the pupa (chrysalis) so that it can become a queen bee . . ." (June 8, 1913).

The *Rundbriefe* imposed a shared interest in the practical matters of the psychoanalytical movement. Aware that he could let his mystical streak run away with him, Freud recognized that the Congress to be held in Berlin would undoubtedly restore his sense of reality. He then turned to another fantasy: it would be nice if some of those rich Americans provided them with money. Lack of money usually gave Freud a sharp and unwelcome jolt of reality.

In a private letter to Jones, Abraham wrote that while he was in Vienna he had had a discussion with Freud about the establishment of standard fees in all the societies. In his *Rundbrief* Jones objected to the idea, because in England there were far higher taxes than on the Continent. To the Committee members Abraham hastened to insist that Jones had misunderstood what he had said in his private letter: there had been no intention of standardizing fees or undercutting foreign colleagues. He simply believed that it would be helpful if they all knew what each was charging so that there would be no wide disparities. Rank in turn chimed in that Freud had no recollection of any such discussion with Abraham, and would never support any proposal for a standard fee. With something as important as money, Freud made it clear that he made his own decisions.

Then it was Jones's turn to be anxious about his status with Vienna. In January, Joan Riviere arrived from England to be analyzed by Freud. She had already been analyzed by Jones, and there is a strong possibility that they had had an affair (this was pure fantasy on her part, Jones claimed). When Jones denied any misconduct, Freud told him that he was relieved to hear it—although he didn't seem altogether convinced.

Riviere had translated a number of Freud's papers and was the translation editor of the *International Journal of Psycho-Analysis*. When Freud expressed his great admiration for her, Jones sent him a number of agitated letters about what a hysterical and unreliable woman she was. This time Freud was determined to speak far more bluntly to Jones than he had done while analyzing Loe Kann. Joan Riviere was a woman of great intelligence from an upper-class background, yet a thread of condescension weaves through Freud's remarks, as though he were speaking about a Viennese *Windbeutel* (cream puff), capable of exerting the same wiles as Spielrein was supposed to have exercised on Jung.

In this very long letter to Jones (June 4, 1922) Freud emphasized that he was perfectly capable of judging Riviere for himself:

> You think Mrs. Riviere has put on her sweetest face and moods, has taken me in completely and seduced me to defend her against you in a chivalrous manner, so that now I am a puppet in her hands, show her the letters I got from you and give you away to her. I am sure you are wrong and I feel rather sorry that there should be a need to point it out to you.

He tried to make Jones see how difficult it was to take on a second analysis. Jones was being unreasonable, he wrote, if he expected Freud and Riviere to avoid any discussion of him. This was the first opportunity Freud had had for judging the therapeutic practice of one of the Committee members, and Freud was happy to be able to pounce on Jones. What he was really attacking was his character. He told Jones bluntly that he was critical of the way Jones had handled the initial analysis and that he was not happy about having to play the role of *Pontifex maximus* between Jones and his former analysands. He would have preferred, he scolded, to see them more closely bound to Jones than to himself; Freud seems to be blurring the distinction here between a therapist and a political leader. It was not the last time he was to express regret that Jones lacked qualities of leadership. But later, when Jones asserted some independence, Freud was to be equally displeased.

By the end of June the Riviere analysis came to an end, and Freud wrote to Jones congratulating himself that their friendship had withstood a severe strain (June 25, 1922).

> Now what made the case so hard for me [Freud continued] was the fact that accuracy and plainness is not in the character of your dealings with people. Slight distortions and evasions, lapses of memory, twisted denials, a certain predilection for sidetracks prevail and whenever I had to examine a case between you and her in detail I had to find that you were to be doubted, while that implacable

woman, over-emphasizing the importance of the slightest features, yet was right and could not be refuted.

In the case of Loe, it was Jones who had said that the friendship had withstood the strain of the analysis. At that time, Freud had felt slightly uneasy about his role in their estrangement. Now Freud could adopt a high moral tone because Riviere, proud and bitter, had confirmed Freud's view of the contemptible side of Jones. Like Riviere, he resented having allowed himself to become involved with Jones, much as he needed him strategically. However, having won Riviere over, he counted on her to report to him on Jones. Sure of Jones's unwavering loyalty, he could afford to bully him. When Jones received this sort of criticism from Freud, given their respective positions, he was unable to respond angrily. As usual, the technique he adopted was to put the incident behind him and to try to win Freud's favor on another front, such as impressing him with the prestigious groups whom he had been invited to address.

But it was difficult to win Freud over because of the continuous difficulties with Rank over the Verlag and the British press. Hiller's installation in Vienna seemed to work well during 1921, but after his return from his Christmas vacation in England, the situation deteriorated rapidly. Hiller (backed by Jones) began to behave in what appeared to be a defiantly independent way, avoided socializing with the Viennese, and did not seem to be making much progress in learning German. Freud informed Jones in no uncertain terms that he believed it was difficult to collaborate with the British. As he had often told him before, Freud felt that Jones did not know how to delegate and that he could not refrain from meddling in every trivial detail. He felt impelled to reprimand Jones harshly because "Rank is too meek to oppose you in these quarters" (April 6, 1922).

When Jones eventually agreed that Hiller had proved a disappointment, Freud graciously acknowledged that he had overreacted in assigning all the blame to Jones (May 11, 1922). He now saw that the basic cause of the Verlag's problems were *Kinderkrankheiten* (children's diseases): inadequate premises, insufficient type, constant trouble with the printers, etc. Again real difficulties threatened the imaginary cohesion of the Committee. Hiller—of whom so much had been expected—had proved inefficient—"yet I do not want to sow discord between you and him." Freud's temporary change of heart toward Jones seems to be a reaction to the latter's fervent declaration that if he could bring out Freud's collected works in English he would feel that his life had been worth living (April 10, 1922). Freud was "deeply stirred" by this declaration. It might have been "a tender exaggeration produced by some sudden impulse," but Freud wrote that nevertheless he appreciated Jones's remarks as "an expression of your unfailing kindness towards me which as you know I always intend to return."

But the center was no longer holding. The group was beginning to break up into dyads of affiliation, with Jones and Abraham standing together and Rank and Ferenczi on constant guard against them. They were all learning the tactics of guerilla warfare. Rumblings of future trouble sounded in June, when Abraham stated that the purpose of the circular correspondence was for open discussion of suggestions and opinions. "Recently we have noticed with regret," he complained, "that our suggestions have been rejected by Vienna without any factual discussion, especially a number of my personal suggestions." Rank replied with a detailed rejection of Abraham's criticisms, eventually concluding with a few ironically friendly remarks.

On July 3 Jones, in his own oblique way, tried to pour oil on troubled waters:

It is certain that Rank's comments could not have been personally intended in the sense Abraham thinks. We must by now all know that it is a quality of Rank's to express his thoughts in a forcible and not always discriminating manner. It is an idiosyncrasy of his that we should willingly allow him if it gives him pleasure. Sometimes the blows fall on Ferenczi's head, often on mine, and at times in Berlin. I have always admired the sunny urbanity with which Ferenczi receives them and have striven to imitate such an excellent ideal. So let me counsel you, my dear Abraham, to smile back and Rank will at once be as amiable as ever.

Freud, vacationing in Bad Gastein, wrote to Rank that he interpreted the exchange as reactions against himself that were being displaced onto Rank (Freud/Rank; July 7, 1922). He added:

> I am never quite sure whether, at the crucial time, I did right in keeping you from the study of medicine. I believe, upon the whole, I was right; when I reflect upon my own tedium during my medical studies I become more certain but when I see you move more fully and rightly into the saddle of the analyst, then the necessity to justify my own action drops away.

On July 20, in another letter to Rank, Freud conceded that Joan Riviere had been entirely right about Jones, and that Abraham's ambition obviously stemmed from his jealousy of Eitingon, whom he had never wanted to join the Committee. "Abraham, is, however, superior to Jones and his irritability isn't of any consequence," Freud wrote. Ferenczi and Gizella had joined the Ranks in Seefeld, and Freud was delighted that a close friendship was developing between them. He wished Rank to discuss the matter with Ferenczi, whose "obvious loveableness intends him for the role of mediator. Also, he has the most influence with Jones on account of his analysis."

Freud also approved of Rank's plan for a Committee meeting in Seefeld in August. Aware that they somehow had to get along, he added that it was probably for the best that he could be there "in spirit only." Abraham and Sachs joined the others in Seefeld in August. By then Freud had moved on to Berchtesgaden, where he was working on his Congress paper on the ego and the id (inspired by Georg Groddeck's work).* Freud confided to Rank (August 4, 1922) that Rank was the only one on the Committee ("the youngest and freshest among us") who knew that Freud had been feeling decidedly unwell for some time. Freud again took up the theme of his regret at preventing Rank from studying medicine. If Rank had done so, he wrote, "I would not be in doubt to whom I would leave the leading role in the Psychoanalytic movement. As it now

*Das Buch von Es (1923).

stands I can't help but wish that Abraham's clarity and accuracy could be merged with Ferenczi's endowments and to it be given Jones's untiring pen." The logic of this is elusive: since Freud was a defender of lay analysis, why would Rank be an inappropriate leader?

Freud really did not want to give a lecture at the Congress. Part of his reluctance was due to his increasing hoarseness. When Ferenczi urged him to disregard his hoarseness and emphasized that the Congress would be incomplete without him, Freud replied (July 21, 1922) that the hoarseness was only a symptom of his resistance. Freud touchingly admitted that things had been fine when they had gone to America in 1909—in Worcester Ferenczi had told him exactly what to say—but since then Freud had felt increasing resistance to attending Congresses. They must accept that there had to be a transition period to the time when he would no longer be able to lend his presence to these occasions. In a sense the existence of the Committee provided Freud with an opportunity to withdraw into himself, and he tried desperately to distance himself from the intermittent squabbles.

But there was no way Freud could remain completely uninvolved with the Committee. Nor could he find in work the tranquility for which he had been longing. On August 18 the daughter of his sister Rosa committed suicide with an overdose of veronal while staying with the Freud family.

The Congress in Berlin in September was a great success, and what Jones later described as "the last amicable Committee meeting"[4] was held immediately afterwards. With Freud present, the illusion of a strong central core was reinforced. The Committee took advantage of the occasion to have a group photograph taken. The subsequent *Rundbriefe* from the various capitals expressed satisfaction with the Congress, although Abraham had missed the intimacy of the meeting in the Harz Mountains the previous year. Jones was reelected president for two years. As early as April 6 Freud had written Jones that he expected him to give the general address in "bold dashing German." And again he reverted to the matter of the future when he was no longer there. "It is time the herd should become prepared to listen to your voice or Abraham's or Ferenczi's as I am getting old and tired and fond of retirement." After the Congress, Jones, always eager for Freud's approval, inquired tentatively (October 2, 1922) whether Freud had been pleased with the way he had conducted the Congress. Freud's reply was not encouraging (November 6, 1922). He had to tell Jones frankly that he had allowed events to drift occasionally "with too weak a hand. Your speech at the banquet was a success however."

By the end of October the crisis of the Verlag exploded again. As Abraham remarked in the Berlin *Rundbrief* of November 1:

> It is strange that our circle is showing the reverse reaction of a neurotic family. They argue when they are together and are full of love as soon as they are separated. But in our circle there is harmony when we are together whereas the correspondence at times is quite different.

The complaints were ceaseless, with Abraham and Jones standing together, and Ferenczi supporting Rank. The dissension within the Committee was a microcosm of the wider world. On October 28 Mussolini marched on Rome and formed a Fascist government. In early November a group of monetary experts met in Berlin to discuss the crisis of the German currency. The economic situation in Austria was even more precarious, and in the Vienna *Rundbrief* of November 1, the idea of moving the operations of the Verlag to Berlin was proposed. As Rank saw it, in Berlin there would be lower production costs and more highly qualified printers. Anxious about the British press, naturally Jones opposed the idea, and in the general turmoil, Hiller resigned.

Reinforced by support from Abraham, Jones explained that the way Rank had handled the uneasy relation between the Verlag and the press was a reflection of Rank's custom of "treating his colleagues as puppets" (November 16, 1922). Plain speaking was necessary, Jones wrote. For the past two years he had been subjected to one complaint after another "in a hectoring tone I would not accept from anyone else." Jones felt that he had exhibited great patience in responding to serious misrepresentations and fictitious accusations, which he had done out of personal affection for Rank and veneration for Freud, "but I must at last raise the question whether this schoolmaster's attitude is really a necessary one towards people who in private life are the best of friends and whose main interests in life are identical . . ."

On November 22, in a private letter to Freud, Ferenczi supported Rank against Abraham and Jones, who, as reasonable men, "must admit their mistakes." Nevertheless, "On the whole, I think that the (often very unjustified) sensibility of A and J has to be taken into consideration *in the interest of the cause* [*im Interesse der Sache*]." It was probably inevitable that cliques would form within the Committee, he conceded, but everything must be done to control the quarreling. Ferenczi found it very sad that their unity could be maintained only by Freud's intervention. He planned to raise the matter in his next *Rundbrief*, but because he was not directly involved in the dispute, he did not expect that anyone would pay much attention to him.

Freud had already defended Rank privately in a letter to Jones (November 6, 1922): "I am of the opinion that some aspects of your behaviour with people create more difficulties than you are aware of." From what Rank told him, Freud was fully confident that Jones was "very incompetent" (September 8, 1922; Freud/Rank). The situation had clearly reached such a crisis that Freud was convinced that his personal intervention was necessary.

Freud's long open letter of November 26 was blunt and conciliatory, a clear exposition of his understanding of the contentious issues. To Abraham's insinuation that Freud had not seen the two previous *Rundbriefe* from Vienna, because he could not believe that Freud was capable of some of the offensive remarks in them, Freud assured the group that all the circular letters were drafted by both Rank and himself, and that he read them before Rank sent them out.

> Consequently there is nothing in these letters for which I would not have to share responsibility. Abraham's assumption, I am sure, was made in a friendly way, but I cannot support any possible tendency from any source whatever to produce affects against Rank which are really directed against me.

The dispute with Jones he considered far more serious. Freud was convinced that Jones's hostility was directed against him and that poor Rank found himself in the position of "a screen which has to catch the negative part of an ambivalent affect." While he had been extremely critical of Jones in recent months, he still valued Jones's merits. "Differences cannot be avoided, not even in a family, but behind them stands the certainty that one cannot get away from one another, and that one does not even want to get away."

In Freud's view, Jones should probably complete the short analysis he had had with Ferenczi. In any event, these issues had brought home to him how important it was for the future of psychoanalysis that the other members cooperate. Accordingly he had decided against participating in the next Committee meeting.

Freud made it abundantly clear that he understood clearly the problems associated with the ambiguous relationship between the Verlag and the British press, and he took responsibility for not clarifying the relationship adequately in the first place. If Jones objected to the removal of the Verlag to Berlin, he had failed to understand that it was still directed from Vienna. The British press was not compelled to move to Berlin, but if it stayed in Vienna, it would no longer receive any assistance from the Verlag. In other words, take it or leave it.

Finally, he saw no reason to reproach Rank for anything, because "as always he had given his best." Nor did Freud want to be like the dying man whose last words were "be united—united—united." "I am still alive," he concluded, "and I hope to see you united by common work and above such hyper-sensitive reactions."

The same day he wrote to Ferenczi an even more personal reaction to the recent events. After a long discussion with Rank, it had been decided that Freud should write an independent letter. He was not particularly disturbed by Abraham because he was a kindhearted and upright [korreckt] man. Freud suspected that Abraham had probably been encouraged by Eitingon, who had exploded with accumulated envy of Rank. Jones was a more serious case because he had profound defects of character.

Freud expressed surprise at Ferenczi's previous report that Rank had been suggesting a change in the membership of the Committee and significant alterations in the *Zeitschrift*. Rank had never mentioned these matters to him, and Freud justified Rank's intemperate suggestions to the fact that the continuous attacks on him could have led easily to rash and embittered statements. Nevertheless, it is possible that this information planted the first suspicion in Freud's mind that Rank was not altogether frank with him. It is also possible that Freud was stretching his memory when he asserted that he had read every *Rundbrief* that had issued from Vienna.

That Abraham still had suspicions on this point was apparent in his reply (December 3, 1922) when he proposed that Freud's signature appear on every letter so that the members could be assured of his approval of their tone and content. He was in favor of a meeting without the "father" in order to restore harmony among the "brothers" on the condition that they subsequently have a collective meeting with the "father."

Jones in turn responded indignantly to Freud's charges that he and Abraham had acted neurotically toward Rank, but professed himself willing to do everything in his power to create peace. In his *Rundbrief* (December 6, 1922), Ferenczi fully endorsed the Professor's open letter. Nevertheless, he advised Rank to be more diplomatic.

The year ended with separate letters to the Committee members from Freud (December 15, 1922) and Rank (December 20, 1922), pleading for the restoration of harmony. Freud's letter was curious. He thanked Abraham and Jones for their "forebearance." He wrote that Ferenczi alone knew that it was his "fanatical sense of justice" that had led him to intervene in the dispute, because psychoanalysis should never be used as a tool for polemics. And it was clear that he did not consider that Abraham and Jones had been sufficiently conciliatory. Jones agreed that if his behavior manifested displaced anger, he probably did need more analysis, but he felt that it was probably even more true of Rank, "who has had none" (December 15, 1922). Freud declared that in the fifteen years he had worked with Rank, such an idea had hardly crossed his mind.* Jones should

---

*. . . , *dass ich in 15 jähriger stetiger und intimer Arbeitsgemeinschaft mit Rank kaum jemals auf die Idee gekommen bin,* der *könnte noch ein Stück Analyse brauchen."*

abandon his grandiose ambitions for the press: it was simply the English department of the Verlag, since there was not sufficient money for it to be anything more than that. To add insult to injury, Jones's only alternative was to accept the situation because, Freud implied, he could not be compared to Rank either as an editor or a businessman.

Rank described his own letter, written five days later, as an "appendix" to Freud's. The bitter feelings he was still experiencing spilled over into it. He reiterated the exhausting and thankless task that had been imposed on him. In moments verging upon despair, he wrote, he had wished that his brothers could have helped him with their friendship "instead of looking on each of my remarks through a looking glass to tell me that it was my fault when everything did not go smoothly." He might remind "dear Ernest" that the press owed the Verlag about seven hundred pounds. There was also so much distrust on the part of the British that further cooperation was impossible, and it would be a good thing for the press to stand on its own feet. Too many people had been involved. "*One* will and *one* hand has to direct everything in an enterprise, then it may turn out either good or bad, but otherwise it comes to nothing. Perhaps you will see in this another indication of my autocratic trends . . ."

The prospects for peace and goodwill did not look promising.

Chapter Eight

Open Warfare

ALWAYS TERRIFIED of death, Freud began to fear he was losing his grip on life. Early in 1923, he confided to Rank that he was feeling particularly indisposed. Why this confidence should have been revealed to Rank rather than to Ferenczi, to whom Freud habitually imparted detailed reports about his health, is puzzling. Perhaps this secret was intended as a means of binding Rank to him even more closely than ever.

Sachs and Ferenczi visited Vienna over the New Year in the hope that harmony would be restored after their discussions with Freud.[1] Rank handed over full responsibility of the *Korrespondenzblatt* (local bulletins) to Abraham, thus eliminating one source of irritation.* Abraham was also optimistic that differences had been laid to rest.[2] Sachs had told him that Freud wished the Berlin letters to reflect a consensual view. To Freud Abraham admitted his difficulties frankly. They both knew how sloppy Sachs had become, and Eitingon was so fixated on his wife (a recurring theme in the letters) that all Abraham usually could get out of him was some meaningless remark.† Sachs's meager contribution was to pass on to the Committee members the information that he had recovered from the flu! "This is the reason," Abraham concluded, "why I attend to most of the correspondence. But I would like to believe

---

*It was the custom in addressing remarks specifically to each group to address members personally as *"lieber."* In this particular letter, Rank writes "1.Karl" and "1.Sandor", but Jones is not even mentioned by name.
†Abraham was perhaps being unfair to Eitingon, who in the course of his frequent travels helped to establish psychoanalytic groups in Moscow and Paris.

that there was very little of any importance that was not approved by the others."

Freud was pleased with the positive reports of the growing strength of the Berlin Society. (Budapest, on the other hand, reported shrinking membership, and Ferenczi feared that he had lost one member, Sandor Rado, permanently to Berlin.) Abraham reported that he had given a lecture on his paper published as "A Short Study of the Development of the Libido, Viewed in the Light of Mental Disorders," a seminal work in object relations theory. Freud was momentarily cheered. "I am glad to note that my paladins, you, Ferenczi and Rank, always tackle fundamentals in your writings instead of decorative incidentals of any kind. That is the case now with your object love. I am very much looking forward to reading it" (April 8, 1923). Jones is conspicuously missing from the list of paladins.

Still smarting from Freud's public rebuke that he needed further analysis, on the first day of the new year Jones confided to Abraham that just before the outbreak of the war Rank had arranged to come to England to be analyzed by him for "a bad gastric neurosis and other difficulties." He concluded gloomily:

> You will see I have renounced the hope of leading Professor to any sort of objectivity where Rank is concerned. One must recognise with regret that even Freud has his human frailties and that age is bringing with it one-sidedness of vision and diminution of critical power.[3]

In the London *Rundbrief*, written the same day, Jones reported that he had been ill in bed during the holidays (a familiar pattern of his in response to a crisis). He conceded that they should all accept that the Rank-Hiller-Jones collaboration had been a failure, but he could not agree with Freud that "friends should judge one another by the same unsparing standards as does fate." They had all done their best, and now they must concentrate on the future. While "the New Year opens darkly for our literary undertakings," he wrote, he was confident that they all could overcome their difficulties with goodwill and cooperation.

The Committee had seemed an ideal vehicle for promulgating

psychoanalysis. But Freud began to fear that Jones, the original proponent of the group, was threatening to destroy it through his personal ambition for the British press and his love child, *The International Journal of Psycho-Analysis*. To Ferenczi Freud confided on January 25, 1923 that he and Rank had "pushed through" the separation of the press from the Verlag, partly because of their own lack of money, but mainly because of "the arrogance and clumsiness of the British." The problem was, as he constantly complained, that Jones simply lacked the qualities of leadership.

Freud sullenly predicted that a British press could not survive more than two years on its own. Jones was determined to prove him wrong. The situation was made even more difficult by the fact that Freud transferred the American sales of his books from Jones to his nephew, Edward Bernays, in New York. Jones, usually so affirmative, seemed unusually depressed. He was frank about the difficulties he was experiencing in finding a publisher, and was shocked when he discovered that Freud had made the American arrangement without consulting him.

Freud continued to be convinced that Jones's constant carping about Rank was displaced anger toward himself. In his self-absorption, Freud was incapable of understanding that Jones and Rank were two incompatible personalities. Jones tried to explain to him (January 14, 1923) that while it was difficult for them to work together, they had no difficulties in personal or scientific matters. "I have every hope that our friendship, which is quite unimpaired on my side and I trust also on his, will be restored to its former harmony" when business complications no longer muddied the waters. Freud had accused Jones of endangering the Committee by making critical remarks about Rank, but Jones claimed that he had done so only after consulting Eitingon, who had felt that plain speaking was necessary for closer collaboration. Rank's reaction indicated that the objective was not attained, and if Freud felt that he was insincere and untrustworthy, "with all respect," Freud's judgment was at fault.*

---

*By March Jones and Freud had resumed an amiable correspondence, and on the 23rd Freud gently dissuaded him from changing his name to the more prestigious Beddow-Jones.

On March 18 Rank suggested that they reduce the *Rundbriefe* to one a month. Ferenczi reluctantly agreed, and Abraham concurred only if the new practice would be regarded as a temporary experiment, with an additional monthly short report.

In the early spring Freud began to live within his own private hell. In his biography of Freud, Jones describes in searing detail the series of operations the Professor underwent during the rest of his life for a growth in his mouth that was ultimately diagnosed as cancerous. But at the time Jones was totally oblivious of the seriousness of the situation. On April 25, Freud wrote him that a leukoplastic growth had been detected in his mouth. He could not swallow and was unable to work, but Freud had not yet been informed that it was actually cancerous. The first official notification of Freud's illness appeared in the May 1 letter from Vienna, in which Rank mentioned that Freud had had "a small operation" caused by too much smoking, and for some days had had difficulties in speaking and eating. It is conceivable that even Rank, there on the spot, possibly refused to consider the implications. The Committee members were not apprized of the truth until they met in August in the Dolomites.

The one bright spot in Freud's life during early 1923 was the presence in Vienna of his grandson, Heinerle, Sophie's second child, who was staying with his Aunt Mathilde. Freud found him the most delightfully intelligent child he had ever known, and was completely devastated when the four-year-old died of tuberculosis on June 19. Usually so impassive, he wept. No death had ever affected him so deeply, and he confessed to experiencing the first real depression of his life.

Actually the depression had been building up since the completion of *The Ego and the Id* in March. Ferenczi had been unusually frank in his criticisms of this book, which formulated a topgraphical model of the mind. Ferenczi was particularly concerned that the title did not reflect the importance of the superego. Freud was not offended by Ferenczi's comments. He felt that he had been walking on slippery ice in arguing the book's thesis (Freud/Ferenczi; April 17, 1923), and that his work had deteriorated since *Beyond the Pleasure Principle*. Except for the basic idea of the id and the insight about the origin of morals, Freud actually disliked every-thing about the work. As for *Group Psychology* (written two years before), he now pronounced it banal, lacking in clarity, and badly written.

He was beginning to understand how important it was that his younger colleagues produce some valuable work. During the sum-mer of 1922, Rank and Ferenczi had worked together on a book on psychoanalysis, sending Freud drafts for suggestions and revisions. At the Berlin Congress they were concerned that there was far too much emphasis on theory at the expense of technique in the dis-cussions and they revised their book to emphasize Ferenczi's "active technique."

Ferenczi was convinced that analysands tended to feel too com-fortable in long-term analysis and develop a sort of dependency upon the analyst and/or the analytic situation. To counteract this complacency and to shorten therapy, he felt that some activity was needed. He advised his patients to leave their "comfortable" state—that is, to do things they didn't like to do (e.g. to expose themselves to their phobic objects, such as streets), or, on the contrary, to abandon their habitual ways of pleasure-seeking (e.g. masturba-tion). For some years he had been experimenting with this active technique method, of which Freud seemed to thoroughly approve.

Jones invited Ferenczi to join him and Abraham in England in June for the International Congress of Psychology. For a time Fer-enczi seemed to toy with the idea of accepting, particularly since Freud had encouraged him to maintain ties with Jones. However, he decided instead to join Rank for part of the summer in the south Tyrol, where they planned to continue working together. Freud urged Ferenczi to encourage Rank to finish the book he was writing on the birth trauma. Ferenczi agreed about the importance of the primal experience, but hoped to persuade Rank not to attach more significance to it than to the Oedipus complex.

It does not seem possible that Ferenczi really had serious inten-tions of visiting England. At the bottom of his *Rundbrief* of March 1, he added a handwritten note for Vienna that Jones had repeated a remark made by Ferenczi in one of his *Rundbriefe* that he con-sidered an English patient of Ferenczi's, a Mrs. Herford, a very difficult case. Jones had also warned Dr. David Eder to stay away from Ferenczi because he was using "a dangerous new technique." The *Rundbriefe* certainly indicate that Jones was constantly making difficulties about admitting to the English group people who had been analyzed by Ferenczi, whereas he had nothing but praise for Edward and James Glover and others who were analyzed in Berlin. Nevertheless, it was not appropriate for Ferenczi to insert a private note to Vienna, and Jones was puzzled when he did not receive the regular Budapest letter.

On March 17 Ferenczi put a question bluntly to Jones: "I should be very interested to hear with which aspects of the so-called active technique you agree [*Dich identifizierst*]."[4] On April 5 Jones replied evasively that his criticism of the active technique was not meant in an adverse sense. "I do not identify myself with any criticism of active therapy beyond what you yourself have emphasized, e.g. caution for beginners, etc." Abraham could see that trouble was brewing, and in a private letter to Freud expressed concern that a Committee meeting should be held as soon as possible in order to reduce tension. The choice of locale would depend on where Freud intended to spend his holidays.

In July a special edition of the *Zeitschrift* honored Ferenczi on his fiftieth birthday. Freud sent him a complete set of the Encyclopaedia Britannica but failed to congratulate him. Eventually Freud apologized (July 18, 1923) for his oversight, giving as his excuse his failing interest in life and the deep depression that had overwhelmed him. "With someone who was more of a stranger, I would not have forgotten the courtesy."

On June 30 Freud left for Gastein with Minna, and in August they moved on to one of Freud's favourite haunts in the Tyrol, the Hotel du Lac at Lavarone on a high peak of the Dolomites above Lake Caldanozzo. Here they were joined by the rest of Freud's family.

Meanwhile Rank and Ferenczi spent a productive summer. They did not allow a short visit from Sachs to interrupt their work. They also received a visit from Brill, who divulged a derogatory comment about Rank that Jones had made in a private letter to him. Brill was somewhat aggrieved with Jones, who he believed was not giving him sufficient support in America; Eitingon planned a visit to the United States to appraise the situation for himself. In Klobenstein Ferenczi managed to finish his book on the genitalia theory, which eventually appeared as *Thalassa: A Theory of Genitality*, a continuation of the Lamarckian views he and Freud had discussed earlier. Here he developed the view that the whole of life is determined by the desire to return to the womb.

It was agreed that the Committee meeting would be held the last week of August. The members planned to meet at Castel Toblino between Lake Garda and Trent, and travel together to San Cristoforo at the foot of the mountain where Freud was staying.* Again Freud emphasized that they must discuss their problems without him, followed by a brief meeting in which they would report the outcome to him (Vienna, June 1, 1923). Rank and Ferenczi had hoped to visit Freud for a couple of days in Lavarone prior to the meeting, but decided against it lest they make the other members jealous. They were relieved that Eitingon would be present as a peacemaker and hoped that differences between Rank and Abraham could be ironed out (or so they told Freud). The situation with Jones they considered more difficult because personal issues were at stake. They didn't want too heated a confrontation with him, "although we do want to reproach him with certain things" (Ferenczi/Freud; August 8, 1923).

This was the first meeting held without Freud, although his presence hovered 2,000 feet above them at the Hotel du Lac. Actually the hotel is situated on the other side of the mountain overlooking its own small lake. Here Freud had been joined by Dr. Felix Deutsch, who, deeply alarmed about Freud's condition, urged yet another, more radical operation.

The news of the seriousness of Freud's growth was revealed to the members by Anna Freud and Dr. Deutsch, who joined them at dinner in San Cristoforo. Rank, according to Jones's account, suddenly broke out in a fit of uncontrollable hysterical laughter."[5] They then launched into an agitated discussion about how Freud

---

*In 1900 Freud had visited Castel Toblino prior to a sojourn at Lavarone. He wrote his paper on Gradiva at Lavarone in 1906. In August 1912, he stayed at the Hotel Seehof in San Cristoforo.

could be persuaded to have the operation. Sachs thought he would listen to Anna; Rank suggested Freud's elderly mother. The others felt that they had no right to intervene. Years later in London, Jones told Freud about the discussion as to whether to tell him about the cancer, and with blazing eyes, Freud exclaimed, "*Mit welchem Recht?*" ("With what right?")[6]

Freud's state of health made a tense situation almost intolerable. Everyone was aware of the implications of his illness. How could he ever be replaced? They knew that none of them would be acceptable to everyone else on the Committee. The center of the group had disintegrated, and they collapsed into infantile behavior by quarreling fiercely among themselves.

Ferenczi and Rank brought up the "certain things" to which Ferenczi had alluded cryptically to Freud. This is Jones's account:

> It appears that I had made some critical remarks about Rank—I cannot remember now to whom—and he at once brought up this unfriendliness on my part. I apologized for having hurt his feelings, but he refused to accept this and demanded that I be expelled from the Committee. This the others naturally would not allow, Abraham in particular defending me, and there was a very painful scene with Rank in uncontrollable anger and myself in puzzled silence.[7]

Jones is being evasive here. He could not possibly have forgotten that Ferenczi claimed Brill had told him that Jones had described Rank as "a swindling Jew." On August 26, Jones wrote to his wife Katharine:

> The chief news is that Freud has a real cancer slowly growing and may last many years. He doesn't know it and it is a most deadly secret. Eitingon is here too. . . . We have spent the whole day thrashing out the Rank-Jones affair. Very painful but I hope our relations will now be better and believe so, but on the other hand expect Ferenczi will hardly speak to me for Brill has just been there and told him I had said Rank was a swindling Jew (*stark übertreiben*) [strongly exaggerated]. Brill of course has gone back to the U.S. without seeing me.[8]

The actual facts were that in the spring of 1923 Brill complained to Jones that he had never received an acknowledgment from Rank for a sum of money that he had sent as an American contribution to the Verlag. On April 9 Jones commented on the situation to Brill:

> Between ourselves Rank has been somewhat deteriorating of late and has not been behaving quite straight. Also his general way of conducting business was distinctly Oriental. For three years the Press was quite unable to get any statement of accounts out of him, so that we did not know where we stood.[9]

Brill in turn expressed surprise:

> I am sorry to hear about Rank of whom I always had such high regard. It is too bad that whatever it is that does it we all undergo changes and have our own peculiarities. Rank I always considered a very fine type of adjusted man.[10]

The eye of God was not on them. With his back turned to them, Freud was wandering in the rolling meadows of his mountain retreat. Rank and Ferenczi seized the opportunity to vent all their accumulated resentment against Jones. That *all* the other members of the Committee supported Jones (as he claimed) is contradicted by the fact that two days later he reported to his wife that they had spent "hours talking and shouting till I thought I was in Bedlam." The group as a whole decided "that I was in the wrong in the Rank-Jones affaire, in fact that I am neurotic." There seems to have been general agreement that Jones needed further analysis. "A Jewish family council sitting on one sinner must be a great affair, but picture it when the whole five insist on analysing him on the spot and all together![11] The serenity of the lake and the beauty of the surrounding mountains were a marked contrast to the rage unleashed by Freud's absence.

Whether Freud in his mountain aerie was informed of all the details is doubtful, although the group made the steep ascent to pay him a final courtesy call. He did not learn until later that Rank wanted Jones expelled from the Committee. In his *Rundbrief* of September 16, Abraham expressed hope for Freud's recovery and also optimism that the days they had spent together would give the inner circle strength for their future tasks. Only Jones wrote frankly about "the difficult days in San Cristoforo" (October 4, 1923). It seemed to him a "bright fact that no others than psycho-analysts could have succeeded in such circumstances to the extent we did, one more reason for being grateful to our science." On September 12 he had written a private letter to Freud expressing his gratitude for the way he had handled the final meeting. Jones had expected that Freud would not want to see them, he told Freud, or that he would simply have turned on Jones for being the "unwitting cause" of the disturbance.

> I should of course have borne that, naturally, but it could not have made the best atmosphere for insight—insight which in any case is not easy, for I knew I had been unfairly treated, and had much right on my side.

Freud's directness, friendliness, and impartiality had helped Jones see things in proportion, and he assured Freud that he would improve because he was not satisfied with "the present unsatisfactory state of my psychology." He added a postscript. On his return to England he had looked up his copy of his letter to Brill and found it "grossly exaggerated." For example, the word "Semitic" did not occur in it. One might wonder why, then, he did not simply quote the passage directly. Whatever construction one might put on Jones's words, they were highly critical of Rank and it would not be difficult to interpret them as anti-Semitic.

In reply (September 24, 1923) Freud assured Jones that he had reached an age when he could not afford to give up old friends. If young people would think like that, it would be easier to maintain good relations. "Now," he concluded, "I hope you will drop the affair and I will do whatever I can to influence Rank in the sense of kindness and tolerance."

When Jones tackled Brill on what was discussed in Budapest to cause such an uproar, Brill (who by then had returned to New York), replied on September 28, 1923:

> We talked about all matters including the statement that you made to me in one of the letters. I was naturally anxious to find out what trouble there was about Rank as you only vaguely hinted at it in a manner that did not seem very pleasing. I am glad to know now that everything has been amicably settled. I feel that men of our type should have sufficient insight and not resort to the resistances commonly seen in the hoi-poloi.[12]

Despite the state of his health, Freud had managed to take Anna with him on a long-anticipated trip to Rome. Although he had suffered a severe attack of bleeding from his mouth en route, it was secondary to the pleasure of sharing with his daughter the beauties of that glorious city. But on his return to Vienna, on September 26 he had a consultation with Professor Hans Pichler, who persuaded him that he must have a further operation the following month.

Nevertheless, his paladins could not refrain from knifing each other. Ferenczi, in reply to a letter from Jones (October 7, 1923) wrote that the wording of Jones's letter to Brill was not so much the issue as its tone. Ferenczi reminded Jones that in San Cristoforo although he had often told Jones that he was not a serious neurotic, nevertheless Ferenczi was convinced that Jones needed further analysis because he seemed unaware of his unconscious motivations.[13] Ferenczi here adopted the superior tone of an analyst to an analysand. He regarded Jones's analysis in 1913 as incomplete, partly because his own technique had not been as refined as it was now (which did not mean that he espoused a short analysis, as Jones seemed to assume). If they resumed the analysis, no date should be fixed for its termination.

In his October 4 *Rundbrief* Jones announced that the British press was in negotiations with the publisher Cape, but how these plans would be affected by the unexpected news of the Professor's transfer of the American rights to his nephew left the British uncertain about the future of the press. Jones's loyalty to Freud was extraordinary. Did he simply suppress his feelings of grievance when he felt badly treated? Certainly the state of Freud's health during 1923 stifled any overt feelings of resentment.

Trouble erupted again at the beginning of November. Jones had published a paper on autosuggestion without making reference to Ferenczi's prior work on the subject.* Ferenczi was only too willing to take offence. In his *Rundbrief* he described himself as insulted that a so-called good friend had done such a thing (November 2, 1923). Abraham reacted in alarm to Ferenczi's accusations (November 7, 1923). Again—as he had done with Jones and Rank—Abraham tried to act as mediator between Jones and Ferenczi. He believed that Ferenczi should have taken up the matter privately with Jones before exploding publicly in his *Rundbrief*. Abraham pointed out that at San Cristoforo he had urged tolerance toward Jones. Like the letter to Brill, Jones's article had been written before their meeting.

> You, dear Ernest, will probably remember our talk on your secret jealousy of Sandor and Otto as the favored oldest and the favored youngest son. In the end it is against the father and we all know that I tend to interpret both incidents as a result of the same affect.

He urged Jones to issue an official letter acknowledging the priority of Ferenczi's writing.

In a long *Rundbrief* (November 12, 1923) Jones passionately defended himself against Ferenczi's accusations. He professed himself grieved that he had "unwittingly" upset his old friend Sandor and expressed astonishment that such an accusation should have been made against him for the first time in his life when he had a reputation for being particularly punctilious in such matters. He reminded Ferenczi that he had done much to publicize his work in English, and if he spoke of the libido theory of suggestion (without naming its original progenitor) it was because it had been incorporated into the psychoanalytic canon. Moreover, he had submitted his paper in advance to Abraham and Freud, and neither of them

*In 1915 Freud and Ferenczi had discussed Jones's tendency to plagiarize. See page 70.

had mentioned his omission in acknowledging Ferenczi's contribution. He expressed himself willing to write a letter to the *Zeitschrift* or the *Journal*, "provided I am not asked to retract what I have never done." What did "dear Sandor" want him to do? It was a storm in a teacup, but the volatile Ferenczi seemed intent on humiliating Jones.

On November 16 Rank announced more grim news about Freud's health. The Professor had had yet another operation, and the painful prosthesis he was now forced to wear had to be adjusted. As for the Ferenczi-Jones imbroglio, Rank had discussed it with the Professor before his operation and they both felt that Jones should have given acknowledgment to Ferenczi. (With the crossing of the letters, it would appear that both Freud and Abraham had forgotten that Jones had sent them the article in advance, and that they had probably not taken the time to read it.)

Abraham in turn (December 2, 1923) informed Jones vaguely that he could not agree with every point in his argument but that he was convinced that no insult was intended and hoped that Ferenczi would be conciliatory. Despite repeated requests from Jones, Ferenczi would not discuss the matter, and by December 15 Jones had decided that there was no reason to continue the debate. Nevertheless, on December 21, Ferenczi finally stated that he would not accept Jones's explanation and demanded a public statement about Ferenczi's prior work on autosuggestion. But by the middle of January he changed his mind after reading an article in an American journal by another writer in which he received adequate credit for his original work. It was clearly a rather feeble way of saving face.

There was a xenophobic dynamic to the Committee. In the eyes of Rank and Ferenczi, Abraham and Eitingon, as Berliners, were snobbish outsiders. In the eyes of all of them, Jones was a Gentile, he spoke German haltingly, he was British, and he had been the enemy during the war. He might protest that he was Welsh and had married a Jew, but the others always seized every opportunity to make him aware that he could never belong. His fantasy of penetrating the inner circle by creating the Committee was an illusion, because he would forever be an unattractive little man with his ferret face pressed imploringly against the glass.

While ostensibly the group wished to extend the frontiers of psychoanalysis, both Ferenczi and Rank exhibited a certain ghetto mentality in belittling all Eitingon's efforts to establish psychoanalysis in Moscow and Paris. After his experience of what collaboration with the state had done to psychoanalysis in Hungary, Ferenczi was strongly opposed to the Russian communist experiment. He also objected to Eitingon's praise of René Laforgue, the rising star of the French psychoanalytic movement, because he seemed to be diminishing the prospects of his own former analysand, Eugenia Sokolnicka, who had been one of the chief figures in the establishment of psychoanalysis in France. The Swiss group appeared to have gone into a complete decline at this time.

Freud must have found his illness in some ways an escape from the problems in which his followers tried to involve him. The events of 1923 were of such a serious nature that the Committee seemed doomed.

Chapter Nine

Dissent and Division

 "EVENTS ARE moving with startling rapidity, and we must be prepared for everything."[1] So Ernest Jones began a letter to Karl Abraham on April 8, 1924. The *Rundbriefe* during the first months of the year convey the impression that relationships were relatively normal, but the agitated private correspondence among the members of the Committee indicates confusion and turbulent passions as the group's carefully constructed edifice began to crumble.

Three books, all originally encouraged by Freud, were responsible for the eventual dissolution of the Committee: the book written jointly by Rank and Ferenczi, *The Development of Psychoanalysis* [*Entwicklungsziele der Psychoanalyse*]; Rank's *The Trauma of Birth* [*Das Trauma der Gerburt*]; and Ferenczi's *Thalassa: A Theory of Genitality*. All three had appeared by early 1924, although Freud had read them in advance. Indeed, Rank had dedicated *The Trauma of Birth* to Freud as "The Explorer of the Unconscious"; and Freud had replied (December 1, 1923):

> I gladly accept your dedication with the assurance of my most cordial thanks. If you could put it more moderately, it would be all right with me. Handicapped as I am, I enjoy enormously your admirable productivity. That means for me too: "*Non omnis moriar!* ("I shall not wholly die.)[2]

Early in January Freud presided over a meeting of the Vienna Society during which Ferenczi lectured on his theory of active therapy. Ferenczi had no opportunity for an intimate conversation with Freud on this occasion, and he returned to Budapest with a sense of foreboding, brooding on a "playful" remark Freud had made in which he described Ferenczi as Rank's "accomplice." On January 20 he could contain himself no longer. He expressed his anxiety that Freud had reservations about his lecture despite his previous frequent expressions of approval of his investigative methods. He begged Freud to calm his anxiety by some words of clarification.*

Freud, who was feeling extremely discouraged by the failure of a regenerative Steinach operation he had undergone a few months earlier, replied vaguely, "I have not completely agreed with your collaborative work although I value much in it. I have spoken critically about some of it with Rank."[3] He had been struck by the fact that Ferenczi's lecture concentrated solely on his own active technique as though he were distancing himself from Rank's theory of the birth trauma. Was it possible, he speculated, that Ferenczi was still suffering from a brother complex?

Ferenczi was dumbfounded, especially as he had heard nothing from Rank about Freud's disapproval. He reminded Freud (January 30, 1924) that in Berlin, Lavarone, and Vienna he had received encouragement for the joint endeavor. Freud had even encouraged them to submit their work for the annual psychoanalytic prize. They had incorporated Freud's suggestions and taken note of his criticisms. Freud had read the galley proofs of their book, and they had followed all his suggestions for structural changes and emphasis on certain points. The only real objection Freud had raised was that there was too much discussion about experiencing (abreaction) rather than remembering. Ferenczi admitted that perhaps they had not included sufficient observational data on this point, but their main aim had been to correct what they had seen as an excess of theorizing.

Ferenczi then turned to Freud's allegation about his brother com-

---

*In the same letter, in a passage on Hungary's precarious financial situation, Ferenczi asks, "Will a 'carpenter' also help us?" This is possibly a reference to Hitler. Later in the year there are references in the correspondence to Hitler's bully boys and their abortive putsch in Munich in November 1923.

plex. He was willing to admit that it had possibly operated to a certain extent in his lecture; but, after all, if he concentrated on the active technique, this was because it was his particular contribution. He had not discussed the question of a fixed date of termination for an analysis since this was Rank's idea, not his.

The thought of a disagreement with Freud was unbearable to Ferenczi, and he pleaded with him for a full discussion among the three of them before the next Congress in April. On the very evening Freud received Ferenczi's letter (February 4), in response to his distress Freud sat down to clarify his objections, although they continued to be as unformulated as before. He had already told Sachs and Rank that what Rank and Ferenczi seemed to suggest was a quick method for traveling salesmen. (The fact that he had discussed the book with Sachs might have had some bearing on Freud's change of heart on the matter. Sachs, who visited Vienna every Christmas, seems to have been a conveyor of gossip between Vienna and Berlin.)

He didn't want to be two-faced, Freud said, but the fact of the matter was that—with distance—he was no longer as enthusiastic about the collaborative work as he had been. "In the beginning, most likely the correction that you made about my timidity to act, tempted [*bestechen*] me too much."

He had been suspicious of Ferenczi's lecture because it avoided the issue of the birth trauma; and Freud had begun to fear that this was a diversionary tactic indicating that both active therapy and the birth trauma implied a radical shortening of the analysis of which Ferenczi knew Freud would disapprove. From Freud's discussions with his own analysands and pupils, he had to say bluntly that he had found nothing to justify Rank's theory that the reenactment of birth would "magically" dissolve neuroses. But, considering Freud's fixation on the Oedipus complex, it is doubtful that he would consider any other sources for neurosis.

Freud always listened very carefully to Eitingon, and he pondered a letter he had received from him from the Riviera, where Eitingon was convalescing from a paralysis of the facial muscles. Eitingon reported that Abraham was seriously disturbed about the direction in which Rank was going, and Eitingon feared that there would be serious friction between Abraham and Rank. Following so shortly upon the contretemps with Jones, Freud felt anxious about the prospects for the Committee. "I had hoped that you would keep together at least as long as I am around."[4] Nevertheless, he did not feel prepared to have a joint discussion with Rank and Ferenczi.

Ferenczi was still confused as to the precise nature of Freud's objections and hurt by the possibility that Freud had been insincere in his earlier assessment of the book. He believed that Freud needed further time to digest the implications of the work. He asked him (February 14) to consider the dates of the respective books. Rank had not "discovered" the birth trauma until after the collaborative book. In the latter book he had suggested the establishment of a termination date in the final stages of analysis. Ferenczi had been led to connect this with the birth trauma, and if he hadn't mentioned this in his lecture, it was solely because it was Rank's idea. On the other hand, they were in agreement about shorter analyses, whereas Abraham was in the habit of prolonging analyses, a lengthy procedure for which Ferenczi could see no scientific justification. Nevertheless, he was convinced that Abraham, "as an intelligent man," would come around to their point of view. He was disturbed by Freud's contemptuous allusion to traveling salesmen, because it was impossible to contemplate either him or Rank slipping away from the fundamentals of psychoanalysis.

As for the Committee, he was convinced that it could hold together provided these petty disagreements came to an end and "the probably non-regainable *friendly* co-operation make room for a matter-of-fact one." It was a feeble hope.

In the Vienna *Rundbrief* of January 4, Rank vented his anger against Berlin because he had heard from one of his former analysands that Berlin analysts had asked him searching questions about Rank's technique and had reacted to the answers with obvious disapproval. Consequently, Rank had no intention of sending any more patients to Berlin. Ferenczi in turn (January 13) reported that he had repeated his Vienna lecture in Budapest. Franz Alexander from Berlin had been present at the lecture and had reacted favorably, and Ferenczi could not help sympathizing with Rank's account of the hasty and tactless way most of the Berliners had responded.

In his *Rundbrief* of January 15, Jones thanked Rank warmly for "his remarkable book on birth traumas and hope also to see the book he wrote with Sandor (of which there are several copies in England). Without pretending to have assimilated all its contents as yet, I am sure that we could all corroborate many of his views at once, e.g. the close connection between psa [viz. psychoanalysis] and repetition of pregnancy and birth." That Rank doubted Jones's sincerity is apparent in a circular letter which, by Freud's request, he omitted to send to England. Here he claimed that Jones had not written immediately to Brill as he had promised to do in San Cristoforo. Indeed, when he did write it was to reproach Brill for divulging a confidence. Rank told them that Brill had apparently replied that there was no question of confidentiality and that he felt that he ought to inform Rank about the matter so that he would be able to judge the situation objectively for himself.*

Berlin in turn (February 18) added a postscript, again excluding Jones:

> We very much regret the news about Ernest's behaviour. The news about this, recently received from Otto, is certainly a compelling reason for a discussion *before* the Congress. Until then, we should be careful about making judgments.

Freud, however, sent Rank a note that his intermediate circular letter "could not have been better."[5] When it came to anything concerning Jones's behavior, Freud was still ready to back Rank to the hilt.

But he was disturbed by Eitingon's report about the hostile reaction in Berlin to the new books and felt impelled to intervene once more in a circular letter of his own sent out early in February.[6] Freud expressed astonishment that the new books had elicited such negative feelings in Berlin, and wrote that if there was any impression that he had disapproved of Rank's theory it must have been

*For Brill's actual reply, see p.135.

conveyed by Sachs. Moreover, the fact that he had allowed Rank to dedicate the book to him ruled out such a possibility.

He then explained that the members of the Committee could not pursue their own investigations freely if they felt that everything they said had to be approved by their leader. They would have his support so long as they did not depart from basic psychoanalytic principles, which of course was unthinkable. As Freud repeatedly emphasized, it took him a long time to understand another person's way of thinking.

The letter was ambiguous at best. Freud seemed to support the new ideas in Rank and Ferenczi's books, only to undercut them immediately. The notion of re-enactment (rather than recollection of experience) Freud considered "a refreshing and interesting attack on our analytic habits." However, he noted that Rank and Ferenczi gave no clear explanation of the technique to be employed in their innovations. Yet he warned the Committee members that new ideas should not be judged in advance as "heretical." Nevertheless, Ferenczi's active therapy would be dangerous in the hands of beginners. He then used an analogy from his own experience. During his illness he had learned that a shaved beard required six weeks to grow in again. Thus he found it difficult to understand how an analysis of four or five months could penetrate the deepest strata of the unconscious and create "a permanent affect." Since he now dealt mainly with students, he would continue to conduct "classical" analysis.

As for *The Trauma of Birth*—the "incomparably more interesting book"—he had not yet arrived at a definitive judgment about the efficacy of re-enacting the experience of birth. Womb fantasies might provide a biological basis for the Oedipus complex. But would these interfere with the incest prohibition? His own explanation had been "historic, social, phylogenetic." The actual father had created the obstacle to incest, and in this crucial issue clearly he and Rank differed. Nevertheless, "What we have here is no revolution, no contradiction of our established insight, but only an interesting enlargement whose value should be recognized. . . ."

He then stated that he failed to see how any possible therapeutic transference to the mother rather than the father could shorten the analysis. Yet finally he concluded: do not pass judgment too hastily.

Rank had expected a more wholehearted endorsement and felt that Freud had failed him. He could see that the letter was intended as a means of maintaining peace within the Committee, but he was disturbed, he wrote Freud (February 15)[7] that his work had been misrepresented. He had not been referring to a womb fantasy but to a re–enactment of a real (though partial) return to the womb. In his own experience the essential factor in impotence was not paternal prohibition but anxiety about the maternal genital.

His work, Rank emphasized, was in no sense a total departure from that of Freud. He believed Freud overemphasized his shortening of the analysis. What he and Ferenczi objected to were interminable analyses, which eventually became ineffective. They did not want the patient to die from the operation, Rank remarked ironically.

Abraham also wanted a meeting of the Committee held before the Congress to discuss the issue, which was fast becoming a crisis. In response to the Professor's circular letter, he joined Jones (always alert to how the wind was blowing), who was beginning to see Rank's book in a new light. "To start with," he assured Freud, "there is no question of hunting heretics."

> Results of whatever kind obtained in a legitimate analytic matter would never give me cause for such grave doubts. This is something different. I see signs of an ominous development concerning vital issues of psychoanalysis. They force me, to my deepest sorrow, and not for the first time in the twenty years of my psycho-analytic life, to sound a warning. When I add that these facts have robbed me of a good deal of optimism with which I observe the progress of our work, you will have to gauge the depth of my disquiet.[8]

The contents and style of the *Rundbriefe* continued to maintain the fiction that life was progressing smoothly and normally. On February 3 Ferenczi reported that after ten years of ostracism, he and some members of his Society would again address a group of

Hungarian doctors. Berlin expressed its gratification (February 18) that such a dramatic change had taken place. But Abraham wasn't at all pleased about the dramatic changes within the Committee. To Freud personally (February 26) he warned that Ferenczi and Rank were repeating the pattern of Jung's behavior. He realized that with all their pleasant qualities, "their actions could not be compared to the deceitfulness and brutality of Jung." But he warned that their deviation from classical technique was closely linked to the disintegration of the Committee. "It almost fell apart last autumn," he reminded Freud. "I may say it was I in the first place who prevented this at the time. I shall now use all my influence once more to avert these dangers, as far as is still possible." His final dramatic point: at the first Congress in Salzburg in 1908 he had warned Freud about Jung, and at the time Freud had dismissed this as jealousy. "Another Salzburg Congress is before us and once more I come to you in the same role—a role which I would far rather not play. If, on this occasion, I find you ready to listen to me despite the fact that I have so much to say that is painful, then I shall come to the meeting with hope of success." The situation was so critical that Jones had assured him that he was willing to travel to Vienna to thrash the matter out in a Committee meeting before the Congress.

Freud replied (March 4) with a heavy heart. He gathered that Abraham had assumed that he was unwilling to have a discussion with him because of his personal intimacy with Ferenczi and Rank. Geographical reasons were responsible for their closeness, and he wanted Abraham to know that "you stand no lower than they in my friendship and esteem." But he would not tolerate the comparison with Jung. Suppose Rank and Ferenczi actually claimed that the birth trauma rather than the Oedipus complex was the decisive factor in development, would the world come to an end? In a last desperate bid for unity, he pleaded, "We could remain under the same roof with the greatest equanimity, and after a few years' work it would become plain whether one side had exaggerated a useful finding or the other had underrated it."[9]

Freud could not possibly bear the polemical atmosphere of a pre-Congress Committee meeting. For the first time he actually admitted that there "lurks a desire to be spared the whole bother of a congress." In any event, he had no intention of giving a paper or attending the large banquet. Abraham then assured him that he had never felt that Freud had slighted him. At the meetings in the Harz Mountains and at Lavarone he had had the impression that Freud had great confidence in him. But, unlike Freud, Abraham continued, he had no difficulty in assimilating new ideas—so long as they "have been arrived at in a legitimate psychoanalytic manner."[10]

Abraham also wanted to have a symposium at the Congress in which Rank's and Ferenczi's ideas would be discussed. Both men were adamant that they would take no part in any symposium, however, and they had no intention of delivering a paper either. Neither of them was eager to be exposed to public humiliation.

Freud invited Rank to dinner in the hope that in an intimate atmosphere they might talk freely and without bitterness. (Naturally Rank passed on to Ferenczi everything that had been discussed.) Ferenczi exploded with rage over what he viewed as Abraham's hypocrisy (Ferenczi/Freud; March 18, 1924). He had always detected signs of ambition and jealousy behind Abraham's veneer of politeness, he wrote. It was these passions that prompted him to blacken [*anschwärzen*] his and Rank's work. He told Freud bluntly that he was not free from blame either: his ambiguous circular letter of February 9 had given Abraham the impetus to exhibit open enmity.

Ferenczi then made some interesting remarks about Abraham's behavior at San Cristoforo. With hindsight he had come to the conclusion that Abraham had decided at that point that the fate of the Committee was sealed. Ferenczi now believed that Abraham's behavior toward Jones had been ambiguous, and Ferenczi and Rank found it difficult to convince him that anti-Semitism could not be tolerated within the Committee. Moreover, Abraham took every opportunity to put Rank in the wrong.

As for the proposal that Abraham become president of the International Association, Ferenczi considered it insulting to impose such a hostile leader on them. If Freud was unwilling to assume the position, he would suggest Eitingon, not only because he was unbiased but because, as founder of the Poliklinik, he had long deserved the recognition.*

Ferenczi wrote as though the cessation of the *Rundbriefe* was inevitable. This would be an advantage to him, because Ferenczi's personal correspondence with Freud could be resumed, and he would visit Freud frequently. The fact of the matter was that Ferenczi and Rank had never been really enthusiastic about the formation of the Committee which Jones had seized upon tactically as a way to exert personal power within the movement.

Freud, too, had missed the personal correspondence with Ferenczi. He wrote an equally long, frank, and detailed letter in reply (March 20).

> My faith in you and Rank is unconditional. It would be very sad if it were possible to find oneself deceived after having lived together for 16-17 years.

But why, he asked, was it imperative to Ferenczi that Freud agree with him on everything? And Rank's rough manner was bound to antagonize people, when he should be comporting himself with the happy confidence that in many respects he was closer to Freud than anyone else.

At this point only Freud and Ferenczi knew that Rank was planning to go to America for a year or so. Freud was concerned that Rank's health was not up to it because he was frequently ill; and, he added ominously, "I am not sure if I will see him again when he comes back in the fall."

A great feeling of sadness had overcome Freud. For the first time he spoke of the "former" [*ehemalig*] Committee. He did not doubt that the members still felt affection for him. But, overcome with self-pity, he complained that they were deserting him in his moment of greatest need. He had survived the Committee, he might survive the International Association, and he hoped psychoanalysis would survive him. What he had to look forward to was a gloomy old age.

*Rank, on the other hand, did not intend to make a public protest about Abraham's presidency, especially as Eitingon offered to take on the secretariat so that Rank would not have to work with Abraham (Rank/Ferenczi; April 3, 1924).

On this occasion he didn't mention the possibility of a release by death, a theme he generally raised on such occasions.

Turning to the question of Abraham's presidency, Freud's position remained the same: Abraham as president, Rank as secretary. After all, the presidency had been promised to Abraham when he took on the position of secretary. "To deny it to him now would look like one was trying to discipline him and to do that—despite his doing wrong—and his unfriendliness against the two of you—I do not believe to be justified."

Freud used a different comparison of Rank to "the blessed Jung" than the one Abraham had employed. Like Jung (and like Freud himself when he first started to practice psychoanalysis), Rank was blinded by his own self-revelations. The Berliners were justified in resenting the uncomplimentary reference to them in Rank's book, and he himself was dubious about the efficacy of a short analysis. It was a splendidly frank letter, and Freud gave Ferenczi permission to show it to anyone he liked.

Rank wrote to Ferenczi the same day, adding some interesting details. Freud had promised to open the Committee meeting ("which will not be a Committee meeting") with the statement that the Committee no longer existed.[11] Rank told Ferenczi that Freud agreed with Ferenczi that Sachs's protestations of friendliness were insincere and that Abraham was undoubtedly hostile. Neither Rank nor Freud felt that they could count unconditionally on Eitingon because he was in the habit of disappearing for weeks at a time, and there were rumors that his health was not good.

Rank and his wife planned to travel to Salzburg on April 18, expecting Ferenczi to accompany them. After the Congress, Rank would proceed directly to Cherbourg where he would sail for America on April 27.

Like Abraham, Jones had been encouraged by Freud's circular letter to unleash his resentment against Rank (February 18, 1924). He wrote that he feared the consequences of "the ulterior tendencies" of the books if they got into the hands of "ambitious or reactionary readers." He also believed that what should have been simply tentative suggestions were expressed in the book in "too dogmatic and even a dictatorial manner." In another letter, following Abraham's lead (February 29, 1924), Jones expressed regret that Rank and Ferenczi refused to participate in a symposium, particularly as all of the other Committee members would have liked some elucidation about their technique, "which is not contained in your books."

Ferenczi defended himself in a *Rundbrief* of March 6. To describe the exact nature of their technique was neither his intention nor that of Rank. He regretted that Jones considered their tone dictatorial, and hoped that once Jones had at least considered the applicability of the birth trauma as responsible for a constellation of drives [*Triebverschränkung*] toward wanting both to return to and to flee the womb, he might modify his views. If they had not presented their work to the Committee it was because they intended to submit it for a prize competition, of which the Committee members were the judges. He also reminded them that the atmosphere in San Cristoforo had not been exactly favorable to scientific discussion. Finally, he expressed displeasure that a public lecture on his genitalia theory was to be given in Berlin by Dr. Michael Balint, who had not yet completed his training analysis. Ferenczi was not aware that in London the brothers Edward and James Glover had made a devastating attack on the birth trauma at a meeting of the British Society.

Rank and Ferenczi were obsessed about Jones. Still harping on Jones's alleged description of Rank as "a swindling Jew," they demanded that the issue be raised again. Abraham wanted further discussion of the Brill matter postponed until after the Congress. In reply to his direct question to Jones as to whether he had written to Brill to clarify the matter as he had promised at San Cristoforo, Jones replied (March 17):

I wrote, of course, as promised to Brill last September, and he sent me a moral lecture by reply. It was evident that he had been in no way influenced by my depreciatory remark. The matter has therefore no external significance whatever. At the same time, we have much more important things to do than to bring up once more this purely personal question. It would be impossible to discuss it fully (which was the reason I could not do so at St. Cristoforo), without exploring very disagreeable financial questions between the Press and the Verlag. This could only lead to further ill-feeling on Otto's part, and no judgment could possibly be arrived at without investigation of many documents and several witnesses. It will be far wiser to relegate the whole matter to the past.[12]

Ferenczi tried to persuade Freud that he had originally encouraged Rank in his speculations. He reminded him (March 24, 1924) of a walk he and Freud had taken in Berlin in 1922 when Freud had revealed Rank's birth trauma theory to him. At the time Freud had said: "I do not know if 33 or 66% of it is true; in any case, this is the most important development since the discovery of psychoanalysis. Somebody else would have made himself independent with a discovery like that." Ferenczi retraced how he had begun to see a close connection between this and his genitalia theory, which he and Freud had initially discussed at length through 1915. He listed the reasons why he supported Rank:

1. He had contributed important facts to psychoanalysis.

2. His theory could not only be incorporated into the existing structure of the psychoanalytic system but act as a confirmation of it.

3. Rank had probably been in the grip of euphoria when he was first formulating his theory, but a careful reading of his book indicated a cautious awareness of this early enthusiasm.

While Ferenczi deplored the negative attitude of Abraham and Jones, he found Freud's ambiguous position "staggering and contradictory." If Freud found it impossible to refuse the presidency to Abraham, Ferenczi wrote him in the same letter,

then some satisfaction would have to be demanded so that Rank could stay in the association. This satisfaction can only be in such a way that *you* characterize Abraham's actions appropriately and show Rank signs of your faith that cannot be misunderstood and that you declare a decision of the scientific question too premature, but worthy of serious consideration.

In reply, Freud finally stated flatly that he was now "66 percent *against* and 33 percent *pro*."[13] His decision had been reached because Rank had not given sufficient illustrative data (e.g. statistics about difficult births, etc.). Above everything else, while Rank did not state it openly, the fact of the matter was that Rank wanted to replace the Oedipus complex with the birth trauma—and everyone realized that. Nevertheless, Ferenczi managed to persuade Freud to postpone publishing a polemic he was writing against Rank's theory.

Always in the past Freud had defended poor, overworked, invaluable Rank. Now—even though he felt Abraham was too hostile to Rank—he was beginning to see Rank in a new light. Instead of protecting Freud as he had done in the past, Rank had introduced dissension into Freud's life; Freud felt he was being torn to pieces by the factions within the Committee. Rank had, for one thing, antagonized people by his aggressive manner. A good example was the *Rundbrief* in which he refused to send any more patients to Berlin. Freud begged Ferenczi to use his influence to mitigate Rank's bitterness against Abraham.

Freud was totally disgusted by this constant quarreling and had no intention of intervening about the question of the presidency. "The circle of our former Committee must sort things out for themselves," because at Easter he planned to take a vacation and would be unavailable for a meeting with them. He wished Rank to take over immediately as president of the Vienna Society in order to give him adequate prestige at the Congress. On March 26, 1924 Freud wrote to Ferenczi:

> I do not have to assure you that my personal feelings for you and Rank remain unchanged. I certainly feel annoyed by the weaknesses that have become obvious in the two of you but that is certainly no reason to forget about services of friendship and co-operation of fifteen years. I just cannot repel the others who might have similar claims. And a little more or less injustice when one lets oneself be led by the passions, is no reason to damn people whom one cares about otherwise.

Freud had been pushed too far. He was sick and tired of the whole business, and feared that it was actually killing him. At the beginning of April he announced that he was not going to attend the Salzburg Congress later in the month but would recuperate instead at Semmering—not because of the quarrels, he emphasized, but because of his "tortured and weakened condition" (Freud/ Ferenczi; April 3, 1924). He had clearly been building up to this decision, but perhaps unconsciously he had never intended to participate. His intention of making Rank president of the Vienna Society might suggest a solution by having a proxy representative.

Freud's warmth for Ferenczi and Rank might have cooled, but he felt no warmer toward Abraham. Indeed, he considered that Abraham was mainly responsible for precipitating the crisis. On March 31 he informed him of his decision to forego the Congress unless his health improved markedly before Easter. However justified Abraham might have felt his reaction to Rank and Ferenczi to be, Freud wrote, it was "certainly not friendly, and it has become clear to me on this occasion that the state of mind is lacking that would make a committee of this handful of people." He believed it to be Abraham's responsibility to prevent further deterioration, and he hoped that Eitingon (who was expected back from San Remo) would help him understand this. Freud found it difficult to think, he admonished Abraham, that it was his intention to cause the total collapse of the International Association. He also informed him that he would wait until a week before the Congress to let Abraham know his final decision about whether he would attend the Salzburg Congress. This was possibly a maneuver to coax Abraham into a more cooperative frame of mind, because only three days later Freud sent letters to all the members of the Committee informing them that he intended to remain at Semmering.

Abraham confided in Jones that he felt unjustly treated by Freud. On April 8, Jones replied:

You have my understanding sympathy in having also to undergo my experience of being unfairly treated by one's best friend, but I am sure you will deal successfully with the situation. It is not hard to make every allowance for him when one considers all the factors, age, illness, and the insidious propaganda nearer home; the deepest reason of all I will indicate in a moment. At all events it shews the imperfection of his objectivity, for no one could possibly have displayed a purer and more loyal attitude than you have done in this difficult year.[14]

Jones listed the warning signs in Rank's behavior: his *Vaterablehnung* (rejection of the father) and flight from the Oedipus complex: the secret way in which he published the book; his evasion of the Committee's questions; the cessation of the *Rundbriefe*; his refusal to take part in the Symposium on the theories and techniques he and Ferenczi had developed; and "his Jung-like decision to go to America without letting any of us know." Jones doubted that Rank would even turn up at Salzburg, but if he did, Jones intended to act in a friendly way toward him. However, he was not prepared to sacrifice his intellectual convictions for any man on earth, even for the Professor.

It would be a strange irony if we lost some of Prof's intimate friendship through too great loyalty to his work, but it may possibly prove to be so. We may possibly have to choose between Psa and personal considerations, in which case you may be sure I for one shall have no doubt.

Then Jones made a perceptive comment on Freud's state of mind. Ten years ago he would have put his work before anything else, he wrote, but now he was old and ill.

. . . he can hardly face the possibility of having once more to go through the Jung situation and this time much nearer home, with someone who perhaps means more to him than his own sons. This thought must call for our deepest sympathy.

It is probably the real reason why he will not come to the Congress, either to the Committee meeting or the Symposium, where there is a risk of his unconscious fears being exposed; and also the reason why he must project his accusations of disruption to a distance, to Berlin or London.

The following day Jones conveyed to Freud his shock at hearing that he had dissolved the Committee, "as I have heard no other intimation in this direction. I am quite in the dark about the meaning of it all."

Only the previous month Freud had described Abraham as his *rocher de bronze*. Abraham felt justifiably aggrieved by Freud's criticism of him because, as he again reminded Freud (April 4, 1924), he considered himself responsible for holding the Committee together at San Cristoforo; and that had certainly seemed to be Freud's view also when they had parted on the Postplatz at Lavarone. And now he was being scolded that he had disrupted the Committee when all his efforts (such as suggesting a meeting before the Congress) had been to preserve it. Abraham recited his contributions to the movement: the organization of the Berlin Society, the International Association, and "the whole burden of preparation for the Congress."[15] It must have been particularly bitter to him not to receive any response from Freud before the commencement of the Congress on April 21.

On April 6 Ferenczi sent out a *Rundbrief* stating the obvious: the Committee's correspondence had splintered up into private letters, and the *Rundbriefe* had deteriorated into "a formality without content." How the relationships among the Committee members might develop would depend entirely on their mutual support of psychoanalysis, he wrote. On the tenth Rank dispatched a letter dissolving the Committee. On the same day Freud wrote Rank approvingly that "Ferenczi's reply is very dignified. Abraham will be astonished by this announcement. Unfortunately he is completely without insight. He writes me, he hopes my 'indisposition' will be over soon and that it will not deter me from coming to Salzburg and also giving a paper. He will not believe that with me it is a new and reduced program for life and work."[16] Freud mentioned the work of Rank's "dear wife" in the preparations for the Congress and urged Rank to come and see him. In other words, he was on a completely friendly footing again with Rank on the eve of the Congress but still furious with Abraham. Freud's wavering reactions suggest that he was momentarily relieved because he had managed to avert a Jung-like confrontation with Rank.

Chapter Ten

Division and Death

THE 1924 Salzburg Congress went off relatively smoothly. Inevitably there was a good deal of speculation about Freud's absence, since it was the first Congress he had ever missed. Ferenczi actually nominated Abraham for president, and Abraham repeatedly begged him to convey to Freud that he had made every effort to reestablish peace. Indeed, Ferenczi found it easier to get along with the Berlin group than with Jones. At the "non-Committee meeting," Jones soon abandoned the idea of the Committee reestablishing itself on the old basis, but in principle the members agreed that they could have a "chairman committee" [*Obmann-komité*] (Ferenczi/Freud; April 26, 1924).* Before the opening afternoon session devoted to a discussion of the active technique and the birth trauma (in which Ferenczi and Rank refused to participate), there was a good deal of tension in the air, and everyone expected some kind of a clash; but apart from an exchange that threatened to become sharp between Jones and Ferenczi, Ferenczi was surprised at the real attempt at objectivity by the Berliners.

Rank suddenly decided to leave the day before the end of the Congress, on April 22, his fortieth birthday. Apparently he remarked that he could not bear to see Abraham elected president (Abraham/Freud; October 27, 1925). Ferenczi wrote to Rank in New York (May 25, 1924) that his abrupt departure had offended everyone, including the Viennese. At the closing banquet, Rank's

---

*Dr. Judith Dupont has suggested that this probably meant an arbitration committee.

"sarcastic" Viennese colleague, Eduard Hitschmann, in what was intended as a humorous speech, made some sardonic comments about "the 'hero' Otto, who, he hopes, will now be rescued from the waters and so will get over the trauma of birth."

> Jones's formal address [Ferenczi wrote to Rank] was nearly a funeral oration for the Professor, very tactless. In closing, *he praised Abraham and the Professor jointly* whereupon Abraham praised *Jones and the Professor*. Very well pre-arranged.[1]

In Jones's life of Freud he explains that Abraham was unable to visit Freud after the Congress because his Austrian visa had expired. The truth seems to be that Freud was still offended with him and did not offer him any encouragement to visit him. Abraham apparently used the excuse of the visa to spare embarrassment for both of them.

On April 28 Freud sent a brief, rather formal letter to Abraham congratulating him on the presidency. He admitted that he was moving closer to Abraham's position theoretically, "but I still cannot take your side personally. I am fully convinced of the correctness of your behavior, but I still think you might have done things differently."

Abraham then prepared a long detailed report about the Congress. Freud was touched by his conscientiousness, and Abraham again resumed his role as Freud's *rocher de bronze;* and by May 15 Freud was praising Abraham to Ferenczi for being clearly responsible for the success of the Congress. Freud wrote Abraham that he was abashed that "of all people it was you, my *rocher de bronze*, whom I had to keep away,"[2] while he had to see people like Jones and van Emden. He was particularly pleased that a reconciliation seemed to have taken place between Abraham and Ferenczi. Freud pleaded with Abraham to try to put himself in his place. He was convinced that he was close to the end of his life. His sixty-eighth birthday was two days away, and he could not help fearing it would be his last because Vienna was conferring the "Freedom of the City" on him, an honor usually reserved for people on their seventieth birthday.

The future of the Committee was left in abeyance for the time being. Ferenczi's career was in a state of uncertainty during that summer. In Salzburg, Siegfried Bernfeld had asked him if he would consider taking over the projected Viennese Poliklinik since Hitsch-mann (the designated director) was very much disliked. At the same time Ferenczi received a letter from a former American analysand, Caroline Newton, asking if he would be interested in participating in an American Poliklinik for two or three years. He reminded Freud that he had barely kept his head above water for some years, but would wait to hear from Rank about the professional possibilities in America before making a decision.

Freud had always opposed any suggestion that Ferenczi go to America, and he assured him that the idea of his coming to the Poliklinik in Vienna had his complete support. Expansively Freud promised to send all his foreign patients to him. Ferenczi would supplant Rank as his successor, he wrote, an action that would be accepted by the Viennese because Ferenczi was a doctor and commanded the authority that Rank lacked. The only obstacle was that Hitschmann had been deeply involved in the establishment of the Poliklinik, so that it might be rather awkward to get rid of him.[3]

Meanwhile Rank was giving well-attended lectures in New York and building up a large practice. He gave no indication that there was opposition to his theories in Europe. Freud encouraged him to charge the "savages" high fees, adding ironically (May 23, 1924):

Nice that you now have nearly all my former analysands whose analyses I recall without any satisfaction. It often seemed to me that analysis fits the American as a white shirt the raven.[4]

Ferenczi found the American financial prospects far more enticing than the vague Viennese offer, especially as Rank enthusiastically encouraged him to join him. Ferenczi then proceeded to tell his patients that he was leaving and refused any new applications. However, he found it difficult to obtain an immigration visa, and he needed all the help Rank and his American associates could give him. He begged Rank to cable him an answer confirming that there was work for him. "I need full assurance in order not to fall between two stools."[5]

After Rank's first euphoria in America, to his discomfiture the queues of patients had begun to disappear, and he cabled back, "Situation uncertain." This disappointment—in which Rank had raised Ferenczi's hopes only to dash them—was the turning point in Ferenczi's loyalty to Rank. "This episode has very much disturbed my summer and my work," a disconcerted Ferenczi complained to Freud (June 30, 1924). He did not add that it was additionally disappointing when the prospects in Vienna fell through as well.

Freud received word from his nephew in New York, Edward Bernays, that Rank had treated him with insolent arrogance. Ferenczi wondered if this was a case of someone being ruined by success. Freud was not pleased by Rank's curt letters and wondered if his "ambitious little wife" was exerting some sort of malign influence on him. He did not agree with Ferenczi's assessment that Rank was spoiled by success, but thought rather that he was failing because he was not using proper analytic procedures. "He remains a problem that will have to be handled with loving hands when he gets back" (August 6, 1924).

Jones was not slow to state his misgivings about Rank's activities in America. Rank offered the Americans what they most wanted: novelty, quick results, and a system that evaded infantile repressions. He had heard that the Budapest group was in disarray because of Ferenczi's views; the Vienna society was unstable, and the Dutch and Swiss groups were of no importance in the outer world. This left only London and Berlin as the staunch defenders of psychoanalysis. He warned Freud, however, not to condemn the Americans too hastily (September 29, 1924):

. . . in fifty years they will be the arbiters of the world, so that it is impossible to ignore them. At all events, I shall persevere to strengthen the slight foothold psychoanalysis has there.

Ferenczi disagreed with Freud about Beata Rank; he felt that she was a moderating influence on her husband.[6] But by the middle of

August Ferenczi's early enthusiasm for the importance of the birth trauma had cooled. He emphasized to Freud that, unlike Rank, he had never abandoned the primal historical importance of the father in his (Ferenczi's) genitalia theory (viz. the universal fantasy of returning to the womb).

In late July, after Freud received a number of adverse reports about Rank from psychoanalysts in New York, a series of increasingly angry letters were exchanged between Rank and Freud. Rank, no longer obsequious, addressed Freud in a tone reminiscent of the final bitter exchange between Freud and Jung. Freud told him that the fantasy of emerging from the womb (in Rank's theory) was in fact simply an expression of the gift of a child from the mother to the father, and that Rank's exclusion of the importance of the father was a reflection of his own early relationships. He was convinced now that Rank would never have written the birth trauma book if he had undergone analysis (July 23, 1924). On August 9 Rank replied that his recent experiences as an analyst had reinforced his view that the physical act of birth was the paradigm for anxiety. He failed to understand why Freud could not accept that since the mother had given birth to the child, the transference manifested in analysis was a maternal one, and that anxiety was attached to the maternal genitals, which was then transferred to the father only secondarily.

> If you interpret the phenomenon of transference starting from the father, with the male, you get the homosexual fixation, with the female, the heterosexual fixation as a result of the analysis; that is really the case with all the patients who come to me from other analysts.

He had not excluded the father, he explained, but simply assigned a correct role to him. Patients hailed him as a "savior," but he was not carried away by such acclaim. As far as his not having been analyzed himself, "what I have seen of other analysts, I can call it only fortunate" (September 8, 1924). Regrettably, he wrote, Freud had been influenced by "noisy ranters" like Abraham. Freud sent the letter on to Ferenczi and Eitingon for their reactions.

Jones and Ferenczi had not communicated since San Cristoforo. When Ferenczi had written suggesting that Jones resume his analysis, Jones did not deign to reply to what he considered an insulting overture. Now, in early August, Ferenczi wrote again in an attempt at a reconciliation. Jones responded (August 7, 1924) in a similar spirit. He admitted that he would like to continue his early analysis with Ferenczi, but could not afford to take the time away from his work. "I can only console myself with the thought that anyone who is so happy in his love-life as I am and able to work so satisfactorily cannot be in any urgent need of further analysis, and I am sure you will agree with this criterion."[7]

By the end of August Freud was sadly resigned to having lost Rank permanently. He asked Ferenczi if he would take over the editorship of the *Zeitschrift*. "I do not have anybody else, and certainly I do not have anyone dearer to me" (August 27, 1924). Two days later Freud wrote him another bewildered letter. He could not recognize the Rank he had known—"tenderly concerned, zealous, discreet, absolutely reliable." To Ferenczi he put the anguished question: "Which is the real Rank now, the one I have known for fifteen years, or the one Jones has been trying to show me for years?"

Ferenczi did not want the responsibility of the *Zeitschrift*. Moreover, his conscience began to torment him that he had betrayed Rank. In a long letter to Freud (September 1, 1924) he tried desperately to act as an arbitrator. Despite the fact that he and Rank had been friends, he insisted that Rank had never confided his ideas about the birth trauma to him, and that it was as much a bombshell to Ferenczi as to the others. But at least he had tried to understand it, which was more than the others (including Freud) had done. Also he had recognized how it might provide a theoretical basis for his active technique. Finally, he felt that Freud should confide in only him and Eitingon about Rank's insolent letters from America, so that there might still be a possibility of reconciliation with Freud and the other members of the Committee. While it was true that Ferenczi held Rank responsible for ruining his American plans, he felt that Rank was irreplaceable and that they should consider seriously how Rank's theories could be incorporated into classical psychoanalysis. He offered to act as mediator. He also had made it clear to Jones that he had no intention of acting treacherously toward Rank. Freud in response found Ferenczi's behavior in the affair "vacillating," but reported to Abraham that Ferenczi was "now retreating from his partisanship of Rank" (September 21, 1924).

Rank realized that Ferenczi held him responsible for wrecking his summer plans, and attempted to explain that he had been trying to spare him from further disappointments (August 10, 1924). His own success had been unique, but it was unrepeatable—mainly because of the jealousy of the American analysts. Those who had been analyzed by Freud were extremely dissatisfied.

> I have given them back confidence in themselves and in the analysis, in analysing them and showing them how one should analyse.

Now the changeable Americans were eager to get rid of him, but perhaps later on there would be a possibility for both Rank and Ferenczi to return. He had heard that Abraham and Ferenczi's "old enemy," Sandor Rado, were attempting to "neutralize" both of them. He was disgusted by such intrigues: "I shall not participate in politics any more but neither will I suffer them to play politics with me; I am really tired of the whole thing and find it repulsive."[8]

Jones was hardly grieved to witness the recurrence of what he called Rank's "wartime neurosis." His diagnosis: Rank was displacing his brother complex toward himself onto Freud, the father figure. Freud urged Jones to seek a reconciliation with Ferenczi, who, he asserted confidently, was "under no suspicion of separation" (September 25, 1924). Jones replied that he was very fond of Ferenczi, with whom he had resumed correspondence, but he believed that Ferenczi suffered from narcissism and poor judgment (September 29, 1924).

Ferenczi meanwhile had heard that Rank was sailing from New York on September 27, and that after taking a short holiday with his wife in the Adriatic resort of Abazzia* he would be in Vienna

*Now called Opatija in Yugoslavia.

again by the end of October. Repeating the pattern of 1913 with Jung, Freud again dictated the sort of letter Ferenczi should write to Rank. Ferenczi sent him a draft to correct and Freud insisted that he be harder on Rank, especially in regard to his disadvantage in not having been analyzed. Freud compared Rank to Adler in his desire to be independent. He was willing to forgive Rank, but had no intention of pleading with him, even though inevitably there would be a scandal. Now Freud became positively paranoid: Rank had fled because it looked as though Freud was going to die; but his recuperation had ruined Rank's American plans. Whatever the outcome, he wrote, the old trust could never be reestablished. Eventually an appointment between the two men was made for October 26. "I nourish no illusions on the result of this interview," a grim Freud told Jones (October 23, 1924).

In preparation for the outcome, Freud sent a letter to the Vienna Society announcing that he would retain the presidency, represented by a deputy at the meetings. Abraham assured Freud that there was nothing to prevent the others from reestablishing the Committee. In retrospect it was apparent to Abraham that Rank had tried to break up the Committee at San Cristoforo.* While they were sitting in judgment on Jones, a "much more serious threat was coming from somewhere else altogether" (October 20, 1924). Everyone had his own explanation for Rank's behavior. According to Abraham, Rank had tried to compensate for his negative tendencies by overwork. His emphasis on money and his increasing irritability indicated a regression to the anal-sadistic stage. He himself felt no hostility toward Rank, but Eitingon and Sachs felt very strongly about him.

The crucial meeting between Freud and Rank lasted for three hours. To Freud's amazement, Rank declared that he wished to stay within orthodox psychoanalysis and that he felt that the birth trauma could be incorporated into existing theory. Freud did not trust his sincerity. When the question of the insulting letters he had written was raised, Rank's reaction was embarrassment. To Freud's blunt question about his American plans, Rank replied that

---

*Ferenczi had already accused Abraham of disrupting it. See p. 147.

he was considering returning for a couple of months, and Freud emphasized that the Verlag could not survive with an editor who was constantly disappearing.

The following weekend Ferenczi and Eitingon met with Rank in Vienna. The discussion was angry, and Ferenczi realized that the former bond between them was broken forever (Ferenczi/Freud; November 15, 1924). He had also heard from Brill that Rank intended to establish his own psychoanalytic school in America, and he warned Freud to be on his guard against trusting Rank again.

After Eitingon's return to Berlin, he met with Abraham and Sachs to discuss the situation. Sandor Rado joined them, and they sadly concluded that Rank was lost to them and that the break would have to appear "as unobtrusive as possible to outsiders" (Abraham/Freud; November 11, 1924). Rado would take over the editorship of the *Zeitschrift*. Abraham tried to cheer Freud with the reassurance that the remaining members were as loyal as ever. He was making plans to revive the *Rundbriefe* before Christmas. They would be sent out once a month and Freud would receive a copy; they would be pleased to hear his comments from time to time, but Freud must not view this as an obligation. Jones declared that he had always been very fond of Rank and was sorry to see him leave: "I still wish him well in his future life though I fear he has not chosen an easy path" (Jones/Freud; November 11, 1924).

On November 28 Rank left for Paris, but within a week he returned unexpectedly to Vienna. Freud recognized that he was suffering from a deep depression. Rank announced that he planned to leave in another fortnight, but, on reaching Paris, he again turned back to Vienna.

Meanwhile, plans for consolidating the Committee on a new basis proceeded. Ferenczi proposed that Anna Freud be brought in as a member. It had been suggested that Brill might also be added, but it was decided to postpone the decision about him until their next meeting.* Abraham was opposed to Brill's inclusion. He felt that the existence of the *Rundbriefe* need no longer be secret, although

---

*Jones suggested as possibilities Anna Freud, Sandor Rado, Franz Alexander, James Glover, or Joan Riviere.

the contents still should be private. He also wanted a clear declaration from Ferenczi about his views on Rank's "scientific innovations" (November 26, 1924).

Ferenczi reverted to his original position that the Committee could only function on as close a basis as possible. Jones suggested that Abraham take over as president of the Committee. He assumed that the members now realized how impossible his position had been at San Cristoforo, when Rank's "skilful manoeuvring" had created unanimous opposition to him. He felt that the original purpose of the Committee should be recapitulated. It had always been clear to him that its purpose was the safeguarding of psychoanalytic doctrine. This could be achieved only by discussing any views about which there might be some doubt before publishing them, yet two members of the Committee had violated that understanding. Finally, he could not agree with Ferenczi that they should aim for intimate personal relationships. Such a desire, while commendable, was impractical because of temperamental differences. "Psychoanalysis should come first and personalities afterwards."[9]

There was then a dramatic change of events. In the middle of December Freud began to see Rank for long daily sessions. In Freud's account to Ferenczi, Rank had suddenly appeared before him "completely contrite, in order to confess" (December 21, 1924). The previous day Rank had sent an extraordinary letter to all the members of the Committee. Its tone, and the fact that it covered all the points of disagreement, strongly suggests that Freud and Rank worked out the letter together. For many years they had collaborated in writing letters, and it is probable that in this case Rank acceded to all Freud's suggestions short of renouncing his theory.

Vienna, 12.20.1924

Dear Friends,

    After all that happened with me and through me in the last few months, I feel the need to inform you, as direct or indirect participants, of the change which has taken place with me, information which, I hope, will justify me in addressing you, the former common friends and collaborators, in the old way, insofar as any one of you was personally hurt, and then to atone for it.

Only after the recent events in Vienna, which you probably know, has my attitude and behavior towards the Professor become clear to me. Obviously certain things had to happen before I could gain the insight, that my affective reactions towards the Professor and you, insofar as you represent for me the brothers near to him, stemmed from unconscious conflicts. For these reactions, I could only give an account of myself and to you after I had overcome them.

From a state which I now recognize as neurotic, I have suddenly returned to myself. Not only have I recognized the actual cause of the crisis in the trauma occasioned by the dangerous illness of the Professor, but I was able also to understand the type of reaction and its mechanism from my childhood and family history—the Oedipus and brother complexes. I was thus obliged to work out in reality conflicts which I would probably have been spared through an analysis, but which I believe I have now overcome through these painful experiences.

From analytical interviews with the Professor, in which I could explain in detail the reactions based on affective attitudes, I gain the hope that I was successful in clarifying, first of all, the personal relationship, since the Professor found my explanations satisfactory and has forgiven me personally. As a further consequence there will be an opportunity for discussion, clarification, and coming together in the scientific field where I shall be able to see things more objectively after the removal of my affective resistance. I confidently hope therefore, to be able to make good again as much as possible.

But before this can happen, I would like to ask every single one of you to understand my affective utterances against him as stemming from this state of mind and to forgive them as reactions not to be taken personally. May I also stress the mitigating circumstances that I have never carried these utterances beyond our most intimate circle, so that they appeared only in the circular letters and sessions of the committee and finally in two letters which I wrote the Professor from America in the summer. Before all I feel in duty bound to give satisfaction to Abraham, whose critical remarks I have obviously used as stimulus to stronger reactions and against whose role as accuser with the Professor I reacted so violently because of my brother complex. I can only hope, dear Abraham, that my painfully won insight into this situation and my most sincere regret will allow you to forgive and forget the insult to you arising from this state of mind.

As far as Jones is concerned I have certainly been in the wrong similarly and out of the same attitude, but I believe that he, on his side, gave me more cause, and with more affective motivation. Nevertheless I ask you, dear Jones, also to excuse the wrong I inflicted on you. I can only hope that you also will set aside the resistances that still exist against me, far enough to recognize and appreciate the sincerity of my apology.

With Sachs, the old and intimate friendship, going back before the founding of the committee, has fortunately prevented you, dear Hanns, from having to be involved in the same affective way with the group of brothers. But should something have struck you without my intention, it was more as against a twin brother and against myself, as perhaps this motive of self-punishment might also have had a part with the older brothers.

As far as Ferenczi and Eitingon are concerned, they have always had for me a separate position; therefore I have written to them separately, although in the same tone, because at the last moment in Vienna they offered me their friendly help, as they wanted to save me, so to say, but I could not understand, therefore could not accept.

I would be glad to hear that my explanations have found with you the same analytical understanding as with the Professor and that they give the satisfaction which, I hope, can afford the basis for the resumption of our group work in a not too distant future.

With best greetings,
Rank[10]

James Lieberman, Rank's biographer, emphasizes that this cringing tone had never appeared in Rank's letters before and would never appear again. What were Rank's choices? He was like a cornered rat. Freud had warned the American analysts that Rank's theories in no way represented his own. The Committee had closed ranks against him, and even his friend and collaborator Ferenczi no longer supported him. Without the imprimatur of official psychoanalysis, scientific journals would be closed to the exposition of his ideas, students would be unavailable, and he would receive no referrals.

Freud seems to have acted as the Grand Inquisitor, and Rank's groveling "confession" could have served as a model for the Russian show trials of the 1930s. Did Rank ever mutter, "eppur si muove"? He believed with all his heart in his theory, but managed to avoid discussing it in the letter. The emphasis is placed completely on his state of mind. He addresses the Committee as though it were a Star Chamber, not a group of fellow analysts. He admits to moral turpitude, but about what? The vexed questions of his theory and technique are totally ignored. Freud wanted to avoid a scandal and to contain the situation for the time being. As he had argued months before, the theoretical issue would take care of itself in time. His subsequent letters to the others were meant as instructions to leave well enough alone.

An astonished Abraham told Freud that he was planning to be conciliatory but cautious. Freud replied that Rank had been cured of his neurosis "just as if he had gone through a proper analysis" (December 29, 1924).* Rank was still very depressed and was planning to return to America in a few weeks to undo the harm he had created on his first visit. Freud begged all the members of the Committee for their tolerance toward a man who was ill and sympathy for the difficulties of his recuperation. He ended his letter to Ferenczi (December 21, 1924): "I am glad though that I haven't given my faith to some unworthy person in the past 15 years, and that I am completely guiltless in the whole matter."† Why did he feel it necessary to add the word *guiltless?*

Ferenczi was puzzled by Rank's refusal to come to Budapest to discuss the situation with him. Jones, too, was unwilling to commit himself until he had heard what action Berlin intended taking. Accordingly Jones wrote Abraham a private letter (December 29, 1924) requesting advice, while at the same time telling Abraham what he thought Abraham should do.[11] His first impulse, he claimed, was to respond generously, and this would be particularly appropriate in his case since he was "the person whom he most injured and against whom he evidently still feels a grudge." Nevertheless, Jones felt deeply skeptical.

> Rank has temporarily regained *intellectual* insight into the situation. That even this is only partial is shown by his infantile attitude that the whole thing is simply a matter of "being forgiven" for being naughty, and also by his clinging to the idea that my opposition to his conduct was dictated by personal reasons on my part, which it never was.

---

*It must have been one of the shortest cures on record, with a fixed termination date, as the matter had to be settled before Rank's proposed departure.
†". . . und das ich am Ganzen wirklich schuldles bin."

17. Freud with Anna at the Sixth International Congress at the Hague in September 1920.

INTERNATIONALE ZEITSCHRIFT FÜR ÄRZTLICHE PSYCHOANALYSE

HERAUSGEGEBEN VON PROFESSOR DR SIGM. FREUD

SCHRIFTLEITUNG: Dr. S. FERENCZI, Budapest, VII. ~~Mszkozkring 54~~ / Dr. OTTO RANK, Wien ~~IX/4, Simondenkgasse 8~~
~~Nagydiofa u. 3.~~

VERLAG HUGO HELLER & CO, WIEN, I. BAUERNMARKT NO 3

ABONNEMENTSPREIS: GANZJÄHRIG (6 HEFTE, 36—40 BOGEN) K 21·60 = MK. 18·—

Budapest I.

Budapest, am 20. Sept. 1920.

Lieber Herr Professor,
Liebe Kollegen und Freunde!

Es sei mir gestattet aus Anlaß des Beginnes unseres regelrechten Briefwechsels Euch Allen meine wärmsten Grüße zu übersenden. Das Beisammensein mit Euch am Kongress wirkte erfrischend auf mein Gemüt, das dieser Belebung schon dringend bedürfte. Ich hoffe, daß der Gedankenaustausch — auf das ganze Jahr verteilt — das Gefühl der Zusammengehörigkeit stets wach erhalten und Ermüdungsgefühle nie aufkommen lassen wird. Da sich unser Briefwechsel ausschließlich mit Fragen der psychoanalytischen wissenschaftlicher Propaganda und mit Mitteilungen persönlicher Natur beschäftigen soll und da unsere Tätigkeit nichts mit Politik zu tun hat, werde ich mich selbstverständlich jedweder Äußerung über soziale und nationale Angelegenheiten enthalten.

18. The first Rundbrief, written by Ferenczi on September 20, 1920.

20. The quiet interior of the Hotel du Lac at Lavarone, far above the squabbles at San Christoforo in August 1923.

19. A. A. Brill of New York. What did Jones say about Rank that Brill repeated to Ferenczi?

21. Abraham with his family in summer of 1925.

22. Rank is banished to the far right at the Bad Homburg Conference in September 1925. Jones, Abraham, Eitingon and Ferenczi seated in the middle, Melanie Klein standing in center behind balustrade.

23. Anna and her father in 1927 at Ernst Simmel's sanatorium at Tegel where Freud sought relief from his prosthesis for his cancer of the jaw.

Jones was convinced that Rank's attitude was motivated by his having burned his bridges in New York and Vienna.

> I distrust Rank profoundly, for I know well how unscrupulous he can be when it suits him and when he has the power, and I feel that we have no guarantee for the future. That he should once more have deceived Professor was inevitable and not surprising, but the question is about the rest of the Committee.

Were they going to forget all that psychoanalysis had taught them about the repetition compulsion? Rank's neurotic behavior would certainly erupt after Freud's death, and if Rank were reinstated in important positions such as Freud's successor, president of the Vienna Society, editor of the *Zeitschrift*, even president of the International Association, consider the consequences!

Therefore Jones advised a cordial reply and good wishes for Rank's own work. He strongly opposed allowing him to resume any of his former responsibilities and was convinced that the question of his readmission to the Committee should not be raised until their next meeting.

> Who is to be man enough to speak out on this disagreeable topic? At all events I, for one, feel it would be dishonest to pretend, in the way Rank wishes, that the past no longer exists and that the skies are all serene. I know this letter will run counter to your temperamental optimism and I do not know what your answer will be; but I am sure you will weigh carefully what I say, for it is based on more knowledge—painfully gained—than anyone else can have.

Abraham sent off a circular letter from Berlin on December 25 without needing to know how the other Committee members were reacting. While the three Berlin colleagues expressed satisfaction at the end of the painful conflict, they stated bluntly that there was a good deal more they needed to know before real confidence could be reestablished. True, they accepted the explanation of the reenactment of early family conflicts, but they wanted more concrete details about how Rank had arrived at this new insight about himself. Had it begun in Vienna before Rank left for Paris or after his departure? What had happened in his last discussion with Freud? What was the immediate precipitating cause for this confession? What were his American plans, and did his success or failure there have anything to do with his change of heart? It was clear that they were not going to let him off easily.

Furthermore, they assumed that he was busy revising his theory. Sachs was writing a report on it, which would be circulated, and this would give Rank ample opportunity to discuss what amendments he wanted to make.* They urged him to visit Berlin, where Sachs would be happy to put him up.[12] Only Eitingon wrote to Rank personally (December 26, 1924).[13] He admitted candidly that, given the emotions of the past months, it would take him time to absorb the sea-change that Rank was supposed to have experienced, but was confident that this could be achieved ultimately.

Jones reaffirmed his enduring friendship, but used the occasion to bring up his old grievances in a letter to Rank (January 3, 1925). He reminded him how he had responded enthusiastically to Rank's plans for the Verlag when they met in Switzerland immediately after the war, but Rank's "secret taciturnity" had made cooperation impossible. While Jones recognized that Rank was in the grip of a neurosis, he was the only member of the Committee to insist on responsible behavior from him. As a result, Jones realized that he was assuming the role of Rank's chief enemy in Rank's eyes. Nevertheless, "May 1925 be an historic turning point is my ardent wish to you for the New Year."[14]

For the next year and a half Rank played his cards very carefully. The crisis had changed him from a highly explosive man to one who was forced to cultivate guile. He avoided a confrontation with the Committee by leaving for America after sending a joint letter dated January 7, 1925, assuring them that his confession was only a prelude to future action. He had found it impossible to leave the Professor "in the lurch—as I was able to do the first time, in a manic state which was to spare me the regret of loss as a direct

---

*The constant harping on technique rather than on the revolutionary emphasis on the pre-Oedipal mother in Rank's (and Ferenczi's) theory suggests interesting questions. The pre-Oedipal mother raised a specter from which the group fled to matters of personal behavior.

reaction to his illness." He had wanted to return to New York in November "because of the success I had had there."[15] This contradicts his advice to Ferenczi not to join him because American patients were disappearing!

Freud, in permitting Rank to go to America—with the ostensibly specious aim of putting right the harm he had previously done—was protecting Rank from the wrath of the older brothers. Freud's denial was extraordinarily naive. Within the fictional family he had created, he could not understand that Rank was fighting for his adulthood. While the situation was contained for the time being, Freud had forfeited the total devotion Abraham and Jones had bestowed on him in the past. In Jones's letters particularly, the tone changes from servility to a note of equality. "You will not be surprised," he wrote Freud (January 10, 1925), "that I also share the purely intellectual reserve expressed by our Berlin friends and am bound indeed to be distinctly skeptical about the security of the future."

Both Jones and Abraham continued to watch Rank with the utmost wariness. (On his return from New York in mid-February, Rank lectured at the Sorbonne and had meetings with the nucleus of the French group: René Laforgue, Eugenia Sokolnicka, and Princess Marie Bonaparte.) Ferenczi assured the other members of the Committee that he had responded in a friendly way to "the recurringly remorseful prodigious child" (January 17, 1925), but that a considerable period of time would have to elapse before he felt the old, unreserved trust.

Ferenczi was making an attempt to write to Freud on his old footing. This emboldened him to ask if Freud would tell him confidentially his impressions of Rank's theoretical and technical views before and after his analytical discussions with Freud. Ferenczi felt that he was entitled to this explanation, since Beata Rank had approached him about analyzing her.

Freud's reply (February 9, 1925) was frank but cautious. He was delighted that the bewildered Beata wished Ferenczi to analyze her. His own attitude to Rank had been determined mainly by respect for a man in a deep depression. He had not tried to extract any revisions of his scientific theories. Rank was aware that Sachs was writing an analysis of these and appeared willing to learn from criticism. Freud felt sure that Rank's future attitude toward Ferenczi and the other members of the Committee would please all of them.

In a *Rundbrief* of March 15, Ferenczi shared with the others his impressions of Rank after a long talk with him in Vienna. He had approached the encounter with great misgivings, but the uncommunicativeness with which they had reproached Rank in November had disappeared. Rank now understood the pathology of his father complex toward the Professor and wished to repair his relationship with him and with the members of the Committee. As for the birth trauma, he adhered to his original position but was looking forward to reading the Berlin critique (then being circulated).

Ferenczi's optimism was premature. Sachs's criticisms made Rank believe that no dialogue was possible. Freud described him as being in a state of lethargic depression, avoiding any discussion about his theory. The people in Berlin were angry because he had never acknowledged Sachs's comments. Ferenczi, too, was offended because Rank had never written to him. A former American patient of Rank's had entered analysis with Ferenczi, and Ferenczi promised to report at the Committee meeting before the Congress on what he had learned about Rank's technique. (He felt negative about what he had learned so far.) In mid-May, Ferenczi and Eitingon traveled to Vienna for a board meeting of the Verlag. They attempted to engage Rank in discussion, but he seemed to have withdrawn completely into himself.

But in the middle of July it was announced that Rank would deliver a paper at Bad Homburg. After a certain amount of vacillation Freud had decided that his health was not up to the Congress, but Rank would discuss his paper in advance with him at Semmering.

Freud received differing reports about the Congress (September 3 to 5), and particularly about Rank and his paper, "The Theory of Genitality." That the Congress succeeded, according to Jones, was due to Eitingon: "He is developing his personality more freely and is in every way exceedingly valuable." People found Rank's paper confused, and Jones described him to Freud as being in a state of hypomania.[16] From Sorrento, where Gizella and Ferenczi had gone on holiday, the latter wrote (September 16, 1925) that in his view, Rank's behavior was "normal and friendly," although his paper was confused and difficult to understand. He described Jones as "caustic and suspicious," and Abraham as preoccupied in a narcissistic state of illness.

In truth Abraham was seriously ill. In June he had choked on an eel bone that had become septic, and pneumonia had developed. He spent the summer in fragile convalescence but summoned up energy to attend the Congress. Conscientious as ever, on September 9 he sent Freud his usual detailed account of the Congress. He was pleased by the modifications Ferenczi seemed to be making in his active therapy.* As for Rank, Abraham had had a long discussion with him and felt that it boded well for their future relationship. However, like Jones, he was concerned about his manic state. Rank had read his paper at such a furious rate that no one could follow him. And here he was going off to America again after Abraham had spent all his energy trying to establish good relations with the Americans, who weren't happy at all about Rank's projected visit. He congratulated Freud on Miss Anna's splendid delivery of her father's paper.† He ended his letter by admitting that the Congress had damaged his health and that he was now being treated by Wilhelm Fliess, and that his illness "has now strikingly confirmed all Fliess's views on periodicity."[17]

Freud was scornful of Abraham's cultivation of the Americans, whom he considered "rather worthless" (September 11, 1925). But he was infuriated by Abraham's remarks about Rank:

> Your opposition to Rank's return is based on the most petty motives, just like your attitude towards lay analysis. Rank's recent trip to America is not a manic symptom, it had a number of important motivations and I had decidedly encouraged him to take it. If I was right will be seen only at a later date.

*He would not have been so pleased if Ferenczi had delivered the paper on telepathic communication, which Freud had vetoed.
†"Some Psychical Consequences of the Anatomical Differences between the Sexes."

Why did Freud vent his anger against Abraham rather than Jones, who held the same views? From the outset he had regarded Abraham as responsible for creating a crisis over Rank's theory. He certainly wouldn't have appreciated Abraham's laudatory remarks about Fliess. But his main bone of contention was the involvement of Abraham and Sachs for the past months in a commercial film about psychoanalysis, despite Freud's unrelenting opposition to the idea.

From his sickbed Abraham defended himself (October 27, 1925). He reminded Freud that when he had first voiced his suspicions about Jung, Freud had accused him of jealousy. Was it not possible that he might be right again? Freud replied (November 5, 1925) that Abraham had been right about Jung, but "not quite right about Rank." The issue might not have blown up had it not been for the attitude of Berlin. "You are not necessarily always right," he snapped.

Unfortunately, these were the last letters they were ever to exchange.

Both men were very ill. In October Freud had to have another operation on his mouth, and although he claimed that he had always taken Abraham's condition seriously, he was so concerned about his own suffering that he did not acknowledge that Abraham's condition was critical until the beginning of December. By then Abraham's death was inevitable, and Freud began to plan with Ferenczi how they would handle the emergency. Freud was too ill to attend the funeral, but Ferenczi promised to be there. Abraham died on Christmas Day. Ferenczi stopped off in Vienna on his way to Berlin. Freud had him check the obituary he had written and also persuaded him to take over the presidency of the International Association. They ruled out Eitingon, who was in Sicily with his ailing wife; they did not know if he would even return for the funeral. As it was, Eitingon did return, and all the surviving members of the Committee gathered for the somber occasion.

Freud had lost his *rocher de bronze*, and for the time being Rank, who had returned to Vienna at Christmas, was the forgotten man.

Chapter Eleven

The Twilight of the Committee, 1925–27

WITH THE DEATH of Abraham, Freud saw no hope for the continuation of the Committee. Jones disagreed: "My Committee, as you call it, will I hope, survive any blow. The need for it will always give it life, though the loss of Abraham could never be replaced" (Jones/Freud; December 25, 1925).

There was no time for a mourning period for Abraham.* While Freud attended a memorial for him in Vienna on January 6, he did not write to his widow until January 17.

Dear Frau Abraham,

Since my telegram on receiving the news of your husband's death I have put off writing to you. It was too difficult, and I hoped it would become easier. Then I fell ill myself, became feverish, and have not yet recovered. But I already see that putting it off was useless, it is just as difficult now as it was then. I have no substitute for him, and no consolatory words for you that would tell you anything new. That we have to submit with resignation to the blows of fate you know already; and you will have guessed that to me his loss is particularly painful because, with the selfishness of old age, I think he could easily have been spared for the probable short duration of my own life.

. . . May you find a new and rich meaning in life from your motherhood. I have no prospect of travelling, so I do not know whether I shall see you

*In an interview of Sandor Rado by Bluma Swerdloff, November 27, 1964, Rado comments on his shock at Freud's refusal to mourn Abraham. "I remember that [Abraham] was just on the verge of conflict with Freud. And my theory, at that time, was that he killed himself to avoid the conflict" (Columbia Oral Archives).

again. Trusting that you will keep me too in your memory, and with heartfelt sympathy,

Your devoted
Freud[1]

It is curious that Freud raised the possibility of never seeing her again, considering that he had two sons and four grandchildren in Berlin whom he visited from time to time.*

The overriding question of the moment was who was to replace Abraham as president of the International Association and president of the Berlin Society. Jones informed Freud that he planned to vote for Eitingon. Freud replied that he would have no objection to Eitingon, but that his ailing wife (whom Freud referred to as his "chain") made too many demands on him. After all, they had been on one of their frequent recuperative holidays, this time to Sicily, for three months. Whether Frau Eitingon was actually unwell is never altogether clear. Certainly there was a prejudice against her because her friends were in artistic circles and she did not become friendly with the wives of the other Committee members or demonstrate their total devotion to The Cause.

Ferenczi stopped off in Vienna on his way to the funeral, and he and Freud discussed how he must be prepared to step into the breach. On January 7 Ferenczi confided in Groddeck that Freud wanted him to move to Berlin and that the younger members such as Simmel and Alexander seemed to support the idea. Ferenczi, desperate to get out of Hungary, was anxious to become the dual president—but Jones also wanted the International presidency. Ferenczi reported frankly and fully to Freud on the discussions held about the succession. Before Eitingon's return, the Berlin group had broken up into various factions. Suddenly Eitingon appeared, cool and clearly in charge of the situation. With his diffident stammer he had always been something of an enigma to the members of the Committee. He was devoted to Freud and to psychoanalysis; his generosity was appreciated, but no one credited him with imag-

*Actually he did visit Frau Abraham at Christmas 1926.

ination. He had never produced a clinical paper and seldom had any analysands.

Eitingon immediately announced that he was willing to take over the presidency of the International. Ferenczi inquired tentatively as to how he would react to Ferenczi's candidacy, to which Eitingon replied that he would consider it a personal insult if the presidency were not given to him. Ferenczi then raised the question of Eitingon's frequent absences because of his wife's health. Eitingon replied that the group misunderstood her; she had reacted "heroically" to the crisis and was totally prepared to subordinate her private needs to Eitingon's work. As for the presidency of the Berlin Society, Eitingon did not want it, and Ferenczi by now realized that the younger members would not tolerate an outsider being imposed upon them.

There was unanimous agreement that Ernst Simmel should take over the reins of the Berlin Society. Ferenczi gracefully conceded to Freud that he considered Ernst Simmel* a talented man who was undoubtedly the best choice. For the time being they agreed that a decision about a replacement for Abraham on the Committee should be deferred. Anna Freud would replace Eitingon as secretary of the International Association. She had already taken Rank's place on the Committee the previous December, and described her excitement at the prospect to Eitingon:

> Sometimes the most beautiful thing is precisely the one that comes unexpectedly and unearned, hence something given truly as a present. Most beautiful, moreover, if it is for Papa's sake. The both of us were pleased together about it, he no less than I.[2]

It was the first step in her growing confidence, and within a few years she was filling the role for which the Committee had been formed—the guardian of psychoanalysis.

The strain exerted its toll on Freud. In the middle of February he suffered two mild angina attacks. This time it was Ferenczi who

---

*Simmel had produced some important work on shellshock. He had also done much to create the Poliklinik in Berlin.

attributed his illness to emotional causes. "Perhaps this is the occasion when I can tell you that I actually find it tragic that you, who presented psychoanalysis to the world, find it so hard, even impossible, to tell someone about your problems" (Ferenczi/Freud; February 21, 1926). As usual Freud insisted that his symptoms were entirely physical, and even implied that Ferenczi was using his illness as an excuse to move to Vienna. As it was, Freud's condition was so serious that he was forced for some weeks to go into a sanatorium, where Ferenczi visited him at Easter.

In mid-April Rank finally left Vienna for good. He took with him all the *Rundbriefe** that were written before he was ejected from the Committee. It is possible that Freud never knew that Rank had purloined the letters. The most obvious motive for Rank was that he wanted evidence that would support his side of the story.

Since his wife Beata refused to live in America, their first destination was Paris, although Freud was convinced that they would eventually settle in the United States. Freud's reaction was philosophical resignation. He wrote to Ferenczi:

> . . . he eventually carried through in an unemotional way what he had tried to achieve through a severe illness: detachment from me as well as from all of us. What is clear is that he was unwilling to renounce any part of the theory in which his neurosis manifested itself; and he did not take the slightest step to get closer to the group here. I do not belong to those who demand that anyone should be chained and sell themselves forever out of "gratitude." He was given a lot but he also worked hard for it. That leaves us even! On his final visit I saw no reason for expressing any kind of special affection. I was straightforward and hard [*Ich war aufrichtig und hart*]. But now he is gone and we have to bury him. Abraham has been proved right.[3]

Anna Freud went into analysis again with her father in the spring of 1924. When she saw Rank also having analysis with Freud late in the year she wrote to Eitingon, with whom she was establishing a close friendship, that she experienced "completely wild feelings of (probably) jealousy, as though I felt that he [Rank] had lost the

---

*Eventually they were bequeathed to Columbia University by the Rank Estate.

right to any closeness".⁴ It was with relief that she witnessed the departure of Rank and his wife. Anna always regarded Beata as a schemer.

With Abraham dead, Rank irretrievably estranged, and Jones always something of an alien, Freud began to revert to his old dependency on Ferenczi. In May some money in von Freund's foundation became available, and Freud gave Ferenczi full credit for obtaining this help for The Cause. Ferenczi also offered to write a critique of Rank's latest work, *Die Analytische Situation* (the first part of *Technik der Psychoanalyse*). This he was pleased to do as a public gesture of ending the collaboration that they shared in "much too brotherly a unity"⁵ for so long. In the discussions about this book, Freud's repressed anger against Rank was finally given full opportunity to vent itself.

One of Freud's most famous cases had been that of the Wolf Man, published as "From the History of an Infantile Neurosis." It was written shortly after the termination of a young Russian's analysis in the winter of 1914–15. The most dramatic aspect of the analysis (started in 1910) was the patient's recollection of a very early childhood dream of six or seven white wolves sitting on a walnut tree. From this Freud deduced that the child had witnessed a sexual act in which his father had penetrated his mother from behind. (The dream is discussed in psychoanalytic literature more for the vividness of the dream itself than for the persuasiveness of Freud's interpretation.)

Rank's interpretation was quite different. He saw it as a genealogical-tree dream provoked by the analytic situation. Probable knowledge that Freud had six children of his own and other patients as well had released infantile jealousy in the patient. Also, from the couch, the analysand would have faced a dark pilaster upon which hung the pictures of Freud's closest colleagues—hence the contrast of the six or seven white wolves against the dark background. He had a view of the trees through the window. According to Rank, birth anxiety was released by the combination of these factors. The patient's sister had occupied his mother's womb once, and further sibling rivals might emerge. He would like to hang these rivals on the tree and perhaps castrate them. Rank believed that the patient identified the analyst with his mother; that is, in the transference the analyst became the mother with a penis.

Freud's outraged reaction was that this interpretation was Rank's way of breaking all bonds between them. Rank seemed to be suggesting that Freud had been taken in by the patient and had mistaken a recollection of a dream from the past as a maternal transference. If Rank believed this at the time, Freud exclaimed, why did he not convey his doubts to him? It was a terrible blow to realize that Rank, who had seemed totally devoted to Freud, had been harboring grave suspicions about him. Rank had seemed very depressed during this period, and it is possible that this was the beginning of his misgivings about Freud and that he simply did not know how to handle the situation. On the other hand, he claimed that he had adopted the idea of eliciting stubbornly repressed material from Freud's practice with the Wolf Man, in which Freud had departed from his usual procedure by setting a date for the termination of the analysis.[6]

Freud wrote in great indignation to Ferenczi (June 6, 1926). He pointed out that the photographs on the wall dated from 1913, after the formation of the Committee. In 1913–14, there were only five pictures on the wall. Ferenczi's was dated 1913, Abraham's 1914. There were also pictures of Sachs, Jones, and Rank. Von Freund's picture had never been hung, and Eitingon did not join the Committee until 1919. In other words, there was a period of only one year in which the Russian could have seen the five photographs— but at no time did he see six or seven. Freud clearly remembered that the dream was reported very early in the analysis. (Freud reckoned that it was early in 1911.)* Moreover, there were not walnut but chestnut trees outside his window. Since the wall was covered with pictures of "hated sister and brother rivals," Freud asked, why had no other patient had a similar type of dream? For someone who placed so much emphasis on symbolism, Freud's clinging to literal facts is surprising here. In his agitation he wrote to the patient, D. Pakojeff, in Russia asking him to confirm that he had related the dream to Freud early in the analysis. The Russian

---

*Apparently it was Freud's custom to destroy his process notes.

acknowledged that this was so. From time to time various members of the Committee had had minor intellectual disagreements with Freud, but no one before Rank had dared to question the very foundations of the interpretation of one of his most famous case histories.

The Committee members assembled in Vienna on May 6 in honor of Freud's seventieth birthday. The following day he spent some hours with them in what was to prove his last meeting with his paladins. It was decided for the present not to add any additional members to the Committee.

Ferenczi and Jones both presented Freud with canes. Jones's had a tortoiseshell handle, but Ferenczi's sounds more elegant, a beautiful malacca with an ivory handle and S.F. engraved on a gold band. (Jones's vivid recollection of this cane suggests his envy of the grander gift.) From Paris Rank sent Freud a beautifully bound set of Nietzsche's complete works. To Jones Freud described the unexpected gift as springing from a mixture of different motives,

> the oppressing feeling of owing so much to me, even in money, a reaction of gratitude, or rather against gratitude, a tendency to boast of his newly acquired riches and a self-destructive impulse to spend all he is earning, which appears also in other doings of his. I am not sure at all what the final result of his career may be, he does not belong to those easy-going scoundrels, to whom success in life is assured.[7]

While in Vienna, Freud and Ferenczi talked again about the possibility of his moving there. However, while Ferenczi was still eager to leave Budapest, his wife was averse to the upheaval because she did not want to be far from her family, or so he said. Consequently he had decided to accept an invitation to America for a few months in order to make some money and to ensure that future patients would come to him in Europe. Ferenczi was also planning to support the views Freud had expressed in his recently written pamphlet on lay analysis.

Freud was not at all happy about Ferenczi's plans to visit "this damned America!" (June 19, 1926). Not only did he despise the money-grubbing Americans, but in part he also blamed them for seducing Jung and Rank away from him, and he feared that he might now lose Ferenczi as well. In his life of Freud, Jones writes: "Eitingon had also felt unhappy about Ferenczi's acceptance of the invitation, though on other grounds."[8] What Eitingon wrote to Freud on June 21 was: "I, too, fear that the President-to-be of our IPV should not be going to America like this."[9] Jones's evasiveness was clearly influenced by his reluctance to accept that Ferenczi was regarded by Eitingon and Freud as the future president of the International Association.

On the same day, Eitingon, in his *Rundbrief* from Berlin, urged Ferenczi to write a severe critique of Rank's technique *immediately*. But in a private letter to Freud, he wrote, "I don't believe he will be in a hurry to do such a thing just now. He still seems inclined to stay fairly close, to distance himself certainly, but not to part company."*[10]

Ferenczi sent Freud a detailed list of the lectures he was to give at the New School of Social Research, to which Freud replied that he hoped he wouldn't allow the Americans to take advantage of him. He also wanted to know exactly when Ferenczi intended to visit him, because he felt they should have at least one meeting before such a prolonged separation. His prosthesis made talking difficult, but he was eager to have as much discussion as possible in an attempt to recreate their former "congresses." Ferenczi arrived at Semmering on August 22 for a week—a week that was, according to Jones, the last occasion when Freud felt really happy in Ferenczi's company. At any rate, just as Ferenczi was about to depart from Cherbourg for what Freud described as "the country of the dollar barbarians," he received an affectionate farewell letter from the Professor with a plea to write as often as possible (September 19, 1926).

Curiously enough, Ferenczi ran into Rank in a travel bureau in Paris and they talked for about an hour. He learned that Rank was

---

*Ferenczi reviewed *Technik der Psychoanalyse* in *I.J.P.A.*, 1927, 93–100. Written mainly at Freud's dictation, the article faults Rank for ignoring the developmental influences in his concentration on the reenactment of birth. He also includes Freud's objections to Rank's interpretation of the Wolf Man dream.

to lecture simultaneously at the *Old* School of Social Research. Rank suggested to him that they at least support each other on the question of lay analysis. He pleaded with Ferenczi not to fight with him in front of the Americans or to attack his book publicly, but Ferenczi assured Freud that "of course I did *not* promise him" (September 29, 1926).

On the ship, Ferenczi wrote Freud, he had recalled "our argonaut trip" in 1909 when he and Jung accompanied Freud to Clark University. He had happy memories of their conversations at that time and of the wonderfully expectant feeling of what lay ahead. He remembered how he had to struggle with his infantile feelings of jealousy of Jung. When he thought of all that had transpired since then, "it makes me very happy to feel that this very long time has passed without anything serious ever interfering or getting between us" (September 27, 1926).

The phenomenon of Rank and Ferenczi lecturing in New York at the same time was bizarre. At first Ferenczi was greeted very warmly, and A. A. Brill, who had become president of the New York Society the previous year, did not seem antagonistic; but it soon became apparent that he and Clarence Oberndorf* were highly critical of Ferenczi's espousal of lay analysis, particularly for his encouragement of the formation of a group in which most of the members had been analyzed in Budapest. Ferenczi's huge audiences dwindled away to a trickle. Freud found the behavior of the New York analysts toward Ferenczi "detestable" (January 2, 1927). Ferenczi explained that Brill was smarting from Freud's reported remark that there were no well-trained analysts in America. "Also the idea that I am here is very annoying to him. Just the idea that someone from Europe is coming over here to teach the people here is an insult in itself. He believes himself to be in possession of a monopoly because of his pioneer work."[11] Ferenczi compared Brill to Jones who was attempting to carve out a monopoly in Britain; in his view both of them felt threatened by the Societies in Berlin, Vienna, and Budapest.

---

*Analyzed by Freud in 1921–22, Oberndorf was one of the stalwarts of the New York Psychoanalytic faculty.

Ferenczi passed on the news that Rank had been boasting that he could "cure" homosexuality in six weeks (January 9, 1927). Freud complained that the tone of Ferenczi's letters was beginning to sound "American" and urged him to come home as soon as possible since he had to have some serious discussions about lay analysis with Anna Freud and Eitingon before the next Congress later that year.[12] Ferenczi ignored this plea and announced that he would be returning in June, planning to stop off in England first and then travel to Baden-Baden to visit Groddeck at his sanitorium.

Jones decided that the Committee would not meet until after the Innsbruck Congress, a decision Ferenczi regretted. Why he regretted this decision is puzzling, since he went on to say that in any event he could not attend a meeting before the middle of June.[13] Since he made no reference to any visit with Freud, it is little wonder that the latter began to become somewhat anxious. Freud continued to press Ferenczi to visit him at Semmering, emphasizing how much there was to discuss. For example, he wanted to tell Ferenczi about Beata Rank's visit to him and her many complaints about her husband. "From Rank," he wrote, "one can learn that it is still the most rewarding thing in the world to be a scoundrel. Not a real cad, indeed, because punishment could be the consequence for people like that, but dirty little tricks are not dangerous."*[14] Ferenczi finally committed himself to making a long visit to Semmering before or after the Congress.

Rank was by now branded as a pariah, for Jones had used his American connections to spread the word that Rank was out of favor. Ferenczi shunned him when they happened to run into each other in Pennsylvania Station. Ultimately Rank was stripped of his honorary membership in the American Psychoanalytic Association in 1930. For some years he moved between Paris and the United States, finally settling in Philadelphia, where he played an active role in the Pennsylvania School of Social Work. Curiously, in America he did not pursue his work on the birth trauma. Freud

---

*"Von Rank kann man lernen, dass es doch am lohnendsten in dieser Welt ist ein Lump zu sein. Kein Bösewicht beileibe, dass könnte Strafe nach sich bringen, aber Lumperei ist ungefährlich."

had effectively silenced him. Rank and his wife were divorced in America shortly before his death.

Freud finally published his rebuttal of Rank's birth trauma theory in February 1926, in *Inhibitions, Symptoms and Anxiety*, which he had been working on for long periods during 1925. While it lacked polemical vigor, it left no room for reconciliation. Freud objected that Rank ignored constitutional factors and offered no evidence that difficult births produced serious neuroses. Rank responded a year later in William Alanson White's *Psychoanalytic Review*. Rank was quick to recognize that he had forced Freud to reverse one of his fundamental positions: Freud had originally considered anxiety to be an expression of repressed libido, but he now described it as a signal of danger associated with earlier trauma. As for the source of his own theory of the birth trauma, Rank had found it in a footnote added to the 1909 edition of *The Interpretation of Dreams*, in which Freud referred to *physiological* anxiety. What Freud did not realize, Rank explained, was that he was describing "the separation of the mother as a trauma of great *psychological* importance." Freud ignored this because his theory denied the significance of the mother. According to Rank: "Not all authoritative persons or figures . . . have a father significance, not even ultimately. For one patient the mother may have been the first authority, indeed perhaps she was for most human beings."[15]

In Jones's comments on Ferenczi's trip to America, he claimed that "Ferenczi was never the same man again after that visit, although it was another four or five years before his mental deterioration became manifest to Freud."[16] He almost seems to suggest that Ferenczi had "caught" some mental illness in the United States. For his part, Ferenczi suspected that Jones was supporting Brill against him—and this suspicion was not altogether wrong.

As always, Jones's relationship with Freud was highly ambivalent. Jones suggests that Freud's feelings for him deteriorated in 1922 when Rank poisoned his mind against him, and that the chill between them lasted for the next ten years. Yet on September 20, 1926, Freud wrote to him:

We may be well satisfied with each other. I have myself the impression that you sometimes over-estimate the significance of the dissensions that have occurred between us. It is, it is true, hard to succeed in completely satisfying one another; one misses something in everyone and criticizes a little. You have yourself remarked that even between Abraham and myself there were certain differences of opinion; with one's wife and children the same things happen. Only the speeches at the graveside deny these indications of reality; the living have the right to maintain that such impairments of an ideal picture do not spoil the enjoyment of reality.

Jones seemed to experience some curious conflicts after Abraham's death, perhaps due in part to the fact that it was clear that Freud did not want him as president of the International Association. On occasion he would indicate to Freud that Abraham had not been a saint who was impossible to replace. At the time of Abraham's death, Jones told Freud that he had lost his "best friend" (December 25, 1925). Yet he felt it necessary to emphasize to Freud that he, not Abraham, was the first to recognize Jung's potential heresy. He also described Abraham as someone whom it was hard to get close to, a view with which Freud concurred: "It is strange that even despite all his simplicity and clarity, the essence of Abraham's being was hard to grasp. There remains something about him as you correctly imply that could not be grasped."[17] In a sense, both Jones and Freud recognized that Abraham's self-sufficiency and lack of neediness made it impossible to manipulate him.

In his realization that Freud did not altogether appreciate his loyalty, Jones began to feel freer about expressing his differences with him. The British Society was going from strength to strength. A Training Institute had opened in London in December 1925 funded by a gift from a former patient of Jones, Pryns Hopkins. A close association with the Hogarth Press (under Virginia and Leonard Woolf) had been established. Jones encouraged his members to obtain medical degrees if possible because he was convinced that this was the only way psychoanalysis would be accepted in Britain. He also continued to twit Freud about his interest in telepathy. Freud told him briskly that he, Anna, and Ferenczi had conducted some startling experiments, but that these were private matters of his own.

The biggest bone of contention between them, however, was the figure of Melanie Klein. Anna Freud had by now entered the field of child analysis, and her pedagogic approach was radically different from Klein's, who attempted to penetrate the deepest recesses of the unconscious in depressed children suffering from the effects of a very early persecutory superego. In July of 1925 Klein was invited to come from Berlin to Britain for three weeks to give a course of lectures. Freud informed Jones curtly that her views were not appreciated in Vienna. Nevertheless, in the summer of 1926 (without informing Freud) Jones invited Klein to London to analyze his wife and two children. Klein was only too eager to accept, because life in Berlin had become intolerable for her since the death of Abraham. He had enthusiastically supported her work, but now formerly suppressed opposition to her theories was being expressed in violent attacks at scientific meetings.

In 1926 Jones published a paper, "The Origin and Structure of the Super-Ego," which was very much in accord with Klein's views. Although he described its approach as speculative, Jones attempted to reconcile the existence of early innate aggressive impulses with Freud's emphasis on the Oedipal conflict in the formation of the superego. Not unexpectedly, Freud strongly disapproved of any modification of this cornerstone of psychoanalysis.

Jones began to envisage London as a pioneering center for child analysis. Matters came to a head early in 1927 when Anna Freud published her first book, *The Psycho-Analytical Treatment of Children* [*Einführung in der Techik der Kinderanalyse*], which was a direct attack on Klein's attempts to penetrate the unconscious mind of disturbed children.

By now Anna had become indispensable to her father. At one point she had approached Eitingon about becoming a member of the Berlin Society, but Freud's cancer forged such a symbiotic bond between father and daughter that there was no question that she would ever leave his side. As far as Freud was concerned, the Committee, even though it continued to exchange *Rundbriefe*, had ceased to act as a viable political unit. He increasingly used Anna as his eyes and ears. Jones was aware of the identification of Anna with her father, but nevertheless refused to publish her book in English because he considered it biased and immature. Moreover, in the middle of May he organized a symposium on child analysis that was in effect a riposte to Anna Freud's attack on Melanie Klein, who was strongly supported by most of the British members. Each in turn concentrated on aspects of Anna Freud's book with which they disagreed. By publishing the proceedings in *The International Journal of Psycho-Analysis*, Jones must have known Freud would interpret the undertaking as an act of hostility.

Freud complained that Jones was launching a public campaign against his daughter. He was particularly upset because Joan Riviere, whom he had analyzed only a few years previously and whose intelligence he admired greatly, had now emerged as a strong supporter of Klein's.[18] Jones replied that he had written to Sandor Rado, the editor of the *Zeitschrift*, requesting that

Anna's book could be simultaneously reviewed, as had been done before, by two people from different points of view, and his reply indicated that only a favourable view of it could be published. There remained only the "Journal," but I promised Mrs. Klein that our pages would also be open to any contribution of hers defining the points of issue between her and Anna and generally clearing up the situation. You may well imagine that it never once occurred to me that Anna would claim immunity from criticism of her writings, still less that you would expect any such immunity for her. Extremely important scientific issues were at stake and an open discussion on all sides seemed the obvious course. I certainly could not sympathise with the possibility of one side of the case being artificially blocked, especially when it was the one that seemed to me to be the more progressive and promising of the two.[19]

Would that he had shown similar tolerance in the cases of Rank, Jung, and Ferenczi!

In his relatively brief contribution to the symposium, Jones refrained from mentioning Anna Freud by name, but he concluded that sufficient evidence from the Kleinian approach to children had accumulated "not only to justify the further pursuit of such investigations with children, but to indicate that the fears of the critics are here as unfounded in fact as they have long been proved to be in respect to adults."

On May 16, between the two sessions of the symposium, Jones sent Freud a flattering letter about his own children's analyses, the amazing success of which he indirectly attributed to Freud. He did not mention the name of their analyst, Melanie Klein, but he wrote that he was convinced that their progress was due to the fact that the analyses were conducted on principles based on Freud's theories—thus implying that Anna Freud was departing from her father's fundamental beliefs. Nevertheless, he concluded his letter in a very straightforward way:

> It is a pain to me that I cannot agree with *some* of the tendencies in Anna's book, and I cannot help thinking that they must be due in part to some imperfectly analyzed resistances; in fact I think it is possible to prove this in detail. It is a pity she publishes the book so soon—her first lectures, but I hope she may prove as amenable as her father to further experience. This hope is strengthened by my admiration for all her other qualities—also analytic ones.

Freud replied that he did not want to take sides, and that Anna worked completely independently, but that so far as he could judge, Mrs. Klein's view of the ego ideal in children was completely different from his own. Jones disagreed. The only difference he could see between them was that Klein dated the Oedipal conflict earlier than Freud; he was convinced that her conclusions were "simply a direct continuation of your own." But Freud could not be dissuaded from his conviction that the superego of children was still under the direct control of the parental figures.* Moreover, he viewed the attack against Anna as a disguised attack against him.[20] Freud confided in Eitingon that he believed Jones needed Klein because he

---

*Actually Freud was right in his suspicion that this was a form of "heresy." True, Klein placed as much emphasis on the unconscious (unlike Anna Freud) as Freud himself. But while Jones might claim that the "only difference" between them was the dating of the Oedipus complex and the inception of the superego, these differences were crucial. To Freud, Jones minimized the fact that primary narcissism had been discarded by Klein and

himself lacked originality and "his application of my ideas has stayed on a schoolboy level. . . . I am a piece of his superego, which is dissatisfied with his ego. He fears to discover this dissatisfaction in me, and, as a by-product of his pathological displacement, he has to take care that I have reason to be dissatisfied" (January 14, 1929).

Before Ferenczi's visit to England, Freud warned him to be on his guard against Jones. During their fortnight's visit, Jones entertained him and Gizella so lavishly that Ferenczi interpreted their apparent kindness as overcompensation for the way he had been treated in America (for which he held Jones partially responsible). At Jones's country home in Elstead, Ferenczi challenged him directly with his suspicions that Jones and Brill had met privately in Italy to plot their strategy against lay analysis at the Congress in Innsbruck in September 1927. Jones categorically denied the charge. He claimed that in the British Society he had found the golden mean with a mixture of medical and lay people. He also felt that Ferenczi identified too much with Freud's position. Ferenczi was shocked to discover the influence Melanie Klein had on Jones and the entire group. He wrote to Freud: "I regard this as a strike against Vienna. In that question as well, Jones was trying to force me to take sides. I refused and said this was a scientific and not a party matter" (June 20, 1927). This letter was written from Groddeck's spa in Baden-Baden, where Ferenczi was recuperating from the strain of the previous year.

While in America Ferenczi had worked with manic energy, but now he realized how tired he was. Nevertheless, on his way to Baden-Baden he stopped off in Paris to meet all the French psychoanalytic figures. In Paris he learned of the princely style in which Rank was living, which he believed was proof of the gossip he had heard from Jones, namely that Rank speculated on the stock market with tips given to him by his patients.

Ferenczi felt too weary to make the trip to Berlin to see Eitingon, but hoped that Eitingon could manage to visit him in Baden-Baden.

replaced in importance by the first relationship at the breast, now seen as the basis of all future relationships. In other words, we see the first form of an object relations theory. In contrast to Freud's instinct theory, which emphasized the subject's need to reduce instinctual tension, here the subject's need to relate to objects occupies the central position.

Once the Congress was over and he felt properly rested, he looked forward to spending two weeks with Freud. Nevertheless, to Eitingon Freud acknowledged that in Ferenczi's delay in meeting with him, "Some sort of emancipation is involved."

Jones, on reading the Ferenczi correspondence for the first time while writing his life of Freud, was probably stunned to learn how violently Freud was opposed to Jones becoming president. Eitingon wanted to step down from the position, and Freud urged Ferenczi to talk to Eitingon before the Congress, even if Ferenczi had to go to Berlin. Despite his fatigue, Ferenczi did rush to Berlin once he learned of Eitingon's antagonism toward lay analysis. Ferenczi felt that if there were a possibility of his assuming the presidency, he could not do so while Eitingon opposed non-medical analysts. After this meeting, Eitingon wrote to Freud that he was alarmed by Ferenczi's stridency. Nevertheless, for a time there seemed a real possibility that Ferenczi would be a candidate, and in that eventuality, he was pleased that he had made the visits to London, Paris, and Berlin. Freud advised him to modify his stand on lay analysis if it meant that he would have to forego the presidency because of his advocacy. This change in attitude was a crucial indication of Freud's priorities.

Eitingon was in favor of Ferenczi as president, but agreed that if they found too much opposition mounted against him by the Americans, he would consider continuing in the post. Freud complained that he found Ferenczi "more reserved" since his return from America. "Damned country!" he wrote (August 2, 1927). To Eitingon, he admitted that "I don't quite understand him."[21] Undoubtedly Freud was paranoid about the effect America had on his colleagues. Ferenczi responded in astonishment to the charge, which he did not believe he deserved. More reserved? "Quite the contrary! My American experiences have probably only enhanced my interest in psychoanalysis (which I think of as an essentially European thing)" (August 5, 1927). There was absolutely no reason why he should be more reserved toward Freud, and the only difference between Eitingon and himself concerned the question of lay analysis.

Freud was delighted with his response (August 8, 1927):

I am more than happy that you contradict me so energetically. Perhaps that was just what I wanted to hear, or perhaps I am just unhappy that I have not seen you yet, although it's been months since you returned from Dollar Country.

Freud continued to press Ferenczi to be president, although he was also telling Eitingon that he would be happy to see him continue in the post. He advised Ferenczi to withdraw only if the opposition was so strong that it appeared that Jones might be elected, an eventuality that must be prevented at all costs.

And this is indeed what happened at Innsbruck during the first week of September 1927. The American opposition to Ferenczi became so apparent that Ferenczi bowed to the inevitable and nominated Eitingon. A meeting of the Committee was held after the Congress. It was decided that since the movement had become firmly established on an international scale, there was no longer any necessity for the Committee to be secret and that it would now consist of the officials of the International Association: Eitingon, Ferenczi, Jones, Anna Freud, and Johann van Ophuijsen (from Holland). This enabled the group to drop their silent partner, Sachs, whom Freud had never considered to be of adequate stature to be a member.

The *Rundbriefe* continued as official newsletters, with a new series beginning in October, but never again were they to have the emotionally charged tone of the original exchange, and they were not sent with the same regularity. Freud said that he would take part in the correspondence "only indirectly" through Anna. Jones and Ferenczi were the two members of the Committee left from the original group of 1912. The fragile ring had splintered into fragments. Its very success in establishing psychoanalysis firmly in various countries was as much responsible for its disintegration as were the departure of Rank and the death of Abraham.

The delegates made their ritual report to Freud after the Innsbruck Congress; afterwards, Freud and Ferenczi shared a happy holiday together. On his return to Budapest, Ferenczi told Freud (October 2, 1927) that the interlude had seemed like the good old days when he and Freud were still discussing the early problems of psychoanalysis, interspersed with minutiae about various kinds of mushrooms. However, he did voice one complaint: the Budapest group was active, but he believed that it would be vitalized by some show of support from Freud, whose pessimism about the political fate of Hungary under Horthy tended to have a paralyzing effect on its members. Freud replied that Ferenczi's attitude indicated that he intended to stay in Budapest. If this were the case, he would give him every possible kind of support: "Since 1909 we have gone a long way together, always hand in hand, and for the short way that remains to be traversed, it will not be different" (October 25, 1927).

One sign of collegiality was the beginning of regular meetings in Vienna with colleagues from Budapest and Prague on Anna Freud's technique of child analysis—in actuality, these were counterattacks on the child symposium in London. At Innsbruck Melanie Klein had delivered a paper, "Early Stages of the Oedipus Complex," in which she agreed with Karen Horney that a girl has an awareness of the vagina, and that when she discovers her lack of a penis she blames her mother, whom she believes is withholding it from her. Jones also gave a paper, "Early Development of Female Sexuality," which supported Klein's contention that the Oedipal situation was galvanized by the oral stage.

Only a few days after Jones's visit to Semmering, Freud fired off a furious letter to him. All his indignation about the "formal campaign" by the English group against Anna was revived. He had never ceased to brood about Jones's insinuation that Anna had not been sufficiently analyzed, particularly as her second analysis had been resumed in 1924. He probably suspected that Jones had heard about this from someone. "Who is really sufficiently analyzed?" he demanded. "I can assure you Anna has been analysed longer and more thoroughly than, for instance, yourself. The whole critique rests on a flimsy preconception which one could avoid quite easily with a little benevolence."[22]

Unfortunately, benevolence seemed in very short supply, even though Jones assured Freud that "The mood here is one of entire devotion to your personality and fidelity to the principles of psychoanalysis."[23] Freud was pleased that he had put Jones in his place, and he wrote Eitingon with some satisfaction about the contents of the letter: "The results of this cold water treatment has to be awaited. As you are now specializing in making peace, I can take over the aggression. Together, then, we will represent the typical father figure."[24]

Gossip was being spread that Ferenczi had had great success with women in America, and from Britain it was reported that he had an American mistress. The antipathy between Ferenczi and Jones was reaching an aggressively infantile stage. The Committee had had a beginning and a middle, but it was to have no definitive closure. It was disintegrating, not with a bang but with a petulant whimper.

Chapter Twelve

The Last Act

 THE SECRET Committee had run its turbulent course. Freud's subsequent gift of rings to Lou Andreas-Salomé, Marie Bonaparte, Katharine Jones, and Ernst Simmel were gestures of personal friendship and gratitude. With the dispersal of rings beyond the inner circle, their inherent symbolism had vanished. The fantasy had been dissolved by the harsh reality of human beings unable to get along together.

But while the Committee existed, it was a means of containing the inflammatory emotions of the brothers. In its new existence as an adjunct to the official body of the international organization the hatred of the two key figures (Jones and Ferenczi) could no longer be formalized within its protocol. Moreover, as Freud's cancer progressed, he lacked the power or energy to restrain his battling sons.

A meeting of the new Committee had been planned for February 1928. Jones was unable to attend because his daughter was dying of pneumonia. He was pathetically grateful for a telegram of condolence sent by Freud. Jones replied, "Although I know that, to my deep regret, I have not found much favour in your eyes of late years, it showed that you retained some affection for me" (February 7, 1928). He added disconsolately: "The politics and personalities of [psychoanalytic] work have brought more pain than pleasure in the last years, and what else is there?"

When Jones wrote in March that his daughter had died at the age of 7½, Freud assured him that he and Jones had had only "a slight family quarrel."[1] As for Jones's bereavement, Freud was convinced that his own griefs had been greater than those of Jones because Freud's daughter and grandson had died when he was too old and frail to absorb his grief. "You and your dear wife are of course young enough to be able to regain serenity in life." Freud suggested that he might be able to get his mind off his suffering if he studied Freud's new theory that Shakespeare was actually the Earl of Oxford. Jones had hoped for more comfort than this, but Freud could only reply: "As an unbelieving fatalist I can only let my arms sink before the terrors of death" (May 3, 1928). Once again, Freud seemed to find it impossible to empathize with the sufferings of another person.

There is no evidence that Ferenczi felt any sympathy for Jones's tragedy either. On February 8 he was complaining about Jones's request that he show him in advance his paper, "The Adaptation of the Family to the Child," which he had delivered in London the previous year and was about to publish in the *British Journal of Medical Psychology*. Jones had said that he would consider this "a great gesture of friendship," but to Ferenczi it appeared as unacceptable censorship. At the end of the year (December 12, 1928) Jones informed Freud that he had not heard from Ferenczi for a long time.

It is difficult to assign blame in a case of such warring emotions. Jones was not an easy man to get along with. From the beginning he was filled with envy toward both Rank and Ferenczi because they were so close to Freud, and there is little doubt that he tried to undermine their credibility. He also felt humiliated because he had been forced to be analyzed by Ferenczi. But, in later years, anything Jones did was interpreted by Ferenczi as guileful or hypocritical. On the other hand, Jones genuinely believed that he was the one who was best serving Freud's interests. His loyalty to Freud cannot be questioned, and, with good reason, he never felt sufficiently appreciated. From the very beginning, he had tried to win Freud's approval; but when he received it, it was generally given only grudgingly.

Freud was convinced that Ferenczi was sulking because he believed that Freud had not thrown sufficient weight behind him for the presidency in 1927. Ferenczi claimed that he had withdrawn from the race when he saw how "tepid" Eitingon had been over

lay analysis. There seems little doubt that Ferenczi's fervent espousal of lay analysis was in part an attempt to convince Freud
that he was his alter ego, but it was also an attempt to prevent
Budapest from becoming isolated entirely from the wider psychoanalytic world. If Ferenczi could attract non-medical American
analysands to Hungary, he could manage to make ends meet.

But the events of the Congress of 1927 were decisive in increasing
Ferenczi's isolation from the mainstream of psychoanalysis. Although he visited Freud on three occasions during 1928, he was
becoming increasingly paranoid in his interpretation of Freud's attitude toward him. Jones, on the other hand, continued to remind
Freud of their close ties in an attempt to heal the rift between them.
On receiving a friendly letter from Freud at the beginning of 1929,
Jones wrote back (January 26, 1929) that he would treasure the
letter because what had made his life most worth living was "my
relationship to you and your work." He recalled that when they
parted at the railway station in Worcester, Massachusetts, in 1909,
he had promised Freud that he would stand firm. Jones also mused
as to whether he would ever write his autobiography. "I could
relate many interesting things."

The 1929 Congress was planned for Oxford in July. Ferenczi
sullenly threatened to boycott the Committee preceding it (sched-
uled to take place in Paris in May), because he and Jones so disagreed
on the question of lay analysis. Ferenczi was also sulking because
Britain had been chosen as the location for the Congress, which
meant that Jones could exert more influence over the Americans.
On March 5 Freud begged him to reconsider. In the first place,
Jones's fiftieth birthday had taken place on January 1, and thus it
seemed appropriate for the Congress to be held in Britain that year.
Secondly, Freud asked Ferenczi to have some consideration for the
family misfortunes Jones had suffered in the previous year. "Giving
in in this matter does not mean that one also has to give in to him
in other respects. Your staying away would be unfortunate, since
the strongest tension in the former committee was the one between
you and him." [*Ihr Ausbleiben würde sehr viel stärkste Spannung in-
nerhalb des einstigen Komites bestaht doch zwischen Ihnen und Ihm.*] Ferenczi finally acceded to Freud's plea that he attend the committee

meeting, but he warned Freud that Jones was "an unscrupulous and dangerous person who is using lay analysis as a pretext to unite the Anglo-Saxon world under himself" (February 17, 1929). In Paris Eitingon had to act as mediator between Anna Freud and Ferenczi on one side and Jones and van Ophuijsen on the other in a heated discussion on lay analysis.

Freud advised Anna to treat Oxford "as an interesting adventure," and to be glad that she hadn't married Jones (July 2, 1929). With Jones's endorsement, the Americans forced the European groups not to accept Americans (physicians or lay people) for training in Europe unless the American Educational Committee gave its endorsement. Thus all Ferenczi's efforts on Freud's behalf had come to nothing, and Ferenczi felt that Freud had ignominiously allowed himself to be swayed by political considerations in making political concessions to the Americans. This was particularly galling, since in principle Brill agreed that the American Psychoanalytic Association should admit some lay people.

"I am extraordinarily pleased," Freud wrote to Jones in August, "that the congress went off in such conciliatory fashion, and brought an unmistakable approach of the New Yorkers to our point of view."

Ferenczi's paper at the Oxford Congress was an expression of the direction in which he had been moving in the past few years. In "The Unwelcome Child and His Death Instinct," he spoke of the deleterious effects of the lack of love on children. In the course of the year his letters to Freud became less and less frequent. On November 6 he suddenly sent an explanation for this neglect. He had found that he was becoming less involved in the psychoanalytic movement than he had been in the past. Moreover, he feared that if he raised the questions he was pondering, he would only meet with opposition from Freud. Finally, he expressed shock at learning that Freud had made the observation that he looked prematurely old and senile.

Freud seemed astonished. He had no recollection of having made such a remark, although he admitted that he might have said to someone that Ferenczi was looking even older than himself. While Freud was accusing Ferenczi of isolating himself, Freud, with Anna at his side, might also have been separating himself from Ferenczi. One indication of this could have been his belief that "my Paladin and secret *Grand Vizier*," was formulating theories opposed to his own.[2] Freud wrote Ferenczi that he realized that he had been deeply hurt when he had not been made president. Surely Ferenczi must realize that this was due to "tiresome politics" because they could not risk antagonizing Jones and creating a possible split in the International Association, even though privately he, Anna, and Eitingon had supported Ferenczi's candidacy at Oxford; but as Freud had occasion to say many times during his life, nothing was as important as psychoanalysis. In other words, from time to time individuals had to be sacrificed.

Ferenczi wrote that he was puzzled and offended by the kid gloves with which Jones was being handled. He knew that he had been pushed aside. At any rate, he rationalized, he was freed from unnecessary responsibilities and could devote himself to real scientific work.[3] But he knew that had Freud fully supported him, the Hungarian group would undoubtedly have gained prestige if their president were also president of the International. After his years of devotion to Freud, he was stunned by what seemed to be an act of betrayal. Clearly Jones was far more important to Freud politically.

Freud issued a warning: if Ferenczi continued to isolate himself like this and to harbor resentment against Jones, it was going to make it difficult for them to vote for him at the next Congress.[4] Ferenczi heeded the warning. In response to a critical letter from Jones, he pleaded that as old friends they should not allow scientific differences to degenerate into personal attacks (January 6, 1930).

Freud tried to deflect Ferenczi's personal bitterness toward him by emphasizing the way the American analysts had treated Ferenczi, and by referring to his feelings about Jones's devious conduct [*an bis zu Jones niedrägen Gesten.*] "If I did not explicitly speak up for you against him, that happened only because I have no interest in stirring up the quarrel, but rather in ignoring it." Freud professed himself unable to understand why Ferenczi seemed to be turning against him personally when his appreciation of him was as high as ever.[5] Ferenczi agreed that their own unclouded relationship should continue without a shadow. They were both by now indulging in a fantasy that their relationship was still what it had been in the past.

Ferenczi's ambivalence toward Freud is reflected in the vacillations of tone in his letters of this period. On January 17, 1930, he finally unleashed all his pent-up resentments. He retraced the history of their relationship. In the beginning Freud was his "adored teacher and unattainable model." Naturally, as an apprentice, his feelings were never entirely unmixed. Then Ferenczi went into analysis with Freud, but it could not be completed for various reasons. Nevertheless, he blamed Freud for never analyzing Ferenczi's negative feelings toward Freud. Years of self-analysis had enabled him to understand that he should not have overestimated his importance to Freud.

He had started his letter, Ferenczi discovered to his surprise, by addressing Freud as "friend" rather than as "Professor." This seemed to him to indicate a decisive change in his feelings toward Freud. Actually he had been suffering distress about him for a long time but refrained from saying anything because of Freud's health. Ferenczi's paper at Oxford was the first public expression of the way in which his views were diverging from those of his former mentor. He realized that he should have been honest with Freud in voicing his uneasiness about what he now considered to be the narrowness of psychoanalysis, but instead he had withdrawn into sulky brooding.

Freud admitted that he had little patience with neurotics, and that there had been a time when he had hoped that he could avoid dealing with deeply disturbed people. He used the analogy of the man who said to his wife after their wedding night: "Now you know what it's like; it will always be the same" (January 20, 1930). In short, he felt he had nothing more to learn from them. His interests now lay in training people to perpetuate his ideas.

Ferenczi responded that he was troubled that Freud was uninterested in psychoanalysis as a means of helping suffering people. Finally, Ferenczi saw little sense in continuing discussions about the presidency, because he realized that he was not a particularly good administrator and that he lacked the necessary diplomacy for

24. Georg Groddeck was now replacing Freud as the mother Ferenczi always wanted.

25. A rejuvenated Melanie Klein (*at right*) with colleague Joan Riviere at the Innsbruck Congress in 1927.

26. Freud with the two problematic women in his life, mother Amalia and wife Martha.

27.   Ferenczi with his wife Gizella at Wiesbaden in September 1932, where he delivered his controversial (and later suppressed) final paper on the sexual abuse of children.

28. Freud arrives in England with daughter Mathilde comforting him, Jones the savior, and Ernst Freud's wife Lucie.

that office. Despite these deficiencies, he wrote, if he possessed other qualities that might qualify him for the presidency, that was up to Freud to decide.[6]

Freud was stung by Ferenczi's reproach that he had neglected the negative transference. He reminded him that the analysis had taken place fourteen years earlier, at a time when such reactions were not anticipated.* And who could have known how long it would take for Ferenczi's hostile feelings to manifest themselves?

That Freud continued to be deeply disturbed by Ferenczi's charge is indicated in the last technical paper he ever wrote, "Analysis Terminable and Interminable" (1937). As James Strachey remarks in his introduction to the paper, "The paper as a whole gives an impression of pessimism in regard to the therapeutic efficacy of psychoanalysis."[7] There is no question that Freud is referring to the analysis with Ferenczi when he defends the fact that negative feelings were not discussed in a specific case:

A certain man, who had himself practised analysis with great success, came to the conclusion that his relations both to men and women— to the men who were his competitors and to the woman whom he loved—were nevertheless not free from neurotic impediments; and he therefore made himself the subject of an analysis by someone whom he regarded as superior to himself. This critical illumination of his own self had a completely successful result. He married the woman he loved and turned into a friend and teacher of his supposed rivals. Many years passed in this way, during which his relations with his former analyst also remained unclouded. But then, for no assignable external reason, trouble arose. The man who had been analysed became antagonistic to the analyst and reproached him for having failed to give him a complete analysis. The analyst, he said, ought to have known and to have taken into account the fact that a transference-relation can never be purely positive; he should have given his attention to the possibilities of a negative transference. The analyst defended himself by saying that, at the time of the analysis, there was no sign of a negative transference. But even if he had failed

---

*The first analysis was conducted during three weeks in October 1914, the second for three weeks (with two sessions daily) in June 1916.

to observe some very faint signs of it—which was not altogether ruled out, considering the limited horizon of analysis in those early days—it was still doubtful, he thought, whether he would have had the power to activate a topic (or, as we say, a 'complex') by merely pointing it out, so long as it was not currently active in the patient himself at the time. To activate it would certainly have required some unfriendly piece of behaviour in reality on the analyst's part. Furthermore, he added, not every good relation between an analyst and his subject during and after analysis was to be regarded as a transference; there were also friendly relations which were based on reality and which proved to be viable.[8]

At the time Freud's diagnosis of Ferenczi's condition was that he had reactivated his neurosis through his paranoia about the presidency. This manifested itself in his touchiness toward his "brothers." Freud told him bluntly that he was too old for such infantile behavior.

Ferenczi would not agree that he was suffering from a reactivation of his former neurosis (February 14, 1930). He was convinced that he had made progress now that he was able to speak openly to Freud not as an analyst but as a friend. (Incidentally, Freud had given him no indication that he wanted to be regarded as a friend.) Ferenczi realized, too, that his reference to Freud regarding him as prematurely old was really a projection of his own anxieties about his health and his anxiety to publish the ideas that had been occupying his mind in the time that remained to him. Freud had not yet seen his Oxford paper, and Ferenczi now felt sufficiently liberated to send it to him. He had also been reading *Civilization and Its Discontents* [*Das Unbehagen in der Kultur*], and for the first time he felt free to tell Freud where he disagreed with him. He believed Freud was mistaken in accepting Melanie Klein's view of a self-destructive tendency in humans. Surely this would be acquired through individual experience, and was there not an innate need for love?*

Anna, concerned about Ferenczi's growing estrangement, trav-

---

*Actually, Jones too had refrained from criticizing the death instinct when Freud first formulated it in 1920, but he was more frank in a letter to Freud, dated January 1, 1930.

eled to Budapest to persuade Ferenczi to visit her father. Freud was immensely grateful for the warm reception she was given. Meanwhile his health had deteriorated and he had to go into hospital. Ferenczi visited him on April 21, and came away confident that his fears about a breach between them were highly exaggerated. But there was nothing concrete he could do to restore the former harmony between them.

Whereas Jones was able to bring out a translation of Freud's collected works through an excellent arrangement with the Hogarth Press, Ferenczi experienced one difficulty after another in doing the same with his Hungarian publisher. Freud, who by July was resting in the sanatorium established by Ernst Simmel in the Berlin suburb of Tegel, brushed these problems aside for a more pressing one: Eitingon was determined to step down from the presidency at the next Congress. Blandly, Freud assured Ferenczi (July 7, 1930): "You also know that we were all aware of the fact that you should have been president, and that we *only* delayed your election for diplomatic reasons." Eitingon had also conveyed his decision to Ferenczi, but had received no reply. What worried Freud was that if Ferenczi had lost all interest in the interval, Jones would be the only available candidate. It went without saying, Freud emphasized, where his preference lay. He resorted to a plea about the state of his health. He would hate to die in the knowledge that Ferenczi had not accepted the post to which he had so long been entitled.

Ferenczi was touched by Freud's expression of confidence in him. He was in a new, conciliatory mood. Six months before he had listed the reasons why he wasn't suited to be president; now he agreed with Eitingon that he was the best man for the job (July 20, 1930). He agreed, too, that they all had to come to terms with Jones. "On the other hand, I can't help looking at the despotism and maliciousness of his character and actions as anything but harmful for psychoanalysis."

On September 12 Freud's mother died at the age of ninety-five. He admitted to both Ferenczi and Jones that he had experienced a feeling of liberation and release at her death. Anna took Freud's place at the funeral. To his brother Alexander, Freud explained that he did not attend the funeral because he could not abide ceremonies. Freud's ambiguous relationship with his mother explains much about his relationships with others, particularly with the members of the Committee. In the Committee he had created an ideal family in which he was both mother and father. Since he had apparently received little tenderness from the stern Amalie Freud, his ability to empathize was frozen. He could understand ambition and rivalry, but not gentle love and concern. He spoke often of the neurosis of the "brother complex," as though it had more reality than actual rivalry between siblings.* He had not understood Ferenczi's sufferings when his mother died, and now he could not mourn for his own mother. In the same letter in which he thanked Ferenczi for his "beautiful words" of condolence, he then immediately turned to the subject of Ferenczi's latest paper†, which he described as "very ingenious" [*sehr geistrich*].[9]

Ferenczi replied that he would have preferred Freud to have described his views as correct, probable, or even plausible. His new theories on relaxation technique were derived from his practice, and he was modifying them constantly. He was offended by Freud's indirect disapproval; but when Freud developed pneumonia in November, Ferenczi rushed to Vienna to see him and again was relieved that Freud didn't seem to find his new views "so revolutionary" (November 25, 1930).

In the meantime another crisis arose. Eitingon's financial support came mainly from his family's branch of the fur business in New York. With the stock market crash, it suffered severe losses, and Eitingon for the first time in his life was without substantial means. He could no longer pour money into the Berlin Society or the Verlag, and he appealed to the individual members for help. Ferenczi replied (June 14, 1930) that it was absolutely impossible for the Hungarian members to donate any more, and he assured Eitingon that his refusal had nothing to do with envy of Berlin or Vienna.

---

*In an interview with Bluma Swerdloff on November 27, 1963 (Columbia Oral Archives), Sandor Rado spoke of how totally uninterested Freud's children (except for Anna) were in his work: "Freud saw the children for five minutes, ten minutes, half an hour, for days, weeks, months, years, and decades." Freud never encouraged any of his sons to pursue medicine or psychoanalysis.
†"The Principle of Relaxation and Neocatharsis."

On December 14 Eitingon and Jones met in Paris and agreed that Ferenczi should be nominated for president at the Congress the following year. But Ferenczi was destined to be frustrated yet again by forces beyond his control. In 1918, when he had been elected president, Freud had predicted a great future for Budapest. By 1920 Freud was persuaded that Hungary was too isolated from the Western world, and that Jones, with his American connections, would be a better tactical choice as interim president. When Abraham died in 1925, Freud virtually promised the presidency to Ferenczi, but was overruled by Eitingon and Jones. In 1927 and 1929 it was again within Ferenczi's grasp, but Freud did not throw his weight behind him. The irony was that Ferenczi had espoused Freud's advocacy of lay analysis to such an extent that he had antagonized the Americans. Yet since the only alternative to Ferenczi was Jones, by 1931 it seemed inevitable that the presidency would be his at last. What none of them had taken into consideration was the world economic situation. After much discussion, at the end of July it was decided that the Congress must be canceled in 1931 because the members did not have enough money to travel. With this decision, Ferenczi's ambitions were thwarted forever.

In the ensuing year Freud was given time to ponder his misgivings about the direction in which Ferenczi was moving. In addition, Jones used every opportunity to undermine him with Freud and to assure him that, like Huxley with Darwin, Jones was Freud's bulldog. Without taking into account the terrible political and economic difficulties in Hungary, Jones stated his opinion that the problems of the Budapest group stemmed from lack of leadership (December 31, 1930). Freud pleaded for cooperation among the three leading members of the Committee. There was nothing Jones wanted more, he replied; but Ferenczi, he insinuated, was the one who had created the difficulty.

Ferenczi has been behaving very neurotically in the last few years towards both Eitingon and myself, and all our endeavours to deal with his resistance were in vain. You know it is not my custom to speak to you about such difficulties among colleagues, but rather to attempt to deal with them myself. I mention them now only because there is no hope that they are at an end. They appear to have been mainly due to my action in proposing Eitingon to be confirmed in the Presidency, which he had been holding in the interim since Abraham's death. I still think it would have been offensive to him to do otherwise and do not at all regret my action, but Ferenczi appears to have felt otherwise. Now, however, I hope that it is a matter of the past. I wrote him a letter at Christmas notifying him of our intention to propose Eitingon at the next Congress and he has, to my great pleasure, replied with a most friendly letter. Incidentally, he now forgives me for the "Groll" (resentment) which he, not I, had been feeling.[10]

After the cancellation of the Congress in 1931, Ferenczi's correspondence with Freud petered out again. On September 15 he asked Freud to forgive his tardiness in writing, but he had been so involved in his work that he could not interrupt it. Freud did not find this explanation satisfactory and on September 9 wrote Ferenczi a sharp letter criticizing him for his remoteness, behavior that Freud described as simply another indication of his immaturity. Freud only hoped that he could get along with the next, "maybe for me last," president of the International. It was hardly a vote of confidence.

Ferenczi replied mildly enough from Capri where he and Gizella had gone on holiday. He described himself as an empiricist, whose ideas would be rejected or confirmed by the progress of his patients.[11] But Freud suddenly discovered a cause to provoke a real quarrel between them from a piece of gossip he had picked up. Ferenczi, he wrote on October 13, had made no secret of the fact that he and his patients kissed each other.* He had heard this confirmed through one of his own patients (via a patient of Ferenczi's, Clara Thompson).† Freud found such procedure "disgraceful," although he had condoned Jung's affair with Sabina Spielrein years before.

*It is not clear whether Ferenczi had actually told Freud this.
†In quoting Freud's letter, Jones omitted the source, Clara Thompson. Thompson had the greatest respect for Ferenczi's technique. See "The Therapeutic Technique of Sandor Ferenczi: A Comment." *IJPA*, 24 (1924), 64–66. According to Ferenczi's *Clinical Diary*, he sat immobile when she tried to provoke him.

Freud had not pressed Rank directly to tell him about his psychoanalytic technique, but now he warned Ferenczi bluntly that he must make his own technical procedures public. When Ferenczi had reproached Freud for not analyzing his negative transference, he was also implicitly criticizing him for withholding the tenderness he craved. Possibly Freud was trying to deny his remorse by seizing upon something for which he could severely admonish and humiliate Ferenczi. In the course of writing the letter (December 13, 1931) he seems to have been carried away by his own sexual fantasies

Now I am assuredly not one of those who from prudishness or from consideration of bourgeois convention would condemn little erotic gratifications of this kind. And I am also aware that in the time of the Nibelungs a kiss was a harmless greeting granted to every guest. I am further of the opinion that analysis is possible even in Soviet Russia where so far as the State is concerned there is full sexual freedom. But that does not alter the fact that we are not living in Soviet Russia and that with us a kiss signifies a certain erotic intimacy. We have hitherto in our technique held to the conclusion that patients are to be refused erotic gratifications. You know too that where more extensive gratifications are not to be had milder caresses very easily take over their role, in love affairs, on the stage, etc.

Now picture what will be the result of publishing your technique. There is no revolutionary who is not driven out of the field by a still more radical one. A number of independent thinkers in matters of technique will say to themselves: why stop at a kiss? Certainly one gets further when one adopts 'pawing' as well, which after all doesn't make a baby. And then bolder ones will come along who will go further to peeping and showing—and soon we shall have accepted in the technique of analysis the whole repertoire of demiviergerie and petting parties, resulting in an enormous increase of interest in psychoanalysis among both analysts and patients. The new adherent, however, will easily claim too much of this interest for himself, the younger of our colleagues will find it hard to stop at the point they originally intended, and God the Father Ferenczi gazing at the lively scene he has created will perhaps say to himself: maybe after all I should have halted in my technique of motherly affection *before* the kiss.

Sentences like 'about the dangers of neocatharsis' don't get very far. One should obviously not let oneself get into the danger. I have purposely not mentioned the increase of calumnious resistances against analysis the kissing technique would bring, although it seems to me a wanton act to provoke them.

In this warning I do not think I have said anything you do not know yourself. But since you like playing a tender mother role with others, then perhaps you may do so with yourself. And then you are to hear from the brutal fatherly side an admonition. That is why I spoke in my last letter of a new puberty, a Johannis impulse, and now you have compelled me to be quite blunt.[12]

Jones, (as Jeffrey Masson has correctly pointed out), in his life of Freud, omitted the penultimate sentence in the paragraph: "According to my memory the tendency for sexual playing about [*sexuelle Spielerei*] with patients was not foreign to you in pre-analytic times so that it is possible to bring the new Technique into relation with the old misdemeanors."[13]*

More than two months elapsed before Ferenczi could control his emotions sufficiently to respond to Freud's fierce denunciation (December 27, 1931). He reminded Freud that he had always advised Ferenczi to reveal as little as possible about one's technique. Furthermore, "youthful lapses" could provide understanding and were an aid to maturity. His work had gone through several phases. He had come to realize the weaknesses of his early active technique, in which he had given patients instructions to act out their repressions. He had then turned to suggestion.

Just as much as Freud, Ferenczi was aware of the dangers in the relaxation technique, but Ferenczi believed that he had been able to mitigate the danger by creating "a mild passionless atmosphere."†

---

*This omission by Jones is understandable, since this was a sensitive area in his own life. It is also not the only change in the letter.

†With certain patients, Ferenczi was experimenting with mutual analysis, wherein analyst and analysand would change places from time to time. Part of Freud's irritation might have been jealousy of Georg Groddeck, who influenced Ferenczi in his views on the psychological origins of many illnesses, and who was in agreement on the benefits that might be gained from mutual analysis. To Lou Andreas-Salomé, Anna Freud wrote (November 29, 1931): ". . . it is not troubling as long as this method is confined to Ferenczi, for he has the necessary restraint for it. I am very much afraid that Ferenczi will draw back from us and close himself off."

Freud's letter had given him pain, but he hoped that their friendly personal and scientific understanding could be restored.

At the beginning of 1932 Ferenczi began to keep a clinical diary. It is an extraordinary document, a blend of observation on the successes and failures of his experiments in mutual analysis, autobiographical material, and a searingly honest reappraisal of Freud as a man and of Ferenczi's relationship with him. On several occasions Ferenczi describes how severe his own mother had been and how she would exclaim that he would be the death of her.* (Did he in some deep sense blame himself for Freud's illness?) As early as 1921 he had confided in Groddeck about how he had been overly respectful to authority figures such as Freud, and wondered whether belonging to a family whose members concealed their true feelings would brew hypocrisy, what D. W. Winnicott was later to describe as the "false self." It would appear that in many respects throughout the years Ferenczi had transferred onto Freud aspects of his mother; Ferenczi had been unaware of how hypocritical he had been in his attitude toward Freud.

But he had not been entirely unaware. He recalled his disgust in Worcester as early as 1909 when Freud, upon receiving his honorary degree, thanked the president, Stanley Hall, with tears in his eyes. Knowing how Freud despised the Americans, at the time Ferenczi suspected that Freud was play-acting.

We learn too that Ferenczi's favorite brother was named Sigmund, and that the name of an older sister with whom he was in love was Gizella. He had tried to make Freud and his own wife into ideal parents, but he now described Freud as a "castrating god" because he had discouraged Ferenczi from marrying Elma, with whom he could have had children. In Georg Groddeck he had finally found a sympathetic friend and mentor, and through the years he would speak warmly of the enjoyment of the familiarity he found in the house and grounds at Baden-Baden.

Ferenczi dated Freud's contempt for neurotic patients from the time he had learned that they lied to him and that he had allowed

---

*An investigation into the early family relationships of the members of the Committee might throw some light on their veneration for Freud.

himself to be deceived by them. ["Die Patienten sind ein Gesindel" ("Patients are a rabble," i.e. a riff-raff) was a remark Freud had once made to him.][14] Ferenczi described Freud's method as having become increasingly pedagogic, and Freud lacked the humility to help his patients in their suffering. Consequently, the last period of Ferenczi's life was spent in an attempt to find a method completely different from that of Freud's.* He tried to offer his patients the kind of understanding and sympathy he could not receive from Freud, to be both a mother and father to them.

In April 1932 Eitingon suffered a mild cerebral thrombosis brought on, Freud believed, by the strain of his financial reverses; and this time it was Freud who offered to lend him money. On April 27 Freud confessed to Eitingon that he himself was suffering a slight attack of "what other people might call depression."[16] The future of the psychoanalytic movement looked desperate. Freud told Ferenczi that the matter of his successor had become absolutely urgent. He hoped that Ferenczi would be willing to sacrifice his isolation and be prepared to take on the responsibilities of a leader. On May 1 Ferenczi replied that there was nothing evil in his isolation, simply that he was experiencing a late (and liberating) creative period. His self-analysis had led him to see that he needed a period of mental relaxation. Was Freud really willing to accept a president like that? If so, he would do the best he could, but he admitted that he was not very adept at handling money. If Freud wanted to consider someone else, he would help him think of the most appropriate person. However, he did not *quite* shut the door on the possibility of becoming president.

On the same day, Ferenczi committed a long analysis of Freud to his diary. He reflected that Josef Breuer had actually discovered psychoanalysis, and that Freud had followed him only intellectually. If Freud was disturbed by the direction in which Ferenczi was moving, Ferenczi was equally disturbed by the distanced superiority Freud had been displaying toward his patients with the

*In Bela Grunberger's view, "By opposing Freud's teaching, Ferenczi was able to show he had not castrated him."[15]

passing of time. His refusal to let anyone else analyze him was an indication of his arrogance.

Freud's response to Ferenczi's ambiguous attitude (May 12, 1932) was that the presidency would bring him back to the real world, and that Anna would be a great help as secretary of the Association. Ferenczi should leave his "fantasy children" and mingle again with real men.

Ferenczi did not appreciate such comments. He found it impossible, he objected, to regard the presidency as some kind of drastic remedy for a neurotic illness from which he was supposed to be suffering (May 19, 1932). But since Freud had promised him a good deal of help, and had accepted Eitingon's suggestion that Brill should be vice-president, he would consider it an honor to be president.

Jones meanwhile was in a disgruntled mood. He was angry with Eitingon for permitting the establishment of the *Psychoanalytic Quarterly* in the United States, because he feared that it would cut into the circulation of the *International Journal of Psychoanalysis*. "We lost our last leader with Abraham," he lamented to Freud.[17] Freud agreed: "I cannot wake him up again, and I can only regret that no replacement has been found for him" (June 17, 1930).

Jones continued to be obsessed with the *Psychoanalytic Quarterly*. He went to Berlin to talk to Eitingon, but he "will never see what he does not want to see" (Jones/Freud; June 21, 1930). But he thought at least Eitingon owed him some loyalty as a friend. One wonders about Jones's reliability when he says, in his life of Freud, that in their discussion about the American journal, "As usual, we reached complete agreement."[18] Jones had tried not to tattle about Eitingon to Freud, he told him, but look at the mistake he had made in concealing from him how dangerous Rank was! The only result was that Freud had been subjected to complaints about Jones, whereas Jones had held his tongue about Rank. How conveniently one forgets one's past behavior!

Ferenczi went on holiday to Venice in May 1932 and did not start to work on his Congress paper until after his return to Budapest. Unlike Jones and Freud, he seemed to be the only member aware of how dangerous the political situation in Germany had become. The Congress was originally supposed to be held in Interlaken, but the German analysts were not permitted to take money out of the country, so the locale was changed to Wiesbaden. Ferenczi thought that it would be problematic if the Congress were held at all. By August 21 he had made a definite decision to reject the presidency. Holding divergent views from those of Freud, he could not in all honesty accept it.

Freud was unable to understand his decision, unless it meant that Ferenczi was planning to form a new school of psychoanalysis (August 24, 1932). Ferenczi assured him (August 29, 1932) that he had no such intention. He simply hoped that he might convince some of his colleagues of his views. He planned to visit Freud on his way to Wiesbaden.

By August 29 Freud must have received Ferenczi's letter renouncing the presidency. Yet in a letter of that date to Eitingon, he still seemed to think that Ferenczi could be persuaded to let his name stand. Aware of the general direction of Ferenczi's paper, "The Confusion of Tongues Between Adults and Children," Freud wrote:

> He must not be allowed to give the paper. Either another one or none. He does not seem disinclined to be chosen as president. Whether he will be chosen by all of you after these revelations is another question. Our behavior will depend, in the first place, on whether he agrees to its postponement, as well as on the impression he makes on all of you in Wiesbaden.[19]

Ferenczi and Gizella visited Freud on September 1. On entering the room Ferenczi, probably very nervous about his reception, immediately began reading his paper to Freud. Within a few minutes Brill (obviously by prearrangement) entered and sat down to listen. Freud did not disguise his impatience. He urged Ferenczi not to consider publishing the paper for at least a year. Ferenczi extended his hand in farewell, but Freud departed abruptly without a word. He smiled at Gizella in passing, and she dissolved into tears. The following day Freud sent Eitingon a telegram: "Ferenczi read me his paper. Harmless. Dumb. Otherwise he is inaccessible.

The impression was unfavorable."[20] Apparently Brill urged both Freud and Ferenczi to withhold Ferenczi's new ideas for the present. Freud's reaction was "What is the use? It has to come out sooner or later."[21]

The evidence seems to suggest that Jones prevailed over Ophuijsen and Eitingon that there would be less scandal if Ferenczi were allowed to give the paper, which virtually reverted to Freud's position in 1896 in "The Aetiology of Hysteria." Its shocking effect was created by Ferenczi's blunt criticism of the superiority, or "hypocrisy," of analysts who acted as though their patients were inferior to them. As a result, they did not really *listen* to what their patients were telling them, particularly in cases of actual abuse. It ended dramatically with a plea to analysts to allow patients to loosen their tongues: "You will hear much that is instructive."[22]

What Freud and the others objected to was that Ferenczi seemed to be rejecting the unconscious. However, the skies did not open at Wiesbaden when the paper was read, and Ferenczi was grateful when Jones agreed to publish it in the *International Journal*. Jones was elected president, and Freud wrote to congratulate him:

> I was sorry that Ferenczi's obvious ambition could not be satisfied, but it really was not in doubt for even a single moment that you could possibly take over the International.[23]

In actuality Freud shared Eitingon's opinion (August 29, 1932): "Jones is hardly a happy prospect for the future."[24] Jones claimed that "the task was not quite welcome to me" because he already had so many other commitments, but he wrote that it would be a pleasure to work with Anna (September 2, 1932).

As for Ferenczi, Jones could have predicted "this dénouement." He had been watching him closely for years. He and Abraham had drawn him back from the precipice during the Rank crisis. But "his exceptionally deep need of being loved, together with the repressed sadism, are plainly behind the tendency to ideas of persecution."

> It is terrible—but also unprofitable—to make comparisons with the brilliant past. One can only accept the facts, do the little possible to

help, and again to learn how one underestimates the difficulties in the way of retaining a full acceptance of the reality of the unconscious; most people seem to have a limit to their power in this respect.

Jones feared that Ferenczi was a sick man—"also physically." He did not tell Freud that Ferenczi had confided in him that he was suffering from pernicious anemia. Even if Jones had told him, Freud would possibly have dismissed Ferenczi's illness as minor compared to his own.

As Sandor Lorand has pointed out, Jones had been trained as a neurologist and would have understood the neurological pathology of Ferenczi's last days, when the spinal column and even the brain might have been attacked.[25]

From Wiesbaden Ferenczi traveled to Baden-Baden to recuperate. From there he moved on to Biarritz and Bagnores-de-Luchon, where he wrote to Freud on September 27. He was still "deeply shaken," he told him, by the cold reception Freud had given him in Vienna, and his present journey was a *"voyage de lit-à-lit."* He was planning to return directly to Budapest and would avoid Vienna.

He wrote that he hadn't been as much disturbed by their scientific differences as by Freud's allowing Brill to be present as a judge or witness at their meeting. He had also been deeply dismayed by Freud's demand that he abstain from publishing his paper.

> You certainly know just as well as I do what a loss it means to both of us that my visit at your house could end that way. You can be sure that I remember all the nice former visits, although I do have to admit that more courage and a greater openness on my part regarding practical and theoretical things would have been an advantage, but unfortunately, the younger and weaker one generally lacks such courage.

Freud was completely uninterested in Ferenczi's illness. Brill was present, he insisted, because only a few days previously Ferenczi had discussed his views with him in Budapest. Brill had also reported to him that Ferenczi had said that Freud had no more insight than a child. Nevertheless, neither of them had been of the opinion that Ferenczi's paper would affect his chances of the presidency. Freud was convinced, however, that Ferenczi was incapable of correcting himself in the way that Freud had done many years before.* One by one his followers had broken away from him, so Freud was prepared to accept Ferenczi's defection in a totally matter-of-fact way.[26]

But neither man wanted the long friendship to come to a bitter end, as had happened with Jung and Rank—and the many others. They exchanged cordial greetings at the New Year. Freud described their relationship as "an affectionate union of life, emotions, and interests." He found some comfort in the fact that there was no way he could blame himself for the change in Ferenczi's thinking. "Some psychological fate has evoked it in you," he wrote (January 11, 1933). On March 20 Ferenczi told Groddeck that he attributed the decline in his health to Freud's deceit.[27] Nevertheless, his concern for Freud's welfare prompted him to tell him on March 29 that he was making an effort to overcome his "childish sulking." He admitted frankly that his illness had progressed to such a point that he had suffered a kind of nervous breakdown. He was also agitated by the widespread persecution of German Jews provoked by the Reichstag fire in March. He had also heard that Eitingon was planning to seek a safe haven in Palestine, and he pleaded with Freud (in what Jones described as "a somewhat panicky letter")[28] to leave Vienna before it was too late, perhaps for a safe country like England. If the Nazi danger got closer to Budapest, he himself was thinking of fleeing to Switzerland.

Freud replied (April 2, 1933) that he had no intention of leaving Vienna, even if he were young and vigorous. He was not at all sure that Hitler would invade Austria, and even if he did, the brutality would never reach the extremes of Germany. He did not believe that he was in any personal danger. He assured Ferenczi that if he

---

*Freud is alluding to his rejection of the seduction theory. Freud could not see that Ferenczi was also being intellectually honest according to his own viewpoint.

thought life would be difficult for the Jews in Austria, it would be nothing compared to the misery of exile.

Eitingon had also tried to impress upon Freud the gravity of the situation when he visited him in Vienna on January 27. The burning of his books by the Nazis in Berlin in May 1933 left Freud relatively unperturbed. In late April the Fascist authorities forced Eitingon to resign from the Berlin Society. Freud's reaction to Eitingon's predicament is not altogether clear. Eitingon paid Freud his last visit on August 5 before departing for Palestine, where his family had purchased land many years before. There he organized a Palestinian Psychoanalytic Society. Jones felt that Eitingon had succumbed to panic, and that he would have been safe in Paris where he could have been of more use to the International movement (Jones/Anna Freud; September 19, 1933). "I fear he is moved by private considerations to do with his wife, but possibly their visit to Paris this autumn may convince her of its [i.e., Palestine's] relative unattractiveness." Even by October Jones continued to believe that it was "unduly pessimistic" to consider the German Society destroyed—even though no Jews were allowed to belong to it. "I think our wisest course is definitely to support Boehm and Müller-Braunschweig in the honest efforts they are undoubtedly making to salvage the situation" (Jones/Anna Freud; October 2, 1933).[29]*

Freud began to be concerned about Ferenczi when he saw how shaky his handwriting had become. In his last letter to Freud (April 9, 1933), Ferenczi thanked him for his "friendly and understanding letter" and agreed that perhaps he had overreacted to the situation. By then Ferenczi's spinal cord had disintegrated and he was unable to get out of bed. On May 24 he was dead. The following day Jones wrote to Freud:

---

*Felix Boehm and Carl Müller-Braunschweig were both Gentiles. They cooperated with the Nazis in the notorious Goring Institute, which was literally purged of all psychoanalytic theory. Both men have been heavily criticized for not following the example of their Dutch colleagues, who resigned *en masse*. The Austrian Society, of course, was completely disbanded.

It can fortunately no longer be said that the event is a blow to the movement itself, but I am sure the shock will have revived in you— as it did in me—the memory of many happy days in the past and the thought of an inspiring figure whom we all loved so much. I am more glad than ever that I succeeded at the last Congress in keeping him within our circle.

Freud replied that for years Ferenczi had not been with them. Basically Freud believed that his illness stemmed from his conviction that Freud did not love him enough, and that Ferenczi's compassion for his patients was an attempt to show Freud that one must treat one's patients lovingly. In his obituary Freud found it necessary to say that in Ferenczi's later years the need to cure had obsessed him. "He had probably set himself goals which, with our therapeutic means are altogether out of reach today." The prevalent view that Ferenczi was paranoid was based on his belief in the stories of abuse related to him by patients, and a myth emerged that Ferenczi's mind had deteriorated at the end of his life. Jones took advantage of Ferenczi's death to break his promise to publish his Wiesbaden Congress paper, and for years it was suppressed.

Ferenczi's death elicited little emotion in Freud. While he agreed with Jones that their loss was great and painful, it was simply "a small indication of the kind of change which overthrows everything that seems permanent and makes room for something new." Ferenczi took some of the past with him, and when it would be time for Freud to depart this life "another period will begin of which you will still be a part. Fate, resignation, that's all" (May 29, 1933).

The subsequent history is well known. In 1938, Jones arranged for the Freud family to flee to England. On September 3, 1939, on the day Britain declared war on Germany, Jones wrote to Freud:

This critical moment seems an appropriate one for me to express once more my personal devotion to you, my gratitude for all you have brought into my life and my intense sympathy for the suffering you are enduring. When England last fought Germany, twenty-five years ago, we were on opposite sides of the line, but even then we found a way to communicate our friendship to each other. Now we are near to each other and united in our sympathies. No one can say if we shall see the end of this war, but in any case it has been a very interesting life and we have both made a contribution to human existence— even if in very different measure.

> *With my warmest and dearest regards*
> *Yours always affectionately*
> *Ernest Jones*

Freud died two weeks later.

After living long enough to see the psychoanalytic movement established firmly in what would become Israel, Eitingon died in 1943. Sachs settled in Boston and, after much discouragement because he was not medically qualified, was finally accepted as the first lay member in the local society. He too died in exile in 1947. Jones, the outsider who proposed a Committee of insiders, lived until 1957, after writing his monumental version of the life of Freud. It must have been an eerie sensation reading what Freud and the other members of the Committee thought of him throughout all those years.

Jones had never felt comfortable wearing his Committee ring, and it was stolen from the trunk of his car after Freud's death. Also stolen was the cane he had given Freud on his seventieth birthday, but it is not known whether this theft occurred on the same occasion.

Epilogue

From one point of view, a committee is simply a group of people who meet at intervals to discuss certain business. It tends to be regarded as an abstraction, but it is actually an interaction of individuals jostling for position, of living people with their own distinctive personalities and aims. Freud made the initial mistake of regarding his Committee as an entity, perhaps in a sense a collective Eduard Silberstein or Wilhelm Fliess, and it is not surprising that he described a group as held together by sublimated homosexuality.

The story of the Secret Committee is one of human frailty. It has no heroes and no happy resolution. In a letter of September 18, 1933, Jones commented that Freud often must have been puzzled by the constant quarreling in all psychoanalytic societies. Why was it that psychoanalysis had not been successful among analysts themselves?

Jones listed three reasons for its failure. First, analysts were generally neurotic people who had chosen this particular profession as a means of controlling their own neuroses. Second, working all day in the realm of the unconscious imposed an intolerable strain on them. Finally, very few of them were sufficiently analyzed, and most should have further analysis.

While this book is based on documentary evidence, it does not have pretensions to dispassion. I cannot help being more sympathetic to Ferenczi than to Jones. And Freud? I am still not altogether sure of my opinion of Freud. He is certainly one of history's great figures, after whom the world was never the same again. His mind explored deep areas of the psyche, from which we are still extracting the gold from the dross. I am also fascinated by the fact that thousands of people continue to idealize and defend him without really knowing anything about him as a person.

It is difficult to assess Freud as a human being because he was a self-created icon who modeled himself on noble figures of the past and was constantly aware of how he would be judged by posterity. He believed that he had discovered the ultimate truth, and he had the ability and personal magnetism to convert others to his vision. Through the Committee, psychoanalysis was institutionalized on a firm basis, but had there been no departures from Freud's Truth, psychoanalysis would have hardened into a fossilized theory. Fortunately, there is no ultimate truth, and dedicated people will continue to search for ways of alleviating suffering.

Freud unquestionably belongs in the tradition of nineteenth-century romanticism. In bestowing rings on his followers, he seemed to see himself as a towering figure in a Wagnerian opera. He created a psychology that undid the values of the Enlightenment just as much as Marx repudiated them politically. Freud legitimized neurosis by labelling the disorders he let into the world when he opened his Pandora's box of the unconscious. By 1930 he vainly tried to shut the lid in *Civilization and Its Discontents* when he asserted that society could operate only when unruly emotions were kept in check. The Committee bears a startling resemblance to the writhing coutours of the Laocoön in which the father and his sons are crushed to death by the retaliatory serpents. Perhaps Freud should have spent more time in Rome gazing on this tragic statuary than in contemplating Moses. The epic story of the Committee evokes Aristotelian pity and terror but, alas, the spectacle does not provide us with any healing catharsis. We are witnessing not actors on a stage but real people wreaking havoc on each other.

Notes on Sources

I have relied mainly on Freud's correspondence with the members of the Committee and on their correspondence with each other as well as on the *Rundbriefe*.

Ernest Jones's *The Life and Work of Sigmund Freud* (Basic Books, 1953–57) I have found invaluable despite his personal bias which I have discussed in the course of this book. I have also been helped by other biographers of Freud: Ronald Clark's *Freud: The Man and the Cause* (Jonathan Cape & Weidenfeld, 1980) and Peter Gay's *Freud: A Life for Our Time* (Norton, 1988). Of a high intellectual caliber are Richard Wollheim's relatively brief but extremely succinct *Freud* (Fontana, 1971) and Frank J. Sulloway's masterly work, *Freud, Biologist of the Mind* (Basic Books, 1979).

A helpful book on the early figures is *Psychoanalytic Pioneers*, edited by Franz Alexander, Samuel Eisenstein, and Martin Grotjahn (Basic Books, 1966), now unfortunately out of print. Paul Roazen's *Freud and His Followers* (Knopf, 1975) remains a groundbreaking work. William J. McGrath's *Freud's Discovery of Psychoanalysis* (Cornell University Press, 1986) is a brilliant analysis of Freud's early relationships, and of course Henri J. Ellenberger's *The Discovery of the Unconscious* (Basic Books, 1970) is a classic.

The Letters of Sigmund Freud to Wilhelm Fliess, 1871–1881, edited by Walter Boehlich (Harvard University Press, 1990); *The Complete Letters of Sigmund Freud to Wilhelm Fliess*, 1887–1904, edited by J. M. Masson (Harvard University Press, 1985); and *The Freud/Jung Letters*, edited by William McGuire (Princeton University Press, 1974) have been indispensable.

There are numerous excellent books on the Freud-Jung relationship: *Freud and Jung: Conflicts and Interpretation* by Robert S. Steele (Routledge and Kegan Paul, 1982), is a book that deserves close attention. There is also *Freud and Jung: Years of Friendship, Years of Loss* by Linda Donn (Charles Scribner's Sons, 1988). For Jung's own recollections, one should read

Jung's *Memories, Dreams, Reflections*, edited by Aniela Jaffé (Vintage Books, 1965).

Much work remains to be written on the members of the Committee itself. Hanns Sachs's *Freud: Master and Friend* (Harvard, 1945) is disappointing in its various inaccuracies in dates. Ernest Jones's *Free Associations* (Basic Books, 1959) ends just when the story begins to be interesting. More helpful is Vincent Broome's *Ernest Jones: Freud's Alter Ego* (Caliban, 1982).

Rank has found a superb biographer in E. James Lieberman, whose *Acts of Will: The Life and Work of Otto Rank*, appeared in 1985 (The Free Press). Anna Freud has been well served by Elisabeth Joung-Bruehl in *Anna Freud: A Biography* (Summit Books, 1988).

Ferenczi has fared best in investigative scholarship: Jeffrey M. Masson in *The Assault on Truth* (Farrar, Strauss and Giroux, 1984), despite its tendentious tone, was the first to publish sections from the Freud/Ferenczi correspondence, which aroused interest in the true story of Ferenczi. Other extremely helpful books are André Haynal's *The Technique at Issue: Controversies in Psychoanalysis from Freud and Ferenczi to Michael Balint* (Karnac, 1988); Pierre Sabourin's *Ferenczi: Paladin et Grand Vizir Secret* (Editions Universitaires, 1985); Judith Dupont's superb edition of *The Clinical Diary of Sandor Ferenczi* (Harvard, 1988); and the Ferenczi-Groddeck Correspondence (1921–1933), edited by le Groupe du Coq-Héron (Payot, 1982).

Scholars have been hindered in their investigations by the absurd restrictions imposed by the Sigmund Freud Archives on the material in the Library of Congress. Copies of many of the letters have circulated widely, but until access to the original documents is permitted, errors are bound to proliferate. Nevertheless, persistence is gradually being rewarded, and it is heartening how much material is coming to light.

There are plans to publish the relevant documents in the next few years. These include the Freud/Ferenczi correspondence now housed in the Osterreichische Nationalbibliotek in Vienna; the Eitingon letters to Freud at the Sigmund Freud Copyrights in Wivenhoe, England; Freud's letters to Eitingon (embargoed until 2000) in the Library of Congress; the Jones-Freud letters in the Archives of the British Psycho-Analytical Society; the unrestricted Abraham papers in the Library of Congress; and the Rank papers as well as the *Rundbriefe* at Columbia University.

Only by the publication of these letters and the removal of all the restrictions at the Library of Congress will we be able to acquire a fuller knowledge of the history of psychoanalysis, one based on facts rather than the mythology, gossip, and rumor that have bedeviled so much writing on Freud.

Acknowledgments

I am grateful to Bernard Crystal of the Rare Book and Manuscript Library, Columbia University, for access to the Rank letters and to the *Rundbriefe;* Dr. Ronald Wilkinson and Dr. David Wigdor of the Manuscript Division, Library of Congress, for access to the Abraham letters; and Pearl King, honorary archivist, and Jill Duncan, executive officer, Archives of the British Psycho-Analytical Society, who have enabled me to examine various items which I have acknowledged in the Notes.

I thank Mark Patterson of the Sigmund Freud Copyrights for access to the Freud/Jones correspondence, which is now in the Archives of the British Psycho-Analytical Society, and David Ross of the New York Psychoanalytic Society for permitting me to examine the early minutes of the New York Society. Richard Welles and Erica Davies of the Freud Museum and Tom Roberts of Sigmund Freud Copyrights were extremely helpful in providing photographs, as was Bernard F. Vieyre for granting permission to publish a photograph of Eduard Silberstein. Diane Thomas of the Farrar Library, Clarke Institute of Psychiatry in Toronto, has always been immensely kind both to me and to my students.

A number of dedicated people have been involved in the translation of material: Jadwige Baranowicz; Matthias Nowack; Petra Fastermann; George Vladar; Tom Roberts; Eva Cooper; Helga Wischnewsky; Barbara Katar. Lisa Pottie was extremely helpful in uncovering arcane information.

I am grateful to Sigmund Freud Copyrights for permission to quote from the Freud letters; to Mervyn Jones for Ernest Jones's letters; and Grant Allan for Karl Abraham's letters. All material by Dr. Otto Rank from the Rank Collection at Columbia University is cited courtesy of the Estate of Otto Rank. All rights reserved. Copyright © 1991 by the Estate of Otto Rank. Used by permission of the Author's Representative, Gunther Stuhlmann.

This book would have been impossible without generous financial help from the Laidlaw Foundation, the Canada Council, and the Social Sciences and Research Council of Canada.

For invaluable help in all sorts of ways I thank Arno and Erika Pomerans; Ruth and Don Rendell; Tom Roberts; Enid Balint; the late Dr. Martin Grotjahn; Dr. James Lieberman; Robert Kramer; Dr. André Haynal; Ernst Falzeder; Professor Hans Fichtner; Dr. Harold Blum; Paul Roazen; Frank Sulloway; Dr. Judith Dupont; Dr. Bela Grunberger; Dr. Alain de Mijolla; Edward Shorter; Miriam Waddington; Brian Grosskurth; Elspeth Cameron; Michael Holroyd; Elizabeth Longford; Goethe-Institut, Toronto.

My agents of the past fifteen years, Jacqueline Korn and Claire Smith, have been my treasured supporters. David Godwin suggested a book something like this some years ago, and the specific idea for the book came from my editor Jane Isay, with whom it has been a wonderful intellectual adventure to collaborate. Cyrisse Jaffee appeared when I needed her to help with the final editing. Tiffany Cobb has been patient and helpful. I am more than happy that Douglas Matthews of the London Library consented to do the index. My husband, Bob McMullan, has been my partner, friend, and critic. My gratitude to him is inestimable.

References

Introduction

1. *The Letters of Sigmund Freud to Eduard Silberstein, 1871–1881*, ed. Walter Boehlich, trans. A. J. Pomerans (Harvard University Press, 1990), p. 56.
2. François Roustang, *Dire Mastery: Discipleship from Freud to Lacan*, trans. Ned Lukacher (The Johns Hopkins University Press, 1976), p. 33.

Prologue: Idyll in the Harz Mountains

1. Freud/Jones, November 18, 1920.
2. October 11, 1921, (*Rundbriefe*, Columbia University).
3. October 11, 1921 (Ibid).
4. October 11, 1921 (Ibid).

Chapter One: Freud's Early Friendships

1. Freud/Silberstein letters, p. 58.
2. Ibid, p. 12.
3. Ibid. p. 16.
4. *Letters of Sigmund Freud, 1873–1939*, ed. Ernst L. Freud (The Hogarth Press, 1970), p. 112.
5. Freud/Silberstein, p. 57.
6. Ibid., p. 126.
7. *Letters of Sigmund Freud, 1873–1939*, p. 113.
8. November 24, 1887, *The Complete Letters of Sigmund Freud to Wilhelm Fliess*, ed. & trans. Jeffrey Moussaieff Masson (Harvard University Press, 1985), p. 15.
9. December 28, 1887 (Ibid, p. 16).
10. August 29, 1888 (Ibid, p. 24).
11. March 8, 1895 (Ibid, p. 118).
12. See Hannah S. Decker, *Freud, Dora and Vienna*, 1900 (The Free Press, 1991), pp. 93, 97, 237, note 43.
13. December 22, 1910, *The Freud/*

Jung Letters, ed. William McGuire (Princeton University Press, 1974), p. 382.

Chapter Two:
The Unruly Son

1. Peter Gay, *Freud: A Life for Our Time* (Norton, 1988), p. 173.
2. Ibid, p. 178.
3. October 5, 1906 (Freud/Jung letters).
4. October 7, 1906 (Ibid, p. 6).
5. January 1, 1907 (Ibid, p. 18).
6. May 3, 1908 (Ibid, p. 144).
7. February 20, 1908 (Ibid, p. 122).
8. April 16, 1909 (Ibid, p. 218).
9. June 4, 1909 (Ibid, p. 228).
10. June 7, 1909 (Ibid, pp. 230, 231).
11. June 21, 1909 (Ibid, p. 236).
12. June 30, 1909 (Ibid, p. 218).
13. Gay, p. 218.
14. December 29, 1910 (Freud/Ferenczi).
15. February 2, 1912 (Freud/Ferenczi).
16. July 28, 1912 (Freud/Ferenczi).
17. August 6, 1912 (Ferenczi/Freud).
18. November 15, 1912 (Jung/Jones) (Sigmund Freud Copyrights).

Chapter Three:
Freud's Adopted Children

1. February 2, 1913 (paraphrase of Freud/Ferenczi).

2. June 8, 1913 (Freud/Ferenczi).
3. June 1, 1913 (*A Psycho-Analytic Dialogue—The Letters of Sigmund Freud and Karl Abraham, 1907–1926*, eds. Hilda A. Abraham and Ernst L. Freud, Basic Books, 1965), p. 141.
4. July 22, 1913 (Jones/Freud).
5. Sigmund Freud Copyrights.
6. June 2, 1914 (Freud/Jones).
7. Archives of the British Psycho-Analytical Society.

Chapter Four:
Years of Hardship

1. December 15, 1914 (Jones/Freud).
2. August 20, 1893 (Freud/Fliess).
3. April 21, 1918 (Freud/Ferenczi).
4. Circa October 4, 1918 (Ferenczi/Freud).
5. October 16, 1918 (Freud/Ferenczi).

Chapter Five:
Mustering the Troops

1. Ernest Jones, *The Life and Work of Sigmund Freud* (Basic Books, 1955), III, p. 12.
2. Sigmund Freud Copyrights.
3. August 8, 1919 (Ferenczi/Freud).
4. Sigmund Freud Copyrights.
5. Jones, III, p. 5.
6. Ibid, p. 19.

7. March 20, 1920 (Ferenczi/ Freud).
8. May 7, 1920 (Jones/ Freud).
9. January 16, 1920 (Archives of the British Psycho-Analytical Society).
10. July 18, 1920 (Ferenczi/Freud).

Chapter Six:
A Band of Brothers

1. Jones, III, pp. 46, 47.
2. Jones, III, p. 47.
3. March (n.d.), 1921 (Ferenczi/ Freud).
4. Standard Edition, VIII, p. 180.
5. Ibid, p. 177.
6. Ibid, p. 181.
7. Ibid, p. 190.
8. Ibid, p. 193.

Chapter Seven:
Squabbles Terminable and Interminable

1. S.E., XVIII, p. 77.
2. Ibid, p. 124.
3. Ibid, p. 134.
4. Jones, III, p. 54.

Chapter Eight:
Open Warfare

1. January 3, 1923 (Vienna *Rundbrief*).
2. January 7, 1923 (Berlin *Rundbrief*).

3. January 1, 1923, Jones/Abraham (Library of Congress).
4. Archives of the British Psycho-Analytical Society.
5. Jones, III, p. 93.
6. Ibid, p. 55.
7. Archives of the British Psycho-Analytical Society.
8. Ibid.
9. Ibid.
10. Ibid.
11. Ibid.
12. Ibid.
13. Ibid.

Chapter Nine:
Dissent and Division

1. Abraham papers (Library of Congress).
2. Rank papers (Columbia University).
3. January 22, 1924 (Freud/Ferenczi).
4. February 4, 1924 (Freud/Ferenczi).
5. January 30, 1924 (Rank papers, Columbia University).
6. February 9, 1924 (Rank papers, Columbia University).
7. Rank papers (Columbia University).
8. February 21, 1924 (Library of Congress).
9. Abraham papers (Library of Congress).
10. March 8, 1924 (Ibid).
11. Rank papers (Columbia University).

12. Abraham papers (Library of Congress).
13. March 26, 1924 (Freud/Ferenczi).
14. Abraham papers (Library of Congress).
15. Ibid.
16. Rank papers (Columbia University).

Chapter Ten: Division and Death

1. Rank papers (Columbia University).
2. May 4, 1924 (Abraham papers, Library of Congress).
3. May 28, 1924 (Freud/Ferenczi).
4. Rank papers (Columbia University).
5. June 7, 1924 (Ibid).
6. August 14, 1924 (Ferenczi/ Freud).
7. Archives of the British Psycho-Analytical Society.
8. Rank papers (Columbia University).
9. Sigmund Freud Copyrights.
10. Rank papers (Columbia University).
11. Abraham papers (Library of Congress).
12. Rank papers (Columbia University).
13. Ibid.
14. Archives of the British Psycho-Analytical Society.
15. Rank papers (Columbia University).

16. September 19, 1925 (Jones/ Freud).
17. August 9, 1925 (Abraham papers, Library of Congress).

Chapter Eleven: The Twilight of the Committee

1. *The Letters of Sigmund Freud and Karl Abraham*, 1907/1927, ed. Hilda C. Abraham and Ernst L. Freud (Basic Books, 1965) pp. 399, 400.
2. Elisabeth Young-Bruehl, *Anna Freud* (Summit Books, 1988), p. 150.
3. April 24, 1926 (Freud/Ferenczi).
4. December 24, 1924 (Young-Bruehl, p. 151).
5. April 23, 1926 (Ferenczi/ Freud).
6. February 15, 1924 (Rank/ Freud), Rank papers, Columbia University.
7. September 27, 1926 (Freud/ Jones).
8. Jones, III, p. 127.
9. Sigmund Freud Copyrights.
10. Ibid.
11. April 8, 1927 (Ferenczi/Freud).
12. January 26, 1927 (Freud/Ferenczi).
13. March 15, 1927 (Ferenczi/ Freud).
14. March 25, 1927 (Freud/Ferenczi).
15. Lieberman, p. 264.

16. Jones, III, p. 127.
17. April 26, 1926.
18. September 23, 1927 (Freud/Jones).
19. September 30, 1927 (Jones/Freud).
20. September 23, 1927 (Freud/Jones).
21. Gay, p. 577.
22. September 23, 1927 (Freud/Jones).
23. September 30, 1927 (Jones/Freud).
24. September 23, 1927 (Young-Bruehl, p. 171).

Chapter Twelve:
The Last Act

1. March 11, 1928 (Freud/Jones).
2. December 13, 1929 (Freud/Ferenczi).
3. February 6, 1929 (Ferenczi/Freud).
4. January 11, 1930 (Freud/Ferenczi).
5. Ibid.
6. January 17, 1930 (Ferenczi/Freud).
7. S.E., XXIII, p. 211.
8. Ibid.
9. September 16, 1930 (Freud/Ferenczi).
10. January 15, 1931 (Jones/Freud).

11. October 10, 1931 (Ferenczi/Freud).
12. Jones, III, pp. 154, 155.
13. Jeffrey M. Masson, *The Assault on Truth* (Farrar, Strauss and Giroux, 1984), p. 159.
14. *The Clinical Diary of Sandor Ferenczi*, ed. Judith Dupont (Harvard University Press, 1988), p. 93.
15. "From the *Active Technique* to the *Confusion of Tongues*," in *Psychoanalysis in France*, eds. S. Lebovici and D. Widlocher (International Universities Press, 1980), p. 131.
16. Jones, III, p. 171.
17. June 13, 1932 (Jones/Freud).
18. Jones, III, p. 169.
19. Masson, p. 170.
20. Jones, III, p. 172.
21. June 6, 1933 (Brill/Jones).
22. Masson, p. 294.
23. September 12, 1932 (Freud/Jones).
24. Masson, p. 169.
25. *Psychoanalytic Pioneers*, eds. Franz Alexander, Samuel Eisenstein, Martin Grotjahn (Basic Books, 1966), p. 12.
26. December 2, 1932 (Freud/Ferenczi).
27. *Correspondance de Sandor Ferenczi et Georg Groddeck*, ed. le Groupe du Coq-Héron (Paris: Payot, 1982), p. 127.
28. Jones, III, p. 177.
29. Archives of the British Psycho-Analytical Society.

Index